URBAN GOVERNANCE, INSTITUTIONAL CAPACITY AND
SOCIAL MILIEUX

Urban Governance, Institutional Capacity and Social Milieux

Edited by
GÖRAN CARS, PATSY HEALEY, ALI MADANIPOUR AND
CLAUDIO DE MAGALHÃES
*Royal Institute of Technology, University of Newcastle upon Tyne,
University College London*

LONDON AND NEW YORK

First published 2002 by Ashgate Publishing

Reissued 2018 by Routledge
2 Park Square, Milton Park, Abingdon, Oxon OX14 4RN
711 Third Avenue, New York, NY 10017, USA

Routledge is an imprint of the Taylor & Francis Group, an informa business

Copyright © Göran Cars, Patsy Healey, Ali Madanipour and Claudio de Maghalhães 2002

The authors have asserted their moral rights under the Copyright, Designs and Patents Act, 1988, to be identified as the authors of this work.

All rights reserved. No part of this book may be reprinted or reproduced or utilised in any form or by any electronic, mechanical, or other means, now known or hereafter invented, including photocopying and recording, or in any information storage or retrieval system, without permission in writing from the publishers.

Notice:
Product or corporate names may be trademarks or registered trademarks, and are used only for identification and explanation without intent to infringe.

Publisher's Note
The publisher has gone to great lengths to ensure the quality of this reprint but points out that some imperfections in the original copies may be apparent.

Disclaimer
The publisher has made every effort to trace copyright holders and welcomes correspondence from those they have been unable to contact.

A Library of Congress record exists under LC control number: 2001096485

ISBN 13: 978-1-138-70409-1 (hbk)
ISBN 13: 978-1-138-70406-0 (pbk)
ISBN 13: 978-1-315-20287-7 (ebk)

Contents

Acknowledgements	vii
About the Authors	viii
Preface	xi

PART I: CONCEPTUALISING INSTITUTIONAL CAPACITY

Editorial Introduction: Collective Action and Social Milieux
Ali Madanipour   3

1.   Transforming Governance, Institutionalist Analysis and Institutional Capacity
Patsy Healey, Göran Cars, Ali Madanipour and Claudio de Magalhães   6

2.   Institutional Capacity Building as an Issue of Collective Action and Institutionalisation: Some Theoretical Remarks
Enrico Gualini   29

3.   Assessing Institutional Capacity for City Centre Regeneration: Newcastle's Grainger Town
Claudio de Magalhães, Patsy Healey and Ali Madanipour   45

PART II: GOVERNANCE IN ACTION IN COMPLEX SOCIAL MILIEUX

Editorial Introduction: The Challenge of Building New Institutional Capacities
Claudio de Magalhães   65

4.   Transformational Pathways and Institutional Capacity Building: The Case of the German-Polish Twin City Guben/Gubin
Ulf Matthiesen   70

5	The Tangled Web – Neighbourhood Governance in a Post-Fordist Era
Judith Allen and Göran Cars	90

6	Is Partnership Possible? Searching for a New Institutional Settlement
Marilyn Taylor	106

7	Governance, Institutional Capacity and Planning for Growth
Christine Lambert and Nick Oatley	125

PART III: BUILDING NEW INSTITUTIONAL CAPACITIES

Editorial Introduction: Creating Milieux for Collective Action
Göran Cars	145

8	Compliance and Collaboration in Urban Governance
Murray Stewart	149

9	A Strategic Approach to Community Planning: Repositioning the Statutory Development Plan
Vincent Goodstadt and Grahame Buchan	168

10	Sustainable Institutional Capacity for Planning: The West Midlands
Alan Wenban-Smith	191

11	Urban Governance Capacity in Complex Societies: Challenges of Institutional Adaptation
Patsy Healey, Göran Cars, Ali Madanipour and Claudio de Magalhães	204

References	226
Index	243

Acknowledgements

A book of this kind involves contributions from many people. We must first acknowledge the ESRC Cities programme and its then Director, Duncan McLennan, for providing a funding contribution to allow us to hold a seminar to develop this book in April 1999. Then we have to thank all those who participated in the seminar in such a stimulating and lively way. We also acknowledge the efforts of all the authors to comply with our continual questions and requests for developing and adjusting the content of the book, so that it seemed to us to fit together reasonably well. We also owe a big debt of thanks to the CREUE Secretary, Yasmin Ibrahim, skilled organiser of Seminar events and careful producer of quality book texts. Without her skills, we would always be lost. Acknowledgements should also be made to Segal Quince Wicksteed, Cambridge, for permission to use Figure 10.2 taken from their report on Regional Development: Can RDAS Make a Difference (1998); and to the publishers of Futura, for permission to use Figure 3.2, taken from Healey, de Magalhães et al. 1999.

Göran Cars
Patsy Healey
Ali Madanipour
Claudio de Magalhães

About the Authors

Judith Allen is principal lecturer in Housing at the University of Westminster. She is presently scientific manager of a major cross-national study of social exclusion and neighbourhoods in the European Union. Her main interests and experience lie in community based politics and housing in a variety of east and west European countries.

Grahame Buchan is assistant manager of the Glasgow and Clyde Valley Joint Structure Plan Committee, and a specialist strategic planner with interests in strategic management, methodology and planning process. Current work themes range from Statutory Development Planning and transportation studies through to benchmarking approaches to strategic planning at the European level.

Göran Cars is an Associate Professor at the Royal Institute of Technology, Stockholm. His professional expertise lies in questions concerning urban governance with special interest directed towards housing and neighbourhood development. Research on this activity has included studies not only on specific housing districts but also of the interplay between neighbourhood development and municipal planning.

Vincent Goodstadt is the Manager of the Glasgow and Clyde Valley Joint Structure Plan Committee and has extensive experience of Strategic Planning processes throughout the UK. In recent years in Scotland, he has been at the heart of building institutional capacity, placing Statutory Planning within the wider corporate context of 'joined-up government'. His UK role has been widely acknowledged professionally and he is expected to take up the post of President of The Royal Town Planning Institute in the UK in 2003.

Enrico Gualini is post-doc researcher at the AME Amsterdam study center for the Metropolitan Environment, University of Amsterdam. His areas of research include innovative approaches to regionalisation and regional governance, local development policies, and strategies for multiple-intensive land-use in metropolitan regions.

Patsy Healey is Director of the Centre for Research in European Urban Environments at the University of Newcastle, and a specialist in cities, urban policy, planning systems and planning theory. In recent years, she has been developing institutionalist approaches to policy analysis and exploring collaborative processes in urban planning.

Christine Lambert is Reader in Urban Planning at the School of Housing and Urban Studies and member of the Cities Research Centre at the University of the West of England, Bristol. Her research interests are in planning for housing, cities and urban governance, especially in relation to the management of urban growth.

Ali Madanipour is Reader at the School of Architecture, Planning and Landscape and a member of the Centre for Research in European Urban Environments at the University of Newcastle. His areas of research include city design and development, culture of cities, urban governance and social exclusion.

Claudio de Magalhães is Lecturer in Planning at the Bartlett School of Planning, University College London. He is a specialist in urban planning systems, property development processes and urban policy. His recent research deals with institutionalist approaches to property markets, capacity building for urban governance, and the relationship between urban governance, urban design and property markets.

Ulf Matthiesen is Head of the Department of 'Planning History and Regional Culture' at the Institute for Regional Development and Structural Planning (IRS) in Erkner (near Berlin) and lecturer in the fields of urban and regional cultural developments at the Humboldt University Berlin. Comparative research activities concentrate on suburbanisation processes, cross border milieux and increasingly on the interrelations between knowledge-based societal dynamics and spatial developments ('knowledge milieux').

Nick Oatley is Principal Lecturer at the School of Housing and Urban Studies and member of the Cities Research Centre at the University of the West of England, Bristol. His research interests are in urban governance, urban policy and neighbourhood regeneration. He is currently on secondment, attached to the Policy Innovation Unit of the UK Government's Department of Education and Employment.

Murray Stewart is Director of the Cities Research Centre at the University of the West of England. He is a specialist in urban regeneration policy and practice, was a member of the Policy Action Team 17 Joining It Up Locally, is a board member of the Bristol Regeneration Partnership Board, and a member of the Government's Regional Co-ordination Unit Advisory Group.

Marilyn Taylor is Professor of Social Policy in the Health and Social Policy Research Centre at the University of Brighton. Her research expertise and interests lie in the fields of neighbourhood renewal and community development, user empowerment in public services, and the involvement of the voluntary and community sectors in policy making and partnerships.

Alan Wenban-Smith is a consultant in urban and regional policy, and planning adviser to MVA Ltd and Segal Quince Wicksteed. He has had previous experience with Birmingham City Council and the West Midlands Forum of County Councils, and was adviser to Yorkshire and Humberside in developing their Regional Planning Guidance.

Preface

The Project of the Book

This book responds to the challenges faced by urban governance across Europe and beyond as city governments, their partners and their critics struggle to transform themselves in the context of post-industrial economies and societies. This context has generated not merely new relations of economic life and social activity to be accommodated in cities. It has also changed expectations of the roles and relationships of governance and the modes of governance. It has changed how the formal organization and procedures of the public sector interact with the wider society. In this context, there is much debate about how the capacity of urban governance impacts on the quality of life and the quality of business environments in different places, and how this capacity is in turn shaped by the social and economic environment, or milieux, of particular places.

In parallel with this practical reality of transformations in the relations of urban governance in diverse social milieux, new conceptual tools for the analysis of these experiences are becoming available. Linked to a broad institutionalist wave of ideas sweeping across economics, political science, geography, sociology, policy analysis and planning, these new tools focus on the dynamic interaction between how particular organisations and actors operate and the wider relations of which they are a part. There are many different strands to these ideas, embodying alternative ways of imagining the nature of such interaction. But they are all concerned, in one way or another, with how governance relations are embedded in the social and economic history of particular places, and how these in turn contribute to moulding social and economic opportunities. Understood in this way, transformations in the relations of urban governance are encouraged and constrained by these embedded relations.

These institutionalist conceptions shift attention in the analysis of urban governance away from an account of formal structures and procedures, and the competences of different sectors and levels of government. Instead, they focus attention on the qualities of the wider milieux in which governance activity is performed and the institutional capacity of different places to act to address matters of collective concern. This critical insight has been developed in diverse ways. A strong strand of analysis within economics seeks to identify elements of such capacity, such as particular knowledge resources, or capabilities for co-ordination, which can then be treated as some kind of input to production processes. Other institutionalists focus their analytical lens onto the dynamic processes involved in the interaction between specific nodes of governance activity and the wider social relations within which they are embedded. This leads to an analytic interest in institutional capacity as a dynamic phenomenon, continually being drawn upon and re-formed. It also has a practical relevance for urban governance policy makers in terms of their contribution, explicit and consequential, to institutional capacity building.

Drawing on this latter tradition within the 'new' institutionalist analysis, and in the context of efforts by urban policy-makers to transform urban governance capacity, this book explores a range of efforts to build new institutional capacities. Our particular concern is to demonstrate the diversity of the social relations between actors, their networks and the social worlds in which they are embedded, the tensions in the ways these social worlds interact, and the complexity of the time-space relations which are drawn into these interactions. Through exploring the relation between transformation processes, institutional capacity and social milieux, we demonstrate the multiple layering in time and space of urban governance relations and the dynamic interactions between local efforts and broader structuring forces.

We are also interested in the implications of the 'new' institutionalist ideas for the practice of urban policy-making and planning. Our focus is on the dynamic processes through which governance capacities are continuously moulded. How should policy-makers imagine their 'place', the territory of the 'urban', in the context of new ideas about the nature of the social milieux of places? How could they understand the dynamics of the way their conceptions, relations and their actions may interrelate with the wider society? Where does authority and legitimacy come from? What does it mean to exercise power in the governance of cities, in a context of multiple, dynamic, transforming processes linking people in specific places to all kinds of other people in other places operating in different social worlds and on different timescales? We seek to show how these new ideas encourage urban policy-makers to widen the focus of their attention to encompass their role in building institutional capacities while engaged in the production and regulation of the material conditions of quality of urban life and business operations.

Underpinning our analytical interest are two general concerns. One relates to our roles as policy advisers. How do these new approaches help to identify what 'makes a difference' to material outcomes, to cultural identity and to the qualities of milieux? The second relates to our normative orientation. What kinds of urban governance in what kinds of context have the potential to contribute to spreading access to opportunities and material welfare and to sustaining community well-being over the long-term? What strategies and practices seem to inhibit such evolutions?

The Organisation of the Book

The Book had its origins in a seminar held in Newcastle in April 1999, part-funded by the ESRC Cities Programme. The authors are a mixture of academics and practitioners from Brazil, Iran, Italy, Sweden, Germany and the UK, representing backgrounds in urban planning, geography and policy analysis. Since the seminar, all the authors have developed their chapters in response to the issues raised in the seminar and in discussion with the editors. In this way, we have aimed for a first level of integration in the parts of the book. Inevitably there are different perspectives and processes emerging in each chapter. To help in developing the argument of the book, we have grouped the papers into three parts, each with a short introduction highlighting the main issues addressed and their relation to the overall argument. This acts as a second level of integration.

The first part expands on the argument outlined above, to set the context of transformation in urban governance, to outline the conceptual ideas that are developed in the book and to suggest ways of translating these into more specific analyses. Part 1 consists of an introductory chapter by the editors. This centres around three propositions: that the widening of government activity to include many more individuals and groups will remain a significant tendency and hence it is appropriate in the contemporary period to focus on governance; that the role of place and territory as a focus for integrating governance activity will present an expanding challenge to the currently well-established sectoral modes of governance; and that the quality of urban governance capacity makes a difference to the social, environmental and economic relations of localities. This is followed by a review of the concepts of institutional capacity building and social capital by Enrico Gualini and an analysis of a partnership case, using the institutional capacity concept undertaken by three of the editors.

The second part explores struggles in different arenas to make sense of, and to create, institutional capacities for acting on and in complex dynamic realities. Ulf Matthiesen unravels the different institutional evolutions in a post-communist context of two sides of a town, long divided by a national border, which has now become an EU border too. Judith Allen and Göran Cars examine the way transforming governance is impacting on distressed neighbourhoods across Europe and how this affects local social relations. Marilyn Taylor reviews the British experience of promoting community involvement in neighbourhood renewal, in the light of the impact on developing social capital and institutional capacity. Christine Lambert and Nick Oatley describe the difficulties of building new capacities at the regional and sub-regional level to deal with exploding growth pressures in southern Britain.

The third part examines attempts to build new institutional relations and create institutional capacity in different arenas in Britain. Murray Stewart provides a critique, from a position of active engagement as a consultant, of national attempts at promoting capacity building in governance structures, discussing the concepts of transaction costs and social capital. Vincent Goodstadt and Grahame Buchan describe how they built an urban region strategy in a context where formal structures and competences for strategy-making had been abolished. Alan Wenban-Smith draws on his experience in a similar situation of the fragmentation of formal government arrangements to develop a practical conception of what institutional capacity building involves.

The book also provides a third level of integration. It concludes in Chapter 11 by summarising what the contributions in the book have to say about processes of transformation in urban governance and the analytical tools available to examine these. It then reviews the three propositions set out in Chapter 1 in the light of the discussion in the book, concluding with an assessment of the implications for urban policy. Overall, we hope the book makes a contribution not merely to the analysis of transformation processes in urban governance, but more widely to the emerging new directions in policy analysis and planning methodology, and, substantively, to the project of imagining and promoting sustainable and socially just cities and territories.

Göran Cars, Patsy Healey, Ali Madanipour, Claudio de Magalhães
Editors

PART I:
CONCEPTUALISING INSTITUTIONAL CAPACITY

PART I:

Editorial Introduction: Collective Action and Social Milieux

ALI MADANIPOUR

The main aim of this Part is to explore the meaning of institutional capacity and provide a theoretical foundation for the book. The Part clarifies the relationship between institutional capacity and related concepts, notably social capital, social milieux, governance and collective action.

The idea of social capital has been increasingly used to express the capacities available within the wider social context upon which governance activity, business initiative and cultural life can draw. It is widely used by the authors in this book. The concept has come to take a central place in social science debates in the last decade, particularly on the impact of social organization and culture on economic and political outcomes (Bourdieu 1986, Calhoun 1993, Coleman 1988, Fukuyama 1999, Lang, and Hornburg 1998, Putnam 1998, Wann 1995, Woolcock 1998). It is, however, a concept that seems to raise as many questions as it tries to answer, a term that appears to refer to a common sense interpretation of social relations and at the same time causing major discussions. In relation to our debates about institutional capacity, social milieux and social capital, a number of questions emerge which need addressing. In the context of what theoretical perspectives and conceptual frameworks are institutional capacity issues being highlighted? What is their focus of analytic attention? What (if anything) is new about them? What is their value orientation and normative 'subtext'? What specific concepts are being drawn into the analysis, for what purposes? Does it help to distinguish the analytical use of the term in research studies and the way the term is being used in policy rhetoric? What specific issues are being/should be carefully thought through if the focus on institutional capacity is to 'add value' to research on urban governance and urban policy? What are the meanings and ingredients of institutional capacity? What is the difference between social capital and institutional capacity? What is the relationship between social capital formation and institutional capacity building? What is the role of institutional capacity and social capital in civic engagement and the development of the public sphere? How far can the application of the concept help a renewal of democracy in the context of globalisation, Europeanisation, and welfare reforms?

Our overall concern in this book is to explore the dynamics of change and transformation in the institutional capacity of urban governance. Conceptually, we see these capacities as evolving in continual interaction between the social worlds of city actors – citizens, businesses, pressure groups, activity groups, political parties, government departments and agencies, etc, and the wider context within which these worlds are positioned. Institutional capacities for governance are thus embedded in the dynamics of the wider social context within which collective action focused at the urban level takes place. It is here that the notion of social milieux plays a key role in describing these relationships and contexts. Social milieux is a term which refers to the complexity of texture and plurality of social life, the social context in its richness. Social capital and institutional capacity, on the other hand, are evaluative and normative concepts, as they refer to particular forms of richness that enable individuals and groups to mobilise resources and perform meaningful action. Several questions arise from these concerns. Under what conditions can collective action emerge from a rich social fabric made of different textures? What is the nature of this collective action and what are its likely directions? How would this collective action relate to the needs and interests of a diverse range of organisations and individuals involved? Who is centrally involved and who is excluded from this process?

The chapters in this Part play two different roles. On the one hand, they analyse the complex processes through which the shape of governance has changed. A significant feature of these processes is a widely-recognised multiplication and fragmentation of agencies involved in the development and management of cities. On the other hand, the Part introduces and develops a normative notion of institutional capacity, which refers to the capacity of these multiple, fragmented agencies to work together. As economic liberalization and civic disengagement put pressure on the formal democratic infrastructure, the question is how this variety of actors engage in collective actions so necessary for addressing their mutual concerns and interests. How, through collective action, can qualities of social milieux be generated? The papers in this part argue that by developing institutional capacity, a new, complementary framework for action can become available to social actors.

Chapter 1 by the Editors briefly traces the changes of local governance and spatial planning dynamics in Europe. It then detects and develops three basic features in this changing landscape. First, it emphasises how the quality of governance capacity in an urban region is significant for its future, in social, economic and environmental terms.

Second, it stresses the significance of the direct involvement of individuals and groups in the wider society alongside the formal processes of representative democracy. Third, it argues that, by moving away from the sectoral organisation of the mid-twentieth century welfare state, place and territory will find a greater role in integrating governance activity. These three notions outline the overall framework in analysing institutional capacity.

In Chapter 2, Enrico Gualini develops the notion of institutional capacity further and explores its links with the notion of social capital. The Chapter asserts the link between institutional capacity and collective action, as they share the same basic theoretical and practical problems. Following Coleman, social capital is seen as a relational asset used by social actors, who construct institutions in pursuit of their strategic-communicative rationality. Institutional capacity is then analysed at the intersection between institutional building and institutional design, i.e., between the process of constructing these institutions and the shape they take. To understand this interplay, the dynamics of institutional change and the forms of institutionalisation find a key role. This, in other words, is an analysis of social action at the interplay between actors and structures. To be able to move away from a static interpretation of institutions, however, Gualini puts a strong emphasis on the autonomy of actors in shaping their actions.

Chapter 3 by de Magalhães, Healey and Madanipour combines a case study with theoretical development of the notion of institutional capacity. The case study concentrates on the historic core at the city centre of Newcastle, where a new urban regeneration initiative has generated a new institutional arrangement between the agencies involved in the process. The chapter then develops the notion of institutional capacity as linking three elements of social interaction: knowledge resources, relational resources, and mobilisation capacity. Each of these elements are analysed further in terms of their constituent parts and dynamics. This conceptual framework is used to analyse the case study.

Together the three chapters provide a platform for understanding and discussing institutional capacity, urban governance, social capital, social mileux and collective action, as developed further in the following chapters.

1 Transforming Governance, Institutionalist Analysis and Institutional Capacity

PATSY HEALEY, GÖRAN CARS, ALI MADANIPOUR AND
CLAUDIO DE MAGALHÃES

Urban Governance in Transformation

Economic and Social Change and their Consequences

Across Europe, those involved in urban government are under pressure to transform their policy agendas and policy networks, their relations with their citizens and their position in the wider regional and European landscape. Underlying these transformation efforts can be seen the impact of the structural economic and technological changes of the last quarter of the twentieth century, which have re-shaped labour and land markets in Europe's cities, demanding new actions in relation to infrastructures, social welfare for those who have lost out from re-structuring, and the management of new nodes and qualities within urban areas. These changes pose challenges for present governance arrangements. In an increasingly globalised economy, cities and regions are often presented as in competition with each other (Pierre 1998). Such competition could be described as a form of 'place wars'. In response to this increased competition, city elites are encouraged to devise strategies to improve the attractiveness and competitiveness of their cities in a globalising world. This often calls for new governance arrangements to co-ordinate public and private investment in infrastructure and other urban investments (Bailey 1995). Socio-cultural changes have co-evolved with these economic developments, diversifying lifestyles and lifecycle dynamics, generating new material demands on urban governments and altering the configurations of values with which citizens judge their representatives. It has been claimed that present governance arrangements are not conducive to the kinds of demands made by citizens of contemporary European democracies and are not sensitive to the voice of citizens (Hirst 2000). It is also asserted that lack of sensitivity to the public undermines the competitiveness of cities in the international market place, and that this contributes to the erosion of confidence in public institutions (Susskind and Field 1996). Today it is understood that widening social polarisation in most European societies cannot be resolved merely by traditional (often individually targeted) social welfare policies. Rather, combating social exclusion presupposes changes in existing governance structures, such as by rethinking mechanisms for delivery of services and providing institutional space to allow residents to act as subjects in decision-making and change in their neighbourhoods (Allen, Cars et al., 2000).

The dynamics of these fundamental changes in social and economic relations within urban regions generates a new context for the political and administrative work of urban governance. Often it seems that changes in the society and economy leave their city governments behind as the relations of urban life transform themselves in diverse, complex and often conflictual ways.

From 'Government' to 'Governance'

On this context, there is a widespread pre-occupation with the transformation of 'traditional' forms of government into what often is referred to as 'governance'. For some commentators, the problem is that changes are happening far too slowly. Traditional ways of managing government functions overall, or in particular areas, are presented as holding back innovation in the economy and civil society. For others, too much is being changed, undermining ways of distributing resources more fairly in society and disrupting the fine grain of social relations through which social support and environmental care are accomplished.

Some analysts describe the changes as inevitable consequences of structural changes in the world economy. Others criticise this, emphasising that this is merely a belated recognition of the complexity of the world in which we live, undermining any assumption that urban governments could be 'in charge' of their territories (Kooiman 1993). Others criticise formal government for its failure to adapt to new realities (Le Galès 1998, Imrie and Raco 1999). Mayntz suggests that such failure arises from challenges of the governability of societies and the acceptance of political leadership; the debate on how welfare policies should be financed and delivered; and the governing capacity of the state, related to inherent shortcomings in the traditional instruments of the state (Mayntz 1993).

Whatever the reasons, many of those working in urban governments have experienced considerable shifts in the tasks they undertake, the policy agendas they are expected to realise, the policy discourses they use to justify their actions, the people and networks they relate to and the ways they are expected to go about their work. In Britain, with its highly centralised and sectoralised state, many of these shifts have been promoted by national policy. In the 1980s, informed by a neo-liberal agenda, national government sought to reduce the activities of local governments through strategies of privatisation and de-regulation, while encouraging 'partnership' between municipalities and other stakeholders, both businesses and local residents, depending on the issue in hand. Spatial planning was reduced to a narrow regulatory role (Healey 1998a, Tewdwr-Jones 1997), dominated by the interpretation of national government policy criteria. Sectorally-organised mainstream programmes were reduced, while areas of industrial obsolescence and concentrated poverty were addressed with special initiatives aimed to 'regenerate' them and re-position people and places in the physical, economic and social fabric of their cities. This resulted in fragmentation and competition between programmes and initiatives. By the late 1990s, with a new, more social democratic government, there has been more emphasis on initiatives to promote 'integration' at the local level, 'joining up' the activities of traditionally separate departmental programmes and co-ordinating activities within local strategies and 'community plans' which are meant to promote 'well-being' of their communities (DETR 1998a) (see the discussions in Chapters 6, 7 and 8).

In Sweden until the 1980s, public authorities, especially the municipalities, were assigned powerful roles in developing and managing cities, within well-developed planning frameworks. Planning was seen as a sequential decision-making process in a rationalist mode. In the latter part of the 1980s, this approach was questioned and challenged. A major reason explaining the shifts that took place was the realisation that an increasing number of stakeholders demanded an active role in the planning process, notably private enterprises, NGOs and organised interest groups. Communicative and collaborative approaches including negotiation and conflict resolution emerged as important features of governance practice (Cars and Engström 1997). Today, urban development and management policies are conducted less through formal rational planning processes than through the informal activities and interplay between actors. Often the role of formal planning processes has been reduced to confirming agreements made in earlier stages of the process. Experiences from other countries in Europe tell a similar story (Blotevogel 2000, Motte 1995).

There are many reasons put forward for these changes. Regulation theorists argue that the welfare state settlement of the mid-twentieth century which served the 'Fordist' patterns of production relations no longer suits the modes of economic accumulation of global capitalism

(Jessop 1991, 2000). Regime theorists make the assumption that the effectiveness of local government depends on the co-operation of non-governmental actors and on the combination of state capacity with non-governmental resources (Pierre 1998). In Britain, arguments are sometimes focused in terms of moving beyond the damaging legacy of the neo-liberal era (Stewart J. 2000). In Eastern Europe, the discussion focuses on the trajectory of post-communist transformation (see the case in Chapter 4). Political scientists discuss the implications of new conceptions of legitimacy and authority and new manifestations of political mobilisation. For example, it is sometimes suggested that one of the key roles played by public-private partnerships is to generate legitimacy for 'fast-track' urban development programmes. In this respect a responsibility of the political/public agencies is to assure that public resources are not spent on partnership projects without some political objective and control (Pierre 1998). Whatever the reasons, the complex, conflicting and co-evolving transformation pressures lead to an experience of multiplication and fragmentation of urban governance effort. Elander and Blanc point out that globalisation and a neo-liberal shift in politics have been accompanied by urban fragmentation and widening economic and social inequalities (Elander and Blanc 2000). These forces have also affected the relative roles of different levels of government acting in the urban arena. Fragmentation implies that the actors involved are spread out not only among a wide variety of agencies but also across public, private and voluntary sectors (Stoker 2000c). This development triggers concerns about how to re-integrate the 'fractals' floating about in urban institutional space.

This fragmentation undermines old certainties, not merely about the structures and functions of government, but about the legitimate boundaries of public action, about the nature of the 'public interest', about where policy directions are articulated and how new ideas get translated into actions which make a difference. It has the potential to generate new arenas for policy development in which new coalitions and policy communities are articulated. At the same time, it undermines the capacity of established policy communities to control agendas, although old ways may persist to 'capture' new initiatives. This is well-illustrated in some of the cases in this book. How these processes play out in particular localities varies widely, depending on the adaptation and adjustment capacities of local elites and the scale of the pressures for change which they face, as the examples in this book from various scales and policy arenas show. In such varied and fluid contexts, it is difficult to make generalisations about emerging patterns of urban governance relations evolving across Europe. In the context of this book, however, we put forward three propositions.

- Firstly, the explicit involvement in urban governance of individuals and groups in the wider society will remain a significant adjunct to the formal processes of representative democracy.
- Secondly, in the struggle to find new foci for integrating governance activity, place and territory will come to play a greater role than in the sectoral organisation of the mid-twentieth century welfare state.
- Thirdly, the quality of governance capacity in a city or urban region, and particularly its ability to act as a collective actor, matters for the future of its citizens, its economy and its ecological relations.

We now expand on these three issues.

Governance: A General Term or Normative Model?

In the discussion above, we referred to the discussion about a shift from 'government' to 'governance'. Following much recent literature (Stoker 1999, 2000b, Le Galès 1998, Crouch et al. 2001), we use these terms to make a simple distinction. By government, we mean the organisations and procedures of the public sector as such, including both formal political and executive functions. Under the mid-twentieth century welfare state settlement, common organisational forms emerged which emphasised a hierarchy of levels between national and local government; a sectoral organisation of competences according to functions; and a clear distinction between politics, managed through the procedures of representative democracy, and experts/administrators, drawing on the manipulation of rational-technical knowledge and/or bureaucratic rule (Esping-Andersen 1990, Jessop 1995a). In this model, the state, as the public sector, was represented as distinct from 'private' interests, both with respect to the individual and as regards commercial interests. The State became the best available locus "for suturing together the distinct forms of sub-national, national and supra-national governance" (Hirst 2000, p 31). This capacity of the state could be related to three simultaneous roles: firstly, the state's capacity as an orchestrator of social consensus; secondly, its ability to become a main focus of political identity for citizens and a main institution for democracy; and thirdly, the rendering of decisions and commitments by national governments in stable democracies as reliable and legitimate (Hirst 2000). The trends discussed above, however, have involved breaking out of these simple distinctions.

Critics of the account of government as a set of organisations and competences driven by representative politics, political parties, experts and officials in the 1970s developed a vigorous debate on the 'relative autonomy' of the state, inspired by marxist analyses of the role of the state in a capitalist economy (Dunleavy and O'Leary 1987). The basic insight of these analyses was that formal government was interpenetrated with economic interests and involved in dominating the citizens it was supposed to represent. The alternative account tended to present society as a whole as organised into three spheres, the state, the economy and civil society. The key debates were over how far the state was a creature of the economy and in what ways the three spheres overlapped (Urry 1981). Much of the subsequent work of urban political economists and their successors has been to explore these overlapping relations in more depth (Judge et al. 1995, Lauria 1997, Le Galès 1998). Some claim that the State has been hollowed out by loss of functions upwards to the European Union and by international interdependencies, sideways through the creation of a range of semi-autonomous public agencies and downwards to special purpose bodies (Rhodes 1997, 2000). The consequences of this development are that "many of the reforms already implemented have helped to create a greater need for coordinative structures and action while at the same time reducing to some extent the capacity of governments to coordinate effectively" (Peters 1996, p 117, referred to in Rhodes 2000).

In parallel with the reality of the creation of new arrangements for partnership and collaboration between government organisations, business groups and community groups of various kinds, these explorations have made visible a reality that always existed. Formal government is linked to the wider society in many ways, while much collective action goes on with little reference to formal government, a point well-illustrated many years ago in the 'community power' literature of the 1950s and 1960s (Hunter 1953, Dahl 1961) and Stone's study of the evolution of Atlanta's political 'regimes' (Stone 1989). From this broader perspective, the mobilisation and management of collective action with respect to the qualities of services, opportunities and places in cities is diffused among an array of actors, in all kinds of institutional positions. It is in this context that the word 'governance' has come to be used in a descriptive sense, to refer to this array of activity, or, as Crouch et al. (2001) argue, to the generation of social order.

But the concept of 'governance' is itself ambiguous and currently carries with it both analytical and normative notions. In new institutional economics, it has been used to refer to activities aimed at reducing transaction costs (Williamson 1996). In the contemporary debate about urban governance, planning and development, the concept has been given various interpretations. It can be seen as a "process in which local political institutions implement their programmes in concert with civil society actors, and within which these actors and interests gain (potential) influence over urban politics" (Pierre 1998, p 5). Thus, Pierre underlines as a new feature, the interplay between public agencies and civil society. Rhodes proposes an even more radical definition, stating that governance "refers to self-organising networks, characterised by interdependence, resource exchange, rules of the game and significant autonomy from the state" (Rhodes 1997, p 15), thereby also underlining that new governance structures do not fit into the formal structures for governance developed in the so-called Fordist era. According to Rhodes, the concept refers to "continuing interactions between network members, caused by the need to exchange resources and negotiate shared purposes....(and) game-like interactions, rooted in trust and regulated by rules of the game negotiated and agreed by network participants". Rhodes concludes that networks are not accountable to the State. Nevertheless, "although the state does not occupy a privileged, sovereign position, it can indirectly and imperfectly steer networks" (Rhodes 1999, p xvii).[1]

Jessop moves explicitly to identify 'governance' with an alternative model for managing collective affairs, a position taken also by Taylor, Lambert and Oatley in Chapters 6 and 7. He contrasts 'heterarchy' with market and state as allocative mechanisms, by which he means "horizontal self-organisation among mutually interdependent actors" (Jessop 2000, p 15), manifest in 'interpersonal networking', interorganisational negotiation and de-centred 'steering' activity. This closely links governance with a 'network' model of managing collective affairs, in the well-established triad of hierarchy, market and network (Amin and Hausner 1997, see also Chapters 6 and 8). In this use of the concept of governance as a distinct model, Jessop argues that self-organising governance operates with a reflexive rationality, avoiding the failures of state and market as ways of organising collective action by:

> instituting negotiation around a long-term consensual project as the basis for both negative and positive co-ordination among interdependent actors. The key to success is continued commitment to dialogue to generate and exchange more information ... to weaken opportunism locking partners into a range of interdependent decisions over short-, medium- and long-term horizons; and to build on the interdependencies and risks associated with 'asset specificity' by encouraging solidarity among those involved. The rationality of governance is dialogic rather than monologic, pluralistic rather than monolithic, heterarchic rather than hierarchic (state-*editors*) or anarchic (market–*editors*). In turn this suggests that there is no one best governance mechanism (Jessop 2000, p 16).

In this account, Jessop comes very near to the accounts of self-organising government developed from research on Californian collaborative consensus-building by Innes and Booher (Innes and Booher 1999). These show that, in certain circumstances, collaborative governance approaches can 'add value'. They can create incentives for the development of alternatives that affected parties assess as preferable to those that could have been achieved by using other, more formalised, methods for decision-making. Thus, a development of dialogic or collaborative governance processes can provide incentives for rethinking the traditional 'win-lose' strategy and if/how it can be replaced by a 'win-win' concept (Susskind and Cruikshank 1987, Susskind, McKearnan et al. 1999, Healey 1999). However, neither Jessop nor these analysts pay much attention to the institutional inheritance which shapes the ways in which such practices may evolve.

Jessop (2000) goes on to analyse the potential for failure in the governance model, recognising that all models are prone to failure. Stoker also addresses the issue of governance failure, claiming that we have to accept these failures. A first expression of failure could be the absence of engagement and commitment among partners. Other explanations lie in complex pressures on a city as a result of market processes over which government actors have little control. Also the prevalent social conflict characteristic of cities can undermine governance. However, Stoker argues that these conflicts can be managed. "Such conflicts lend themselves to compromise and the art of bargaining... The cumulative experience of muddling through numerous of such conflicts is the heart of an effective governance system" (Stoker 2000c, p 105).

Critics of the normative use of the term 'governance' fear, however, that the promotion of 'governance' as a model condones the tendencies to offload areas of government activity back onto citizens, and to develop more or less formal ways in which privileged groups, usually from the business sector, are able to influence how public agendas are set and public funds spent, escaping the constraints of accountability which operate within formal government arenas (John and Cole 2000). Elander and Blanc (2000) summarise this critique in a number of 'democratic' concerns. A first issue is transparency. New forums for decision-making are often not as open and transparent in the way that traditional government decision-making is now expected to be. Real decision-making often takes place behind closed doors. Second, partnerships and other 'new' governance forums for decision-making often do not include any mechanisms for democratic accountability. Third, new forms of partnership tend to build fortresses around themselves, i.e. some groups and interests are excluded from participation (see the discussion of UK policy and practice in Chapter 6). Elander and Blanc conclude that governance does not replace government. Rather, it is complementary and should be subsumed under representative democracy. John and Cole provide empirical support for this conclusion in their account of the significant role of formal urban government bodies in France and England in initiating projects and building networks. In parallel, critics from the business community have argued that the contemporary transformation in governance arrangements may lead to economic ineffectiveness. Decision-making processes will be more time-consuming. Conflicting interests will make the development of strategies and detailed decision-making process harder to handle. The likelihood of implementation will be reduced (Stoker 2000a). In other words, transaction costs for business are increased.

These discussions about emerging modes of governance and their normative consequences reflect significant struggles occurring in reality (see, for example, Chapters 6 and 7). However, our interest in this book is to explore transformations in governance and their consequences for the 'steering capacity' of collective actors concerned with urban management and development. In the context of transformations, established modes and models are dissolving and the outlines of new ones are hard to see and may never reach sufficient stability to be identified. As Offe argued in the 1970s, the enterprise of governing involves a continuous search for ways of reconciling inherently contradictory forces (Offe 1977). This is amply illustrated in recent empirical analyses of governance change (see for example John and Cole 2000, Healey, de Magalhães et al. 2001, forthcoming, MacLeod 1999, Raco 1999). These reveal a complex picture of change and continuity, operating at different scales and different speeds. When comparisons are made between one situation and another, it becomes clear that the particular mixtures in each place are highly contingent on specific institutional histories and geographies. What 'patterns' arise are the contingent consequence of the interaction between broader driving forces affecting many places and local specificities. Standing back, and focusing the optic on the driving forces, it is possible to make some generalisations about the 'patterning power' of particular forces, such as economic globalisation and the de-centring of the welfare state model. Much of the reality discussed in this book illustrates processes of 'dis-integration' of formerly taken-for-granted ways of thinking (discourses) and ways of doing things (practices), the experience of 'de-centring'. But it also shows all kinds of inheritances from the past which live on in memory and organisational routines, as well as efforts to invent and re-compose relations in new ways. What 'patterning' will result from these active invention processes can only be 'read' through analysis of situated relations as they evolve. It is here that the concept of 'milieu' has its attraction. It suggests the ethnographic understanding of a 'habitus' (Bourdieu 1977) or dwelt-in world (Ingold 2000, Chapter 10), involving culturally-situated dwelling in interacting material and mental worlds, without any connotation of 'coherence' in governance relations.

We therefore maintain our use of 'governance' as a general heuristic term to encompass all these modes and models. It represents a wider optic with which to explore the transformations we are interested in (Crouch et al. 2001). Used in this way, it serves to highlight processes as much as organisations (Pierre 1998); active agency as much as formal structures; and roles, relationships and mobilisation capacity (the power to act) as much as power over resources and regulations. It explicitly recognises that the activities of formal government are never hermetically sealed from the outside world. Therefore analysis needs to focus overtly on the complex relations between formal government and the wider society. "Governance is about ... how the challenge of collective action is met and the issues and tensions associated with this shift in the pattern of governing" (Stoker 1998, pp 34-35). It is about how collective actors form within contexts which involve both forming collective actors from diverse local groups and about the relation between these, economic interests and government bodies operating at various scales (Le Galès 1998).

Our interest in this book is to finds ways of getting an analytical and evaluative 'handle' on these processes of decentering and re-composing the relations of governance as they are evolving. This requires a focus on *dynamics*, change through time; a focus on *relations*, the links, gaps and boundaries in the social relations, which embed governance processes in the wider society; and a focus on *capacity*, what particular configurations of governance relations can do and what they seem unable to accomplish. The evaluative interest is then at two levels. The first is about 'what makes a difference' to material outcomes, to cultural identity and to the qualities of the 'milieu'. The second is a normative concern about who gets to benefit, and how far the evolution of governance processes seem likely to sustain or to restrict the opportunities available for human flourishing in civil society.

Place and Territory as a Focus of 'Integration'

The welfare state settlement, which was so influential on governance forms in Western Europe in the second part of the twentieth century, divided up the work of government into functional sectors, linked to the world of business and work, the world of home and housing and the world of welfare, particularly education, health and social benefits. Complex policy communities were built up around the delivery of services in these sectors. The role of 'local' government was to co-ordinate these services within localities. 'Town planning' had a role in this task, developing and safe-guarding 'place quality' as a 'local amenity'. Whereas national governments dealt in important issues of the delivery of economic stability, education and health, local governments were expected to deliver local services and amenities. In this hierarchical conception, people were sliced up into a range of different needs to be catered for by service departments and delivery agencies, while place qualities were largely considered as marginal concerns of government.

Always a difficult task, the delivery of this 'local amenity' became acutely difficult in countries such as England, with highly centralist government and politics, accentuated in the later part of the century by the moves to privatise local government services and reduce the role of local government overall. This resulted in persistent criticism, not only of the neglect of place quality, but of the failure to deliver services in ways relevant to citizens in their daily life experiences. It is partly in this context that the idea of 'joined-up' thinking has been promoted (Wilkinson and Appelbee 1999, Social Exclusion Unit 1998), particularly as regards the delivery of programmes to avoid social exclusion (see Chapters 6 and 8). In the wider context of the economic importance of the qualities of milieux, these difficulties become more serious. Although less centralised, many other European countries have experienced sectorally-organised government and face similar problems. The resultant critique has highlighted a number of issues. Failure to attend to the relations of programmes in places produces inefficiencies and blindness to potential synergies. A study of poor neighbourhoods in eight EU countries concluded that the effectiveness of localised services is not only a question of *what* is delivered. Of equal or greater importance is *how* and by *whom* programmes are delivered, that is, the mechanisms of governance in the areas concerned. Services were often poorly matched to the needs assessed as most urgent by the residents. Often service provision created dependence rather than independence, and to large extent residents were regarded as passive consumers rather than active subjects (Allen, Cars et al. 2000). Similar critiques of the failure of sectorally-organised government to be responsive to need, to operate in co-ordinated ways and to promote the 'city' within a perceived geography of competing cities and regions in a global context have been made by analysts of the relations between government activity and economic interests (Leitner and Sheppard 1998).

Where things happen thus becomes important for governance efforts directed at both economic and social support. The 'place' focus brings attention to all the relations which transect a particular geographical space, the patterning of nodes and peripheries in each relation, the extent to which they link to each other, the significance this gives to geographical spaces which become nodes of intersection, and the values that are placed on the qualities of these 'locales'. In this conception, it is no longer possible to allocate concern with place quality to a particular level of government. Just as the relations which transect a geographical area may have all kinds of spatial dimensions, from very localised time-space relations to those with a global reach, so in most geographical areas, many relations of governance are manifest, even in the smallest community development initiative (Healey 1998b). This means that parallel conceptions of nested hierarchies of place and of levels of government need to be replaced with multiscale conceptions of governance relations (McLeod 1999).

A number of tendencies have fostered this shift of attention to recognise the importance of place quality and its manifestation in all kinds of governance relations. One is the increasingly acute crises of co-ordination in government programmes, with ever more strident calls for attention to improved linkages between sectorally-separated areas of activity (Pierre and Peters 2000).

Behind the co-ordination problem lies the recognition already referred to that 'geography matters' to economic performance (Storper 1997, Boddy 1999, Kotkin 2000). In some analyses, 'place quality' is treated as an asset, made up of attributes such as labour market quality, research and development capacity, physical infrastructures, social networks and governance quality. Some places seem to have attributes which foster economic innovation or attract inward investment. Others do not (Putnam 1993, Belussi 1996, Asheim 1996, Amin and Thrift 1994).

The territorial innovation literature however argues that what is important about innovation capacity is not just the collection of assets but the way they mesh together to produce a 'culture', a way of thinking and going on (Moulaert 2000). Place-focused governance thus pays attention to both the specific material assets of localities and to the cultures of places and the way people use these as cultural resources in identity formation (Madanipour, Hull et al. 2001).

The role of a focus on place quality in collective mobilisation is also promoted by the environmental movement, particularly that associated under the banner of 'sustainable development' (Haughton 1999, Low, Gleeson et al. 2000). This has not only generated an additional moral dimension of environmental care across the spectrum of government. It has also favoured forms of politics based on local grassroots action, which intensify political mobilisation in defence of environmental qualities and relations. Detached from much of the formal world of politics and government, citizens increasingly deploy their often considerable knowledge and skill to challenge and object to proposals for changes in localities. The resultant vigorous politics of defence of place then generates strategic problems for those pursuing sectoral agendas. The quality of place has also been a focus for stakeholders representing cultural activities and preservation of the built environment. The promotion of cultural activities is increasingly incorporated in the policy agendas of urban economic strategies, on the premise that a rich array of such activities attracts companies because their workers enjoy the facilities, and in turn provide a source of economic dynamism. An issue of increasing interest is how to generate collective action to promote cultural development and preservation (Ebert, Gnad et al. 1992, Du Gay 1997).

All these forces combine to emphasise aspects of place quality, as a new integrative force in re-configuring and re-composing policy agendas and relations for collective action within the urban arena. The focus of mobilisation may be a single objective (to obtain a health centre or resist a road project) or a broad feeling for the promotion and defence of milieux. It may involve a few activists or a broad alliance. It may be promoted from the grass roots or initiated from municipal or national government. But such efforts all convert place, whether neighbourhood or city, locale or region, into a significant node of action in urban politics. They create a 'voice' for place. The increasing visibility and leverage of the politics of place is evident in initiatives to give more attention to cities and the urban in the European Union and in the national policies of member states. It is manifest in city governments' attempts to re-make and re-express themselves to their citizens and the outside world, and in recent emphases in public policy on integrated area development (Mouleart 2000) and strategic spatial frameworks (Healey, Khakee et al. 1997, Salet and Faludi 2000).

However, these ambitions for place-focused governance still run against the grain of the institutional discourses and practices inherited from the welfare state settlement. They also challenge the position of national governments as the prime arena for articulating both urban policy agendas and the institutional design of structures, competences and processes. Any transformation towards a more 'place-focused' governance is therefore likely to involve all kinds of struggles with inherited centres of power over agenda formation and with competing initiatives for transforming governance. The cases in the following Chapters provide ample illustration of these struggles.

Our objective in this book is not merely to observe how these struggles play out. We are also interested in the capacities of the governance relations available in different localities to mobilise themselves to give 'voice' to valued place qualities and to act *for* their neighbourhoods, locales, cities and regions, however understood. This leads to our concern with the institutional resources for urban governance and its interaction with local social milieux as this relation evolves and changes through time.

The Capacity for Collective Action at the Urban Scale

We have argued that creating the capacity for collective action in a dynamic, dispersed power context is a challenging enterprise. The formation of urban regimes is one possible response to this challenge. Urban regimes as discussed in the US literature are informal but yet relatively stable coalitions, typically including both public and private actors (Stone 1989). Stoker notes that a crucial role of the regime is to "blend" capacities between actors involved in governance to achieve a governing task. Thus, regimes are given their character by who is included or excluded (Stoker 2000a). But whether or not sufficient stability and integration in urban governance relations is present to constitute a regime is an empirical question, relating to the institutional histories of particular places. Research in the UK suggests that 'urban' regimes as such have been difficult to establish in a context of centralised and sectoralised government (see for example, Painter and Goodwin 2000).

Another possible organisational response to collective action is create a range of 'partnerships'. There is no legal or clear-cut definition of partnerships. The concept is used in various ways depending on the issue addressed, and the legal and other contexts discussed (Bailey 1995, Peters 1998). Peters develops a set of characteristics that 'appear' to be involved in most partnership arrangements. These include a mix of public and private actors, that partners are principals, i.e. capable of bargaining on their own behalf, that the partnership is an enduring relationship, that each partner 'brings something' to the partnership and finally that partners have some shared responsibility for the outcomes of their activities (Peters 1998). But whether a 'partnership' arrangement is capable of mobilising collective action and who gets involved in it are matters which can only be resolved empirically (see the example in Chapter 3). Attempts at generating 'partnership', as with the promotion of 'urban regimes', also raise difficult questions of inclusion and exclusion, legitimacy and transparency (Stoker 2000a, Pierre 1998, Riley 1999). Nor is there any necessary reason why partnerships *in* cities should have the capacity to act *for* cities.

In times of economic, social and political stability, the scope and structure of formal arrangements for collective action may take on a taken-for-granted stability, a 'naturalness' which precludes challenge. This is what Stone describes as a 'regime' in his study of Atlanta. In contrast, in the contemporary European context, everything seems to be up for challenge and in a less coherent and unified way. In such fluid and fragmented contexts, with diffuse pressures to change coming from many directions, impacting on different groups within cities in diverse ways, is it possible for collective action programmes to be articulated and sufficient support for them to cohere to enable any kind of such action at the urban level? Maybe an array of semi-autonomous partnerships is a reasonable reflection of this 'no-one in charge' situation. In this context, how can 'cities' become collective actors? How can the capacities of their governance relations create a 'voice' and 'identity', with meaning and relevance for the lives of citizens, for local businesses, for ecological relations, and with a capacity to position the city and its complex layers of relationships within a wider economic, social, political and environmental landscape? What kind of 'intelligence' is embodied in such collective action capacity and what sorts of relations bind those involved to the wider social relations within and beyond an urban area?

These kinds of questions raise the possibility that governance *as such* at the urban level, especially for large cities and urban regions, is unachievable in the contemporary context. If so, there is no collective actor 'for' the city, merely an amalgam of collective actors working in and across cities and regions, sometimes in partnership but often in conflict with, or ignorance of, each other. Some analysts suggest that this is the reality in British cities in recent years (John and Cole 2000). Yet the capacity of urban governments to focus on and develop the qualities of a territory or place, on the multiple dimensions of the 'milieux' in which citizens, firms and ecosystems co-exist, is asserted in many contemporary literatures, as we discuss below. These qualities relate not merely to the material assets of neighbourhoods, cities, rural settlements and territories. They relate also to the significance of place/locale in people's sense of identity, in terms of the cultural and material meaning of the 'habitus' of daily life (Bourdieu 1977). From the literatures on regional economic innovation, on health and welfare and on the management of environmental qualities, there is an increasing emphasis on the qualities of 'milieux', a concept which combines the material and mental experience of place, and the role of governance relations in sustaining and promoting these qualities (Amin and Hausner 1997, Moulaert 2000, Hassink 1997). Some areas seem to bask in milieux sustained by positive governance capacities. Other areas suffer from governance relations which are stuck in a past which no longer has such significance for local economies and civil societies. Some governance relations act to privilege only strong economic interests. Others are so riven with conflict and tension that concerted governance action is difficult to achieve. In this book, through the concept of institutional capacity, we seek to explore not merely what urban governance capacities there are in particular places, but how positive capacities evolve and the role of the structures and practices of governance in promoting them. In this way, we seek to move beyond simple typologies of regime and partnership when describing instances of urban governance and their capacity to act *for* the city.

Institutionalist Analysis and Institutional Capacity

Institutional Capacity and Social Milieux

We have argued so far that governance capacity 'matters' for economic, socio-cultural and ecological reasons. We have sought to show that this capacity is to be found in the complex relations through which collective action is mobilised and organised to give 'voice' to particular qualities of places which some people desire or seek to defend, from ease of transport movement, to protection of valued habitats, to delivery of health care in convenient ways for busy people or helpful ways to ethnic minorities, to the re-visioning of their city in the minds and lives of citizens, to opportunities for young people, and to promotion of an urban ambience attractive to dynamic innovators in the expanding 'high tech' industries. We have emphasised that these relations encompass not merely the arenas and practices associated with formal government but are to be found in all kinds of niches and networks in the social worlds which co-exist in urban areas. Governance capacity is thus embedded in complex local milieux whilst interacting with all kinds of external influences. It is not something which is a fixed asset, but evolves through time.

This implies that urban governance capacity varies through time and across space. This also means that transformations in governance have variable trajectories and are to an extent continuously ongoing projects. Governance relations transform as broader structuring forces interact with local histories and specificities. Capacities to act are moulded by the ongoing efforts of active agency in maintaining, re-interpreting and building new dimensions to these capacities.

The phenomenon of governance capacity is sometimes referred to as the social capital of places (Putnam 1993). Other analysts equate Putnam's work with the concept of territorial milieux (Malmberg and Maskell 1997). However, in our view these uses collapse all attributes and relations of places into a single phenomenon. Our preference is to separate out from a broad conception of 'social milieux' a specific set of relations focused around the performance of governance. We use the term institutional capacity, which we have developed from the work of Amin and Thrift (1995) on the wider relations underpinning the economic performance of so-called industrial districts (Healey 1997, Healey 1998b). Our interest is in how, as governance relations evolve, the store of institutional capacity in localities shapes that evolution, and new capacities are built. We are thus not merely interested in the 'path dependency' of transformations, to use North's concept (North 1990). We are interested in the extent to which pathways can be changed by the creative work of active agency engaged in collective action processes. Analytically, our concern is to develop ways of identifying and evaluating institutional capacity-building processes. Normatively, our interest is in ways of promoting institutional capacities which are desirable from the point of view of distributive justice and human flourishing.

Our focus on institutional capacity parallels an emerging focus in the British local governance literature, which refers to the comparative qualities of governance capacity (John and Cole 2000), and, developing from a starting point in regulation theory, to local regulatory capacity (Hall 1998, Painter and Goodwin 2000). We expand on our own use of these concepts later in this Chapter. To introduce this discussion, we locate our approach within the broad wave of ideas associated with the *new institutionalist* interpretations of economic and social relations. In the final section of this Chapter, we outline our own approach to the analysis of institutional capacity and institutional capacity building processes in urban governance, within a broadly 'constructivist' institutionalist frame of reference.

Analysing Governance Relations

Clearly, the kind of understanding implied by the above is a long way from traditional accounts of the formal structures and procedures of government, though these have an importance in shaping governance capacity. It approaches governance activity as a relational process, far from the kind of input-output system with a 'black box' in between described by the influential political scientist, David Easton (Easton 1965). Nor is our understanding encompassed readily in models of government and politics as constructed by Machiavellian struggles between individual actors and organisations to capture control of the machinery of government, though some governance contexts may encourage such struggles (Flyvbjerg 1998). Nor again is it expressed easily in the language of rational choice or game theory, which describes episodes of governance in terms of the playing out of interest conflicts on relatively stable and well-known gameboards (Dowding, Dunleavy et al. 2000, Scharpf 1997).

Our interest is in how governance capacity emerges, shifts, changes and transforms, and in doing so creates or reduces possibilities to mobilise and maintain a voice as a collective actor for issues to do with qualities of life in places. However, accomplishing collective action is not a goal in itself. When reconsidering governance arrangements, it is necessary to consider the purposes of such activity and its legitimacy. Governance processes are in any case complex and contain the potential for multiple fractures and conflicts. To analyse transformations in this context, we therefore need analytical tools which focus on how structures and procedures, and the practices which build up around them, are made more fluid; on how the inside of the 'black box' of governance practices interacts with the wider context in a process of mutual constitution and transformation, not a linear process of agenda formation, output and impact; on how particular modes of doing governance build up in particular places and times, with their routines and rituals, and how these are changed, rather than assuming that a specific mode or way of doing politics is 'natural'. Similarly, we need to be able to see the complex interactions between the playing out of broader forces, such as changes in economic processes and relations, or in people's lifestyles and aspirations, and the diverse ways these are expressed and 'represented' in urban governance processes.

This implies an analytic approach which focuses on process dynamics, that is, change in processes, practices and modes of governance through time. It needs to focus on the interactions between those involved in governance as much as on the individual players. It needs to consider how values, preferences, interests and ideas about place qualities are constituted in these interactions and translated into policy agendas around which actors congeal to mobilise as some kind of collective actor. It should be capable of recognising the complex interplay of active agency and broader forces which provide opportunities for, and constrain, what specific governance projects can achieve. It requires an awareness of the potentially multiple social worlds which shape the ways of thinking and ways of acting of those who get involved in governance activity and their connection to the social milieux of urban life in particular times and places. It should recognise the diversity of the time-space relations which are brought into play in governance activity and the many arenas which act as nodal points in governance relations.

We thus conceive of urban governance processes as a complex and conflictual flow of multiple social interactions through time, shaped by their histories, creatively adjusting to the flowing and changing context, each seeking to create and maintain particular imageries about what needs collective attention and for whom, and to mobilise to promote those evolutions that seem promising and close off those that seem threatening, in the process giving rise to, and re-shaping alliances and consensual projects.

There are many recent attempts to articulate analytical windows on urban governance processes which reflect some of these attributes. The major proponent of the urban regime approach, Clarence Stone, concludes that the outcome of governance should be understood by analysing the composition and policy of the governing (regime) coalition (Stone 1989). We share many of Stone's concerns, particularly his emphasis on the changing relations between urban governance elites and the shifting social context. However, given our focus on change through time and transformation, the enterprise of analysing whether regimes exist and what their characteristics are focuses too much on particular patterns and over-emphasises the visible dominant forces. Our concern is more with the dynamics of transformation and the multiple potential patterns which emerge, come to flourish or get closed off in transformation processes.

We also share some common emphases with work in urban political economics, with its emphasis on the playing out of structuring forces in localities (Lauria 1997, Fainstein 2000), with recent attempts to undertake local studies within the framework of regulation theory (Jessop 2000, Painter 1995, Painter and Goodwin 2000), and the analysis in politics and policy analysis of policy implementation processes (Sabatier and Jenkins-Smith 1993).

All these evolving strands of work have provided feeders into the broad wave of conceptualising which these days tends to co-habit under the banner of 'new institutionalism'. As Gualini argues in Chapter 2, 'institutional change is notoriously the crux of institutionalist analysis'. To this we would add that so too is the appreciation that social actions of any kind need to be understood in the context in which they are embedded. However, the range of contributions within this wave is diverse, both in terms of contributing disciplines and in terms of epistemologies (Peters 1999, Gualini 2001). Within institutional economics, the trajectory of 'transaction cost analysis' associated with the work of Oliver Williamson (Williamson 1996) seeks to draw the institutional context into conventional economic analysis and to give much greater attention to the time dimension of decision-making (Scharpf 1997, Alexander 1995).

In contrast, contributions from interpretive policy analysis, communicative planning theory and actor-network theory adopt a much more relational and social-constructivist position, which shifts analytic attention from actors-with-interests to the way relations are formed and sustained through time. It emphasises the networks and frames of reference within which the identities of those involved in collective action are constructed, repertoires of action developed and material tasks accomplished. It focuses on the social processes of identity formation and the social practices of activity performance. It highlights the importance of interactive practices in framing ideas and modes of thought (discourses) and of culturally formed social actions which shape organisational routines and bodily practices. It emphasises the social processes through which material realities and mental constructs are formed (Healey 1999, Hajer and Wagenaar, forthcoming).

On the way between these two epistemologically distinct contributions, the range encompasses North's discussions of the 'path-dependency' of economic activity in particular places on its institutional history (North 1990), Putnam's identification of the way historically-formed social capital shapes contemporary governance responses to external forces (Putnam 1993), and the discussion in European regional development literature of the significance of local social relations on the business performance of urban regions (see above). Institutionalist analyses are by now well-established in organisational analysis (Powell and Di Maggio 1991), in political science and policy analysis (Hall and Taylor 1996, Scharpf 1997, Muller and Surel 1998, Peters 1999, Gualini 2001, Hajer and Wagenaar forthcoming), and in planning theory (Alexander 1995, Healey 1999). Our own approach, and the contributions in this book, tend more to the social-constructivist position, though moderated with an appreciation of both the interaction between the material (struggles over resource allocation) and the mental (struggles over identity), and the interplay between structuring forces and active agency.

A Relational Understanding of Governance Processes

Research on governance conducted from this viewpoint tends to focus on micro-social relations. It is sometimes criticised for paying too much attention to the world of agency and too little to the wider context, and the structuring forces which shape the world of agency. We counter this by asserting the linkage between structuring forces and active agency, drawing on Giddens' structuration theory (Giddens 1984). This argues that what are experienced as abstracted structuring forces are formed through continual interaction with the worlds of agency. Agency relations simultaneously shape and are shaped by structuring forces. These forces, powerful though they be, are but accretions of past relations, expressed through resource flows, regulatory principles, discourses and practices which become accepted, taken-for-granted and embedded in the everyday worlds of micro-social relations. This provides a way of understanding the social processes through which Putnam's 'social capital' gets formed and 'sedimented' in the social relations of a locale and how institutional capacities evolve.

This approach complements a relational view of social interaction with a relational view of structuring dynamics. It situates the analysis of social relations within the context of structuring dynamics, as well as in specific times and places. What happens in any instance is portrayed as the outcome of multiple interactions, operating at many different spatial scales and at different speeds. In any interactive instance, maybe the development of a new policy, or the work of an urban regeneration partnership, a range of geographical and institutional referents may be called up as actions are designed which will impact on particular localities. Comparisons are made with other places and other ways of doing things. Similarly, past and future are called into play, as symbols of cultural memory to be conserved or visions to be promoted. Instances of governance action, in this relational viewpoint, reveal the complex interplay of multiple forces, made active through micro-social relations which themselves generate processes of invention in response to the complexity of situations in which actors find themselves.

This kind of analysis emphasises the potential for multiple conflicts operating at different levels, from specific visible issues, to the more hidden struggles 'behind the scenes' and the deeper struggles between culturally-embedded assumptions about what should be done, by whom and how (Lukes 1974, Schon and Rein 1994). In these struggles, different relations and referents are mobilised, each having differential power both internally within networks and between networks. As Dyrberg (1997) argues, power can be conceived both as the power to control the actions of others and as the power to act, to build a business park, or deliver a home-help service, organise a transport system or find a self-organising way of managing a neglected public space. In the social relations of governance processes, these two forms of power are often in obvious tension. Politicians and officials fear to let go their role in regeneration partnerships (see Chapter 3). What analytical tools might help in describing and evaluating emergent governance relations and power dynamics and the impact of governance initiatives on emerging trajectories of material urban development?

Building Institutional Capacities and Transforming Governance Trajectories

Finding ways of 'capturing' these evolving, dynamic, complexly-interweaving relational processes in analyses of how and how far transformation in urban governance is taking place presents formidable challenges. Yet such analyses are important to help those involved in attempts to shift the trajectories of their cities and build new governance capacities to 'see' new foci for their policy agendas and mobilisation activities. In this book, we explore the leverage of the concept of institutional capacity and institutional capacity-building as an analytical tool in this context.

The previous section emphasised the broad social dynamics within which the concept of institutional capacity could be formulated. Amin and Thrift, in their work on the qualities of economic milieux, have provided more specificity to the idea. They were concerned with how local governance could get to play a role in reducing the vulnerability of local economies, societies and environments to damaging external pressures while at the same time promoting local economic health and quality of life. Drawing on a rich Italian literature, they argued that localities which could deliver this beneficial nexus were characterised by four factors: a plethora of civic associations, a high level of interaction between social groups, coalitions which crossed individual interests, and a strong sense of common purpose. These four factors generated a quality of 'institutional thickness', or richness, within which firms and households were embedded, and an institutional capability to mobilise to sustain supportive conditions for both (Amin and Thrift 1995, p 101). Other researchers have pointed out that the four factors do not necessarily lead to the beneficial trajectories which Amin and Thrift seek, as they can be found associated with dominatory local elites and with failures in economic innovation.

These ideas link to the rapidly expanding but diffuse literature focused on trust, social networks and social capital (Wilson 1997). These terms are being used in the literature within different conceptual perspectives and epistemologies, reflecting the broad sweep of the current interest in institutionalist approaches and social 'embedding' discussed above. Our own preference is to maintain an analytical distinction between the qualities of social relations (the nature of bonds of trust and norms in the networks which link people together) and the knowledge resources which flow around and are developed through these relations. Following Innes, Gruber et al. (1994), we distinguish between three forms of resources which are deployed in interactive governance contexts: intellectual capital (knowledge resources), social capital (trust and social understanding which build up through face to face encounter) and political capital (the capacity to act collectively). We use the term 'institutional capital' to cover all three forms. How then is this institutional capital created? Innes' work shows the way her three forms of capital are generated through particular kinds of consensus-building process (Innes, Gruber et al. 1994, Innes and Booher 1999). This has led to an interest in evaluating the way in which such governance initiatives create new knowledge resources, relational resources and mobilisation capabilities and how far these governance innovations are likely to be sustained (Healey 1998b, Healey, de Magalhães et al. 1999, Wilkinson and Appelbee 1999). We elaborate on this approach as applied in a case study in Chapter 3.

In this book, therefore, we seek to make a contribution to understanding the complex processes of transformation being experienced in urban governance across Europe. We are motivated by the recognition that the qualities of urban governance capacity have significant impacts on the economic, socio-cultural and biospheric qualities of cities and regions and that, among these qualities, the ability to articulate a collective voice for qualities of place and territory is an important resource. Institutional capacity, as we use the term in this book, may thus be considered as a 'public good', to use the language of the economists, or, from policy analysis, a major part of the collective 'infrastructure' of city life.

To understand the nature of this capacity, we have argued from a position within the broad range of 'new' institutionalist analysis, and we hope to show how this helps to get some kind of analytical leverage on the issues at stake. However, we also believe that the focus on governance capacity, as defined in the previous paragraphs, implies re-defining urban policy agendas. In Chapter 11, we attempt to develop the policy and practice implications of our analyses.

Note

[1] Others have taken up the game-like qualities of urban politics, making links to game theory in economic analysis (see Scharpf 1997).

2 Institutional Capacity Building as an Issue of Collective Action and Institutionalisation: Some Theoretical Remarks

ENRICO GUALINI

Introduction

This Chapter addresses the issue of institutional capacity building according to two basic assumptions. First, the constitution of institutional capacity is considered as sharing the same basic theoretical and practical challenges as the constitution of forms of collective action. Second, a specific critical dimension of the constitution of collective action, affecting its effectiveness and ability to sustain itself as well as its openness to adjustment and evolution, is identified in its dynamics of institutionalisation and institutional change.

Both assumptions arise from a critical confrontation with debates on the essence of democracy and the public sphere in late-modern democracies and on their reflections in concepts such as 'civil society', 'social capital', or 'institutional capacity', which paradigmatically frame discourses on the prospects of 'democratic governance'. My position is that a commitment to institutional capacity building should refrain from an a-critical, heuristically poor, and definitely ideological reification of what is, in fact, the problem to be explored. In this sense, the essence of the concepts addressed may be identified with the processes by which, through action and discourse, the 'public sphere', the meaning itself of what is 'public', is renewed in everyday practices, rather than with a pre-condition for a democratic public life. Conversely, such a commitment should not overshadow, but rather overtly address the tension between normative inspiration and analytical consistency inherent in these notions in an experimental way, in a perspective of action-research.

First, the terms of this vocabulary of policy analysis and political debate (governance, social capital, and institutional capacity) will be briefly examined in order to recognise the questions they address and why they are currently attracting our interest. This will lead to a critical appraisal of the heuristic potential of these notions. Finally, a tentative proposal on how this potential may be operationalised in a fertile strategy of inquiry is presented.

Social Capital, Governance and Democracy

> Democracy is a 'translation circle'. Should the translation stop, so would democracy end. Unless it is to betray its essence, *democracy cannot understand any of its translations as completed and no more amenable to negotiation*. A democratic society may hence be recognised by the fact that it can never fully overcome the suspicion that its task is not yet complete – that it has not yet become democratic enough emphasis added (Bauman 1999, p 2).

Discourse on democracy is beset today with ambiguous concepts. These have often developed as derivatives of preceding ones, like the concept of 'community'. As old concepts have exhausted their explanatory viability, new concepts emerge in the social sciences which inherit a similar contradictory tension between an analytical ambition and a socio-ethical orientation. According to a metaphor taken from the vocabulary of physics, they represent 'tracks', observable trajectories taken by (conceptual) particles after the disintegration of a (conceptual) nucleus (Bagnasco 1999). As such, while often analytically weak, if not dubious, they nevertheless highlight the value of their normative bias in 'imagining possible worlds'.

Social capital is such a concept. Research on social capital expresses a basic concern for the re-construction of conditions for democratic life, a concern already central in Coleman's comprehensive attempt to understand the viability of social bonds in the framework of increasingly differentiating processes of socialisation (Coleman 1990). It is the expression of a fundamental quest for the sense of democracy and for the effectiveness of democratic processes, for an understanding of 'how democracy works' and of what 'makes democracy work' in a changing, challenging governance environment. Comments on its normative overtones (Edwards and Foley 1998) and on its theoretical shortcomings (Levi 1996) – particularly in its most popular version (Putnam 1993) – cannot therefore deny that, precisely through their normative commitment, notions like social capital raise important, unavoidable questions.

Social capital is a concept which has become one of the most paradigmatic and popular expressions of a theoretical attitude towards a reversal of traditional institutionalist assumptions, interpreting institutions as *constraints to action,* as *regulatory principles* or as *persistent models* of behaviour.[1] Its strategy of inquiry is rather defined by a bottom-up bias.

Social capital, in Putnam's terms, is a crucial condition for the viability and effectiveness of institutions. It refers:

> to the norms and networks of civil society that lubricate co-operative action among both citizens and their institutions. *Without adequate supplies of social capital* – that is, without *civic engagement, healthy community institutions, norms of mutual reciprocity,* and *trust* – *social institutions falter* (Putnam 1998, p v; emphasis added).

It is, as such, a 'public good', the erosion of which jeopardises institutional life. Its ingredients are seen as the conditions for institutional performance and for the reproduction and maintenance of institutions, as explanatory variables of institutional life.

Social capital thus ideally addresses a reinterpretation of the role of politics in organising society and in shaping the social fabric: a crucial issue, in face of the decay of dominant modes of regulation and of the reframing of the role of institutions in democratic life. In this context, investigation of social capital is apparently very much akin to questions of 'democratic governance' (March and Olsen 1995).

As with the concept of social capital, the notion of *governance* is set in a tension between its analytical and its normative stance (see Chapter 1). It does not only respond – despite its polisemy and imprecision – to a need for new conceptualisations of emerging trends. It also bears reference to the need for redefining conditions for effectiveness and legitimacy of governing activity in a voluntarist and normative perspective, and hence for innovating institutions in the face of shifting state-society relations. Thus, as has been noted, '[i]n 'governance', ideas of leading, steering and directing are recognizable, but without the primacy accorded to the sovereign state' (Le Galès 1998, pp 494-495). Governance studies have been accordingly defined in general terms:

> as concerned with the resolution of (para-)political problems (in the sense of problems of collective goal-attainment or the realisation of collective purposes) in and through specific configurations of governmental (hierarchical) and extra-governmental (non-hierarchical) institutions, organisations and practices (Jessop 1995b, p 317).

In this perspective,

> the various approaches to governance share a rejection of the conceptual trinity of market-state-civil society which has tended to dominate mainstream analyses of modern societies (Jessop 1995b, p 310).

They also express a dissatisfaction with top-down explanations of the exercise of power and an interest in forms of socio-political co-ordination which broaden the field of traditional relations between the public and the private, constituting new forms of interdependencies in defining the public sphere. The shift from *government* to an enlarged conception of *governance* is marked by the demise of the alleged grounding of public action in traditional conceptions of institutional sovereignty (Kooiman 1993, Rhodes 1996).

Accordingly, governance signifies a governing practice in which the achievement of an effective coherence of public action is no more entrusted to an élite and to relatively homogeneous, self-centred political-administrative patterns of agency. It is rather the outcome of multi-level and multi-actor forms of co-ordination,

> the result of which, always uncertain, depends on the capacity of different public and private actors to define a space of common-sense, to mobilise expert forms of knowledge from different sources, and to establish forms of commitment and legitimisation of decisions which may operate in the meantime in the sphere of electoral politics and of the politics of problems (Muller and Surel 1998, pp 96-97).

The guiding function of formal governmental institutions is therefore set in a tension defined by both issues of effectiveness and legitimacy. The availability of formal-institutional structures that may 'link the various public and private-sector forces that can influence change and make their efforts coherent' (Harding 1997, p 293) cannot be anymore taken for granted. As their authority and effectiveness are being narrowed by growing factors of interdependence, though, their steering potential extends in terms of the ability of mobilising social stocks of knowledge and resources from a broad field of societal forces. Political regulation trespasses the boundaries of hierarchical settings and impinges on processes of restructuring of relationships between formal-institutional settings and social actors. The emergence of systems of governance may be thus interpreted as a process of the articulation, throughout different social sectors, of different modes of regulation (Le Galès 1998), the dynamics of institutionalisation of which are both path-dependent and situational.

The concept of governance hence tendentially assumes a radical interactionist stance, marking a paradigmatic shift from a traditional conception of relationships between the domain of political and administrative institutions and civic life. Its focus is rather on the potential dissolution of distinctions between the state and civil society: '[t]he state becomes a collection of inter-organisational networks made up of governmental and societal actors with no sovereign actor able to steer or regulate' (Rhodes 1996, p 666). The challenge for governing and managing action becomes that of *co-production*, of the pursuit of joint results from the activity and initiative of multiple social actors. While this questions the idea that civil society may be understood in a dualism with the sphere of the state, it points to new potentials for self-regulation. This goes as far as to render conceivable the possibility of 'governance without government', in specific spheres of activity, when effective even if not formally legitimated regulatory mechanisms are enacted.

Governance does not only entail new opportunities, though. As a reality, it also challenges our common understanding of democratic representation and accountability. Particularly through new forms of territorial governance, significant potentials for empowerment, but also new conflicts of representation and interests may develop Governance settings may thus resist democratically legitimated forms of control and regulation (Rhodes 1996), as well as reinforce structurally unequal distributions of opportunities (Painter and Goodwin 1995, Mayer 1995). They highlight, as such, our deficits in the renewal of democratic theory and practice.

Apparently, it is precisely in the face of such challenges to 'democratic governance' that applications of the concept of social capital reveal their shortcomings. The crux of the matter lies in a theoretical framework that often tends to assume institutions as a dependent variable. Criticism of social capital as an explanatory concept, particularly in the version put forward by Putnam (1993), is well known.[2] Basically, what we share with it is a criticism of the assumption of its components as *heritage*, *historical deposit*, *shared cultural background* (Bagnasco 2000), as a "native soil in which state structures grow rather than one shaped by patterns of [institution] building and [institutional] strategy" (Tarrow 1996, p 395).

As has been noticed, the main consequence of this bias is an inherently determinist pattern of causal explanation (Pasquino 1994, Tarrow 1996, Bagnasco 1994, 2000). The generalisation of microanalytical aspects (the 'symptomatology of civicness' (Tarrow 1996)), bypassing macro-phenomena like the dynamics of institutionalisation and institutional change, forces into a unitary interpretive framework phenomena which, on the contrary, grow out of increasingly differentiated forms of social structuration (Bagnasco 2000). Most significantly, this attitude focuses on a reified understanding of the informal dimensions of political and institutional life that ignores their rooting in the interplay of formal and informal social phenomena, and hence leads to a basic underestimation of the dimension of political action (Pasquino 1994).

This criticism appears the more significant under conditions of 'reflexive modernisation', as politics is increasingly understood as an activity that contributes to creating images for alternative collective ends and to defining collective identities, and as practices of collective sense-making within policy processes are recognised as a major challenge for 'democratic governance'. As the rationale of institutions themselves is changing, and as mechanisms for their production, maintenance, and effectiveness become increasingly uncertain and ambiguous[3] (March and Olsen 1989, 1995, Giddens 1994, Weick 1995), relationships between institutions and social capital become an issue of research in itself, rather than an explanatory variable.

Significant in this sense is a reappraisal of the heuristic potential of Coleman's agency-based paradigm of social capital (Bagnasco 2000). In Coleman's work (1990), the notion addresses the question of the relationship and the tension between formal and informal social structures, whereas social capital (in analogy with the idea of institutions as 'public goods of a second order') is intended as a by-product related to the development of (relatively) informal patterns of agency connected to (relatively) formal ones.

Social capital is hence understood as a relational notion, as a *resource for action* inherent in relational structures. It is therefore not intended as a specific object, as reified, but rather as a way to understand social phenomena in their making. In this sense, social capital is seen as an outcome of *generative matrixes* (like social rules, roles, and networks) that are formed as they are concretely activated by social actors through their interactions. It is intended as an *appropriable social structure* of a basically emergent kind, distinct from intentional constructs, and thus inherently embedded in its 'institutional conditions' of emergence, but never reducible to a static framework. Social capital is rather a relational asset that allows strategic actors to play in relative autonomy with the set of social relations available, 'shifting' from codes to codes rather than being defined by given, dominant cultural frameworks. In this sense, social capital (as culture) is for Coleman more an issue of on-going production than of reproduction.

Moving from Coleman's position (and perhaps beyond it) makes it possible to identify two important heuristic directions. His relational conception allows us to understand cultural constructs as creative means for the development of actors' identities and volitions (Swidler 1986, Melucci 1996a, 1996b). Furthermore, bridging micro- and macro-levels of analysis, such a relational conception helps towards understanding institutions as patterns of social agency affecting the definition of the actors' identities and volitions while being enacted, reproduced, and possibly redefined, through the actual interactions deployed in the pursuit of their strategic-communicative rationality.

Institutional Capacity Between Institution Building and Institutional Design

A few consequences may be drawn from this in terms of our understanding of *institutional capacity* and of its relationships with concepts such as social capital. If we in fact agree on the 'pluralist challenge' represented by social practices that are changing our policy-making agendas, and on the need to address issues of institutional effectiveness and legitimacy in terms of innovative responses to the challenges of 'democratic governance', then the issue of institutional capacity should be traced back to some fundamental questions concerning its nature and possibility of emergence. For this purpose, building on a reified conception of its conditions – as expressed by summary concepts like 'social capital' – may not be heuristically useful, as the shortcut they establish between explanatory function and normative aims may overlook the reflexive nature of the relationships between institutions and social action. The likely consequence is a failure in addressing the need for a renewed understanding of institutions themselves, of their making, and of the co-evolution between social dynamics and institutional rationales through concrete processes of institutionalisation.

The issue of institutional capacity should rather be defined as the subject of a dual strategy of inquiry. On the one hand, it should explore the processes through which the mobilisation and commitment of individuals, the contingent unity of meanings, and the constitution of collective forms of action may emerge and possibly develop into stable institutional patterns (Melucci 1987, 1988). As an operationalisable explanatory tool, a notion like social capital should be accordingly broken down into the social mechanisms which nurture and sustain new forms of collective action and define their trajectories of institutionalisation. In this sense, social capital – rather than as a premise or a condition – would be seen as a set of 'abilities' at play in building institutional capacity. The focus would be therefore on the processes of its formation rather than primarily on its persistence and reproduction, and emphasis would shift to its 'generative' dimension. We may call this a focus on the dimension of *institution building*.

On the other hand, a shift in focus towards the 'generative' conditions for institutional capacity should lead to address the mutually constitutive relationships between social capital and its institutional determinants. It should address, in other words, the *enabling* dimension of institutions, inquiring into "how [...] institutional arrangements affect the interpersonal, inter-temporal and substantive quality of policy choices", assuming institutions 'as configurations of organisational capabilities (assemblies of personal, material and informational resources that can be used for collective action) and of sets of rules or normative constraints structuring the interaction of participants in their deployment', creating 'the power to achieve purposes that would be unreachable in their absence' (Scharpf 1989, p 152). We may call this a focus on the dimension of *institutional design*.

Inquiring into the constitution of institutional capacity as an interplay between processes of institution building and institutional design is a task which should thus be addressed in a co-evolutive and incremental perspective, rather than within an analytical framework which defines their relationships in a linear, determinist way. Exploring this interplay, however, entails addressing the complex dimension of *institutional change*.

Institutional Capacity Building as an Issue of Collective Action

Institutional change is notoriously the crux of institutionalist analysis (Di Maggio and Powell 1991, Zucker 1991, Ostrom 1990, Meyer and Zucker 1989). Addressing institutional capacity building as an issue of collective action may thus offer a fertile theoretical inspiration as long as reference is made to contributions which – on the background of an assumption of the mixed motives which define the preferences and behaviours of social actors – have shifted from the traditional question of the (rational) motivational conditions (or the *why*) of collective action towards a new-institutionalist interpretation of the possibility and the dynamics of emergence (or the *how*) of collective action.

Whilst classic contributions traditionally subordinate the possibility of collective action, intended as an arrangement realising a stable balance between individual and collective benefits, to conditions which imply the adoption of exogenous solutions (i.e. external sources of enforcement in the framework of hierarchical or quasi-hierarchical settings) that is, the existence of social relationships of a communitarian kind (Olson 1965, Taylor 1987), new-institutionalist approaches stress the possibility of their endogenous development, focussing on their dynamics of emergence rather than on their static conditions. Accordingly, the issue of the constitution of collective action is reframed as a process constitutively related to a dynamics of *institutional change*.

Parting from paradigms of resource dependence or exchange, as well as from assumptions of self-interested actor rationality still dominant in game-theoretical models (Schelling 1978, Axelrod 1984), new-institutionalist theories share with recent trends in research on social movements and collective mobilisation (Melucci 1987, 1988, 1996b, Snow, Zurcher et al. 1980, Snow, Burke Rochford et al. 1986, Tarrow 1994) an interest in the symbolic-cognitive and cultural dimensions at play in the development of collective forms of action. At the core of this research stand processes of cognition, learning and identity formation and their interplay with institutional conditions in building structures of opportunity for collective action and in eventually developing trajectories of institutional change.

As a consequence of this strategy, new-institutionalist approaches (Ostrom 1990, 1992, 1994) introduce a shift in focus from social capital – intended as a necessary condition for initiating collective action – to the notion of 'institutional capital' and to 'the *process of accretion of institutional capital*' that results from 'the *incremental self-transformations* that frequently are involved in the *process of supplying institutions*' (Ostrom 1990, p 190; emphasis added).[4]

The explanatory focus for the emergence and self-sustainment of collective action turns hence to the relationship of co-production and co-evolution between social capital and institutional settings. What may be called *institutional capacity building* is seen as eventually emerging as a result of incremental, self-transforming and self-policing processes. In this conception, traditional exogenist perspectives on institution building – according to which it is the availability of appropriate institutional structures that sets the conditions for collective action – are reversed. Rather, collective action becomes an emergent, incremental outcome that may itself retro-act on the conditions for the constitution of new institutional settings, and thus originate processes of institutional change. Micro-constitutional forms of choice, based on available amounts of social capital, may be the origin of the constitution of forms of collective action and contribute to the establishment of macro-constitutional settings which, as 'second order public goods', retro-act on the possibility of their production and reproduction.

Appropriate solutions of the 'dilemmas of collective action' (in classic terms, the problem of the supply of adequate institutions, the problem of credible commitments, and the problem of mutual monitoring) may thus emerge as an incremental outcome of this process, based, again, on the sharing of information, on networking relationships, and on conditions of mutual trust built through on-going interactions.

Thus, social capital is reinforced by the very enactment of the conditions for collective action it contributes to define. It is not to be seen only as a starting condition for collective action. It is, at the same time, a by-product disposable for further action.[5] As such, social capital constitutes a 'public good' which, as it enters a dimension of institutionalisation, innovates in the institutional conditions for its production. It becomes a 'public good of a second order', allowing its enhancement, reproduction and self-sustance.

Institutional Capacity Building and the Constitution of the Public Sphere

The dynamics of institutional change and the forms of 'institutionalisation' become thus central for an understanding of the interplay between *institution building* and *institutional design*. Their process of mutual reinforcement reverses determinist assumptions on the primacy of structure on action, rather emphasising conditions (as well as constraints) for change that may be found at the threshold of their conjunction.

A significant aspect of this conception of institutional capacity building is a revision of its relationship to 'public goods'. Building institutional capacity implies focussing on the processes through which public goods are constituted. Constructivist and interactionist approaches to collective action develop an attitude towards processes of collective sense-making and learning that rejects both subjectivist or reified conceptions of social identity and its formation. The reference for such a conception is not given by either communitarian identities or instrumental definitions of social practices. Attention is rather directed towards the character of social and emergent constructs of commitments to collective action, and towards the cognitive dimensions of processes of interaction and exchange among reflective, knowledgeable actors.

In this perspective, the question of collective action is reframed in terms of the processes of the constitution of concrete systems of action. Concepts such as 'collective identity', or 'social capital', far from constituting a given pre-condition for action, point to "an interactive and shared definition which groups of individuals develop about the directions of action and the field of opportunities and constraints in which it is situated", where the terms "interactive and shared mean negotiated through an on-going process of enactment of relations which reciprocally bind the actors" (Melucci 1987, p 46). Local institutional settings appear thus as 'never static, nor self-stabilising, but being built continuously by a process of rational bargaining and negotiating', through which 'the categories of political discourse, the cognitive rules of the social order, are being negotiated'. In this perspective, 'the whole system of knowledge is seen to be a collective good that the community is jointly constructing' (Douglas

1986, p 29). Social behaviour requires accordingly to be interpreted in conjointly transactional and symbolic-cognitive terms, aiming at understanding "the role of cognition in forming the social bond" (p 19), that is, in constituting that particular 'public good' which is represented by the shared social acknowledgement of the nature of goods around which action develops (Giglioli 1989).[6]

Assuming a constructivist and interactionist stance leads hence to rethinking public goods in terms of the processes of constituting a sense of what is 'public'. The 'public' character of choices, in this perspective, depends on the process of situating policy issues 'in the sphere of social visibility', making them matters of public discourse on collective ends (De Leonardis 1997, p 174). The public character of goods is freed from features inherent to the good itself, rather emphasising the process-like relationship that the public establishes to it. In this sense, potentially everything may be assumed as a public good, and the concept may thus break the ethnocentric borders into which the opposition to markets has confined it, unveiling its cultural-political dimension (Douglas 1992, Malkin and Wildavsky 1992). A public sphere is thus given:

> in every social process in which goods and interests are developed and acknowledged as such to the extent they are shared, and in which action is constitutively interaction (De Leonardis 1997, p 169).

Institutional settings, accordingly, may be seen as 'public goods of a second order' (Ostrom 1990, De Leonardis 1990, Donolo 1997), mediating the production of public goods and acting as 'formative contexts' (Lanzara 1993) for public choices, as well as being re-generated through their very enactment, in a constitutive relationship between regulatory patterns and social action (Giddens 1984). In this conception,

> institutions do 'matter' not only as far as [...] they pre-define the framework for actors' choices, but also – and in the context of this reflection, even more – as they shape the inter-subjective texture of interactions and communications on matters of collective relevance (De Leonardis 1997, p 185).

Institutional Capacity Building in an Action-Research Perspective

The concept of institutional capacity building highlights the social-constructivist dimension of institutions, their rooting in the 'everyday life of the public sphere' (De Leonardis 1997). In a perspective of 'democratic governance', however, institutional capacity building faces multiple challenges. It faces the challenge of *pluralism*, as no statutory institutional settings within patterns of modern governance ensure stable conditions for accessing and influencing policy-making arenas. It faces the challenge of *mobilisation*, as the shared and negotiated definition of action orientations becomes the necessary means for possibly achieving the effectiveness of public policies. It faces the challenge of *collective sense-making*, as policy-making increasingly unveils as an activity which – beyond the mere definition of solutions – entails the social construction of problems, setting the discursive and symbolic-cognitive conditions for effectively and legitimately addressing possible solutions. It faces, finally, the challenge of *institutional change*, as the aim of the effectiveness of public policies is set in a tension between the resilience, the power of conformance of institutional settings, and their amenability to change, between a perspective of institutional persistence – or 'permanent failure' – and a perspective of *innovation* and *discovery*.

In coping with these challenges, the building of institutional capacity is continually set in a tension between the enabling and constraining features of the institutional dimensions of social practices. The pursuit of institutional capacity should consequently address such challenges through an experimental commitment.

Such a commitment entails a basic meta-theoretical assumption about institutional capacity building as a framework for action. In addressing the aims and possibilities of institutional capacity building, I have moved from observing the inherent tension between analytical attitudes and normative commitments that nurtures the vocabulary of 'democratic governance'. My own view is that the tension inherent in these notions is hermeneutically unsolvable. Rather, their usefulness resides in a coherent assumption of this tension, acknowledging the hermeneutical bond between the observer and its subject, and the impossibility of reducing the experiential dimension of agency to a categorisation of social phenomena (Crespi 1992, Emirbayer and Goodwin 1994).

The refinement of conceptual tools, in this sense, may become normatively meaningful as far as it is consistent with an experimental commitment to action and change. Such a commitment calls for a critical-pragmatist perspective of inquiry, inspired by principles of action-research (Peters and Robinson 1984, Marshall and Peters 1985, Whyte 1991).

In such an experimental perspective, the interplay between processes of *institution building* and aspects of *institutional design* plays a key role. Processes of institution building and inputs of institutional design are set in a dual relationship in the co-evolution of social action. On the one hand, around experimental practices, processes of problem-setting and problem-solving may develop into arenas of micro-constitutional choice, displaying forms of reciprocity, mutual commitment and recognition among involved actors, developing self-policing organisational and monitoring abilities. On the other hand, in the framework of innovative measures of institutional design, these arenas may enable the development of embedded reflective attitudes, linking everyday issues with a consciousness of their structural determinants through processes of institutional learning.

A possible approach to an operationalisation of such an experimental commitment strategy may be hence, again, envisioned in a dual focus. First, a strategy for institutional capacity building should stress the social mechanisms and processes through which social practices may develop into effective forms of collective of action and through which these may enter a dimension of institutionalisation. Processes of institutionalisation, developing at the threshold between the constraining and the enabling dimensions of institutions, are crucial in defining paths of social innovation. As such, they may act as factors of resilience to change as well as become mediums of the emergence and diffusion of processes of change. New-institutionalist analyses indicate some of the most crucial of those mechanisms in interactive processes that enhance the development of networks, the sharing of rules, and the interplay of social roles. While recognising the incremental, emergent, and definitely non-intentional nature of collective action, a commitment to such key social mechanisms and to their paths of institutionalisation into structured interactional patterns may help in experimentally targeting the areas of everyday social practice which are sensitive to the cross-cutting and cross-fertilising of aspects of institutional design and institution building.

Acting on processes of institutionalisation represents hence a crucial factor for the co-evolutionary development of collective action and institutional capacity and, finally, for a *generative* perspective of politics. But, in order to favour such a perspective, a strategy for institutional capacity-building should further develop within a framework for policy design that may allow the deployment of experimental paths of institutionalisation.

The evolution of actual forms of territorial governance seems to provide an extraordinary ground for developing such experimental opportunities. A crucial, and indeed highly critical, implication of emerging governance settings is in fact the reframing of their territorial domain according to pluralist patterns of regulation and to flexible combinations of their spatial, sectoral and functional connotations. The local forms taken by these combinations assume the features of largely policy-led processes of territorial identification. Territorial governance, in this sense, rather than being defined as a spatialised function or domain of governmental activity – and as an expression of a 'Westphalian' conception of the state –

becomes growingly understandable as a complex cluster of policies or, in different terms, as a set of 'policies of policies', that is, of meta-policies overarching and combining different policy rationales as well as different policy arenas, according to different 'local' rationales – and thus also implying a re-conceptualisation of the territorial dimension of the state. The new 'politics of scale' related to the changing geographic dimension of socio-economic regulation and to the emergence of new 'spatio-temporal fixes' is a relevant expression of the development of tentative institutional settings (such as new forms of regionalisation) for coping with the dialectics of 'embedding' and 'disembedding' which frames the challenges facing territorial policy-making (see Jessop 2000).

Building on the notion of active policies, we may think of the design of *active territorial policies* as a reference for directing actual governance processes along experimental paths of institutional change and for turning dynamics of spatial disembedding into opportunities for new forms of territorial identification. By 'active policies', an ideal-type of policies is intended which "conceive their intervention on concrete processes not only in terms of handling them as objects, but also of valorising as much as possible their actual dynamics and their latent resources" (Donolo 1997, pp 97-98). In pursuing their action-orientation, thus, active policies intersect different regulatory settings, combining the aims of different strands of social, economic, and institutional policies, and cast them into complex 'environments of scope' which may induce effects of retro-action on the constitution of preferences and on the definition of policy goals, and possibly enhance reflexive attitudes. While their "design rationality" (Schon and Rein 1994) is put at the service of effective policy outcomes, their evolutionary path hence bears potentials for learning and for realising feedback loops retro-acting on the institutional settings which define their conditions for effectiveness.

The territorial dimension of policies, however, is crucial in establishing a common symbolic-cognitive ground and an operational and procedural linkage among the actors, preferences, modes of regulation and policy rationales which contribute to define their active orientation. Only in their territorial grounding, on the basis of place-boundedness – and of its redefinition 'in action' – may active policies enable the combination of three potential dimensions of institutional innovation: a dimension of *enactment* of policies, rooting policy development and implementation rationales into concrete spatialised social practices; a dimension of *mobilisation* of resources, bundling the traded and untraded interdependencies between resources of a material, relational, knowledge- and power-based kind embedded in locales; and a dimension of *collective sense-making* and *learning*, as a condition for the reflecting processes of social identification on the institutional settings of policy-making, for turning everyday social experience into an institutional 'capital'.

The 'active' dimension of public policies is thus the dimension where innovative institutional design and social reflexivity may fruitfully hybridise. But it is within the territorial dimension of active policies that the "intelligence of democracy" (Lindblom 1965) may cross-fertilise with the "intelligence of institutions" (Donolo 1997).

Notes

[1] Reference is made here to different lines of institutional analysis, typified according to their prevailing assumptions on institutions and processes of institutionalisation, contrasted with sociological streams of new-institutionalism. Such a typification, as should be clear, is not intended as alternative to other possible, more discipline-centred representations of institutionalism (e.g. Ostrom 1995, Hall and Taylor 1996, Peters 1999): it should rather be understood as a generalisation of evolutionary trends in institutional theory. A more extensive discussion may be found in Gualini (2001).

A first line of analysis primarily addresses the structural features of institutions, understanding institutionalisation as a *property* of societal structures (rules, procedures, and organisations), and the dynamics of institutionalisation as the reproduction of the properties of discrete institutional forms. Expressions of this prevailing focus on the relative degree of social objectivation of institutions, intended as *constraints to agency*, and of a consequent emphasis on their *formal-juridical* component, are contributions from classical institutional economics as well as public choice and specific strands of new institutional economics.

A second line of analysis, rooted in classical sociological thought, addresses the structuring features of institutions rather through an understanding of institutionalisation as a *process* of a continuous, path-dependent kind, leading to the development of institutions as the reproduction of *valid and persistent models of behaviour* defined by different and evolutive degrees of formalisation. Representative of this attitude are contributions by the founders of modern sociological theory of institutions, exchange theories, as well as the so-called positive political economy of institutions.

A distinctive shift towards an understanding of the *subjective* foundations of institutions and of their structuring function in defining societal order – thus relaxating assumptions on the formal nature of institutions while keeping to rather functionalist patterns of explanation – is expressed by a third line of analysis, which understands institutions as *regulatory principles of behaviour*, emphasising their *prescriptive-normative* component, as embodied in contributions from classical sociology as well as in certain developments of new institutional economics.

Sociological new-institutionalism represents a distinctive attempt to combine the macro-sociological dimension of institutionalisation processes with a micro-sociological analysis of their interactional foundation in understanding the dynamics of institutional persistence and change. Its origins may be traced back to sociological reactions to the determinist assumptions of both functionalism and behaviourism and to the inspiration of phenomenology, symbolic interactionism and ethnomethodology, cognitive psychology and the sociology of organizations, combined with more recent contributions to sociological theory. Institutions in this line of analysis are understood as *constitutive elements of social reality*, with an emphasis on institutional phenomena which stress their *symbolic-cognitive* component and their features of *dynamic* and *co-evolutive collective constructs* and of outcomes of *experiential processes*.

2   It may be remembered here that the philosophically grounded – and theoretically much more ambitious – notion of social capital introduced earlier by Bourdieu (1979) has been largely relegated to a marginal position within recent debates, which have focussed mainly on Putnam's contribution.

3   'Ambiguity' is intended here, according to March's definition, as a status defined by 'a lack of clarity or consistency in reality, causality, or intentionality', referred to 'situations that cannot be coded precisely into mutually exhaustive and exclusive categories' (March 1994, p 178), thus supporting at the same time several different interpretations (Weick 1995).

4   In general terms according to Ostrom (1990, p 190, emphasis added), [s]uccess in *starting small-scale initial institutions* enables a group of individuals to *build on the social capital thus created* to solve larger problems with *larger and more complex institutional arrangements*. 'Small scale', in this formulation, is not to be intended in the sense of a primacy of community-like social settings, however. It is rather a hint to the everyday dimension of agency. For debates on the scale or on the 'communitarian' requirements for collective action, see in particular, Douglas (1986) and Ostrom (1992).

5   In analogy to this conception, discussions on consensual approaches to planning underline that, besides their achievements in terms of problem-setting and solving, i.e. beyond of their goal-orientation, successful consensus-building processes may favour the emergence of important 'by-products', defined as *intellectual, social,* and *political capital* (Gruber 1993, Innes, Gruber et al. 1994).

6   In other words, as Douglas (1986, p 45) puts it, "how a system of knowledge gets off the ground is the same as the problem of how any collective good is created".

3 Assessing Institutional Capacity for City Centre Regeneration: Newcastle's Grainger Town

CLAUDIO DE MAGALHÃES, PATSY HEALEY AND
ALI MADANIPOUR

Introduction

It is now widely recognised that, from the late 1970s onwards, governments in more advanced economies have sought to reconfigure their relationship with society and its various sectors, redefine their spheres of influence vis-à-vis economic forces and with citizens, and their mechanisms for accountability and legitimacy (see Chapter 1).

Urban policy has not been an exception in this wider picture. In the UK, reconfiguration was manifest in private sector-led initiatives in the 1980s and early 1990s, partnerships and competition in the mid-1990s, place-focused 'joined-up', 'enabling' interventions in the late 1990s (Bailey 1995, Oatley 1998, Stewart, Goss et al. 1999). The unifying characteristic of these changes has been a shift of State delivery of policy from universally-targeted, needs-linked mainstream expenditure programmes, to differentiated ad-hoc public-private arrangements based on time-limited, issue- or place-specific programmes. The implications of these changes have been widely debated, and whatever the conclusions, it is now clear that they are very unlikely to be reversed (Stoker 1995, 2000b).

In this context, the need has risen to understand what can be achieved through these new institutional arrangements. The evidence that some localities have done better than others has led more recently to a focus on issues of 'institutional capacity'. Assessing and evaluating the efficiency and effectiveness of these arrangements implies looking not only at outputs and outcomes, but also at issues of process, participation and accountability. How far are these new structures likely to achieve their claimed objectives? How far are the outcomes sustainable in the long term?

What are the distributive patterns associated with the outcomes being produced? How and how far can good practices be transferred and generalised?

This Chapter discusses some of the issues involved in assessing 'institutional capacity' and the processes of building such capacity. It does this through examining an urban regeneration initiative in Northeast England, in order to explore ways in which these concepts can be operationalised and their qualities evaluated.

The next section describes and situates the Grainger Town initiative in Newcastle upon Tyne. We look at how 'new' governance forms have emerged, what they respond to, and what they intend to deliver. We also situate these forms in their evolving context. We then discuss a conceptual framework for investigating institutional capacity building. We relate this to the history and recent developments of our case study and in the last section we draw some conclusions on both the case and on assessing institutional capacity in general.

The Grainger Town Partnership[1]

The Grainger Town Partnership was set up in the mid-1990s to regenerate the economy and the physical fabric of the heart of Newcastle city centre. It has involved the creation of institutional structures which these days are associated with British urban regeneration funding regimes – formal partnership with the private sector with some community participation, local-central government collaborative arrangements, output-focused management with some degree of autonomy in relation to the local authority, etc.

Historically, the area now known as 'Grainger Town' was the core of nineteenth century Newcastle, the result of 1830s speculative development (Pendlebury 1999) (see Figure 3.1). As the city's main office and retail location, the area kept its economic dynamism until the late 1960s. However, its fortunes started to decline in the 1970s and 1980s as a result of structural problems, aggravated by the impact of disconnected urban regeneration strategies in the context of a weak economy. Firstly, there was the development of Eldon Square Shopping Centre in the 1970s just west of Grainger Town. Meant to counteract the impact of a huge out-of-town shopping complex in a neighbouring district (Gateshead's Metro Centre), its success contributed to changing the map of retailing in central Newcastle. It accelerated a historical trend of dislocation of the retail gravitational centre away from its traditional location towards the new shopping centre and the Northern edge of the city centre. Secondly, the activities of the Tyne and Wear Development Corporation on riverside sites

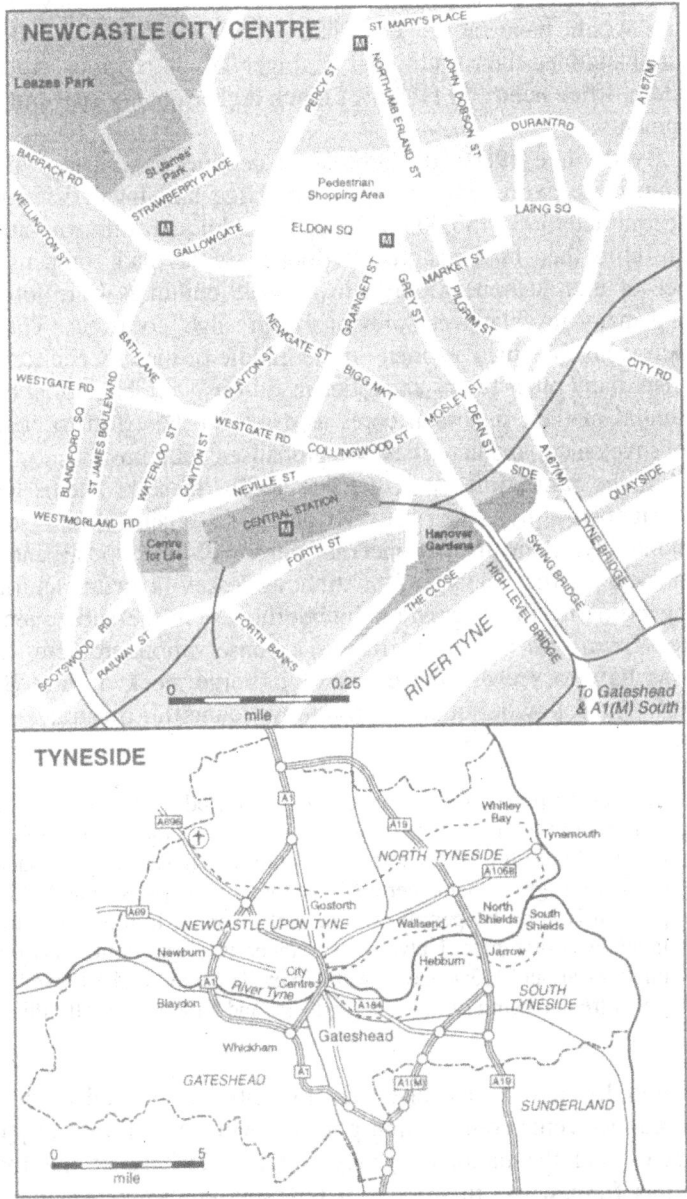

Figure 3.1   **Newcastle City Centre**

from 1988 to 1998 led to the provision of a considerable amount of modern office space to the south of the Grainger Town area. The availability of such spaces might have helped to keep many firms in Newcastle that otherwise would have moved elsewhere. However, many did stay in the city, but abandoned their traditional Grainger Town locations, ill-equipped for modern office needs, in favour of much higher quality space in the new developments.

By the late 1980s, the process of decline was all too visible. Its most immediate expression was the very large amount of vacant upper-floor accommodation (153,000m^2 in 1998). Although this was not a new problem, until then bustling ground floor activities had compensated the existence of unused upper-floors. Now whole buildings were left vacant, including many in what were previously 'prestige' locations. The overall result was a hole of disinvestment in the middle of the city centre, just at a time when many other towns and cities in Europe were beginning to realise the potential of their historical cores as assets in the effort to capture the flows of investment and activities of a globalised economy.

At the same time, until the late 1980s, these problems had been largely ignored by the City Council's regeneration strategies. Understandably, their main concerns were with the social and spatial consequences of the heavy and continuous losses in manufacturing jobs affecting primarily the riverside neighbourhoods. In the subsequent years, Grainger Town was seen primarily as a conservation problem. The key issue was how to prevent the decay of its large stock of fine Georgian buildings. The following quote from a City Councillor illustrates well this process:

> The central part of the town has been neglected for many years now, you can see it in the fabric of the buildings; certainly the buildings themselves are fine buildings, perhaps the reputation of Newcastle as a place [...] to come to neglect them, certainly above the shops, which I think were previously used by people who actually worked in the shops, they have fallen into disrepair. I always remember walking along Clayton Street, this was about a year ago, towards Neville Street, and I looked up and I saw a tree growing out of the windows, and I thought, really this can't be right.[2]

Initially, it was envisaged that this situation should be dealt with through public-sector conservation policies, with the relevant city council departments and the national agency English Heritage at the forefront. Within this framework, there were a few attempts to engage the private sector in limited partnership exercises focusing on public realm improvements. It was only in the mid-1990s that conservation efforts were subsumed into a broader agenda of economic regeneration, through the window of opportunity provided by increasing policy interest on the economic and social viability of town centres. Instrumental to this development was the realisation by the main players of the sheer amount of resources that would be needed to tackle the problems of the area.

Delivering Regeneration in Grainger Town

By 1997, the momentum generated by this wider nexus resulted in a successful bid for a slice of national government urban regeneration funding (the Single Regeneration Budget, Round 3) and a substantial commitment to invest from the regeneration quango English Partnerships, to add to the resources already committed by English Heritage. With active encouragement from the Government Office for the North East, a partnership was formed to tackle the physical and economic regeneration of the area. The vision and strategy for this was consolidated in 1996 (EDAW 1996), and a dedicated structure was created in late 1997 to manage the resources and deliver the outputs. This was configured as the Grainger Town Partnership, an arm's-length company whose board includes representatives of Newcastle City Council, the private sector, various public and semi-public bodies and area residents. At the executive level, the Partnership consisted of a project team, including staff seconded from the city council.

The agenda of the initiative is essentially similar to that of many other recent town centre regeneration programmes in the UK. It involves property development and renovation, public realm improvements, job creation and support for the arts and cultural activities. Its uniqueness lies in the weight given to the conservation issue, the large proportion of English Partnerships funding and the absence of a significant resident population (only 1,000 people lived in the area in the mid-1990s).

In an effort to spread the ownership of the initiative, the partnership set up two formal advisory fora. One (the Business Forum) congregates the different businesses perceived to have an important role to play in reviving the area, and was organised through a top-down selection by The Newcastle Initiative (TNI), a private-sector promotion body, with close links to the local Chamber of Commerce (Bailey 1995). The other includes the area's residents (the Residents Forum), with participation on a voluntary basis. There are also two panels, without formal advisory roles. The Urban Design Panel is made up of design professionals and conservation groups, and functions as a sounding board on design matters (in relation to buildings and the public realm). The Arts Panel includes members of the arts industry in the city and performs a similar function for arts and culture policies and interventions.

The nature and shape of these institutional arrangements are the result of three sets of overlapping determinants. Firstly, there were the requirements of the funding regimes that were being tapped (English Partnerships, the national Single Regeneration Budget, English Heritage), which favoured specific delivery arrangements (a public-private partnership to secure leverage of private sector funding; a dedicated delivery agency to monitor outputs; community representation, etc.). This led to the formation of a body separate from the policy-delivery structure of the local authority, jointly-controlled by the main sponsors and the holders of statutory powers.

Secondly, although less explicitly, they are the result of a history of mutual accommodation combined with distrust between the private sector and the local authority, built over many years. In this sense, the arm's length partnership was a way of creating a relatively autonomous arena where the City Council and businesses could decide on an equal footing how to regenerate Grainger Town. This was seen as particularly important, since the success of the initiative depended directly on the commitment of private sector resources, most of it local. In this context, the creation of the Business Forum on the one hand provided a way of broadening the formal involvement of local businesses, especially those not directly related to the TNI – Chamber of Commerce nexus. On the other hand, it provided further demonstration of the partnership's willingness to listen to the private sector and to develop agreed strategies.

Thirdly, there was the need to secure legitimation for public sector spending in Grainger Town. The weak political clout of the city centre put it at a disadvantage in relation to the politically strong working-class neighbourhoods in the city's West and East ends, whose structural problems of economic decline, unemployment and physical dereliction had made them the traditional focus of most of the Council's regeneration strategies. The creation of participatory structures and especially the residents' forum, despite the small resident population, could be seen in this light.

The initiative has not evolved in a context characterised by a fixed landscape of governance practices. On the contrary, it has grown in a highly changeable environment. This generated tensions between partners, between different funding regimes, and between the initiative itself and the evolving governance context of the city and the region, which became more evident as the project began to materialise.

The public-private partnership overseeing the regeneration of Grainger Town was in many respects one outcome of a long and difficult change of attitude within Newcastle City Council. This involved abandoning entrenched hostility towards business and a monopolistic conception of policy-making and delivery, and accepting a re-definition of its role as an enabling agent in governance processes with an increasing regional dimension (Healey, de Magalhães et al. 2001). As in other places where this move happened, the drivers for change were a mix of opportunistic pragmatism and genuine effort to adapt to a changing context, and it was full of tension and back-turns (Stewart 1999). In this context, Grainger Town represented for some within the Council the opportunity to consolidate links with the influential businesses articulated around TNI, and to exercise a more modern political discourse. It is perhaps no coincidence that this should be done in an area relatively free from the 'turf' politics of other parts of the city.

However, by 1999 Grainger Town had become a contested part of the city council's politics. There was now a city-centre wide plan that re-affirmed the direct role of the council in managing the whole of the city centre. This plan however lacked detailed specification and referred ambiguously to the Grainger Town partnership strategy. Also, Newcastle had just established a partnership with neighbouring Gateshead, an embryonic arrangement between the two municipalities and TNI which sought to create the maximum of synergy from developments currently happening or programmed on both banks of the river Tyne. This shifted the relative importance and position of Grainger Town in the agendas not only of the council but also private players, as it put the relationship between the council and TNI on a different footing.

A similar analysis can be made of the involvement of other key partners. In the mid-1990s, English Partnerships was trying to position itself in the new urban policy agenda. In this context, its involvement in a large city centre initiative such as Grainger Town offered the opportunity to demonstrate the organisation's potential in a brownfield, city centre-focused urban regeneration strategy. This was also not a conflict-free evolution, as it involved changing long-established practices within the organisation itself. However, as the urban policy field evolved, new initiatives came to occupy the centre stage (such as the promotion of Millennium Villages – new complete, sustainable settlements on brownfield sites (Urban Task Force 1999). Moreover, by the end of the 1990s English Partnership had been caught up in the national process of regionalisation. It was dismembered and partly merged into the new Regional Development Agency.

However, despite the shifting institutional context, by 2000 the Grainger Town Project was in its fourth year and its success on the ground was beginning to show. Considerable progress had been achieved in increasing and renovating the housing stock, through the activities of housing associations and the private sector. A number of major 'flagship' commercial development projects were under way, which provided a boost of confidence in the prospects of the area. Some office activities were being attracted back into the area. The Project was having less success in meeting employment targets, although projects in the pipeline were expected to improve achievement. Overall, the Project was managing to re-establish the area's value as a city centre location, for retail, leisure and commercial activities and to develop a significant housing market in the area. It was aided in this by contextual factors, including a national uplift in the property market and a new interest in city centre living nationally. Nonetheless, there remained questions about how far the concentrated attention on the city centre would remain once the funded Project period was completed and how durable would be the changes the initiative has introduced.

Evaluating Institutional Capacity Building in Practice

There are obviously deep and more general causes for Grainger Town problems, in which a localised partnership is unlikely to make a difference. The fragile nature of the region's economy is one of them, and any critical look at a partnership exercise of this kind has to consider these limitations. However, a considerable part of what it can achieve is linked to how the partnership is inserted into local governance processes.

How can we actually begin to see whether an institutional arrangement of the kind described above, which by no means is exclusive to Grainger Town or Newcastle, can be effective in transforming places in more inclusive and sustainable ways? And how do we interpret this? What are the qualities of the institutional capacity drawn upon and developed through this particular initiative and how do they influence its outcomes? Do they contribute towards a long-lasting transformation of the area? Do they lead to a broadly-shared project for change and effective collective action?

The notion of 'institutional capacity building' is not a new concept. It has been used to highlight the need to build up individual capabilities of firms in a competitive environment, as well as those of public administrations. In the former case, the focus has been on the institutions that help to develop such capabilities; in the latter, the emphasis has been on the attributes of particular organisations. However, the very nature of the institutional arrangements in current urban governance requires an approach to the concept that accounts for the capacities of the array of stakeholders involved – wherever positioned among government organisations, the private, voluntary and community sectors – and their ability to mobilise and co-ordinate for collective purposes.

In this Chapter we are interested in the capacity of stakeholders to mobilise *within* a locality and to focus on action programmes aimed at improving the qualities of a *locale* or place. This is a challenging agenda if the geographical space of cities, regions and neighbourhoods is regarded as a surface cut across by multiple relational networks, whose diversity and spatial reach seem to be more diverse than ever before (Healey 2000). Spaces become 'places' because they are acknowledged as such by those living there, doing business there or involved in governance activities in some way. The relative importance of a city as a 'place' varies among stakeholders, networks and social worlds, depending on their systems of meaning. This can generate synergies or clashes of place conceptions, which may lead to mobilisation to generate new conceptions, new resources and new activities of place making. The ability of those involved in places to act to manage and develop their 'qualities' is therefore linked to the relational dynamics within which the city/region/neighbourhood is located. It is also linked to the capacity of those networks to shape and mobilise resource flows, regulatory powers and ways of thinking (Giddens 1984) and to focus on the agendas set by nodal points in networks within the 'space/place'. Besides, the idea of 'place' has a key role in defining the identity of social groups, and this collective identity may contribute towards generating social cohesion. Therefore, place management depends upon an explicit 'sense of place' and conscious collective identity, which resonates with the meanings of the social networks which transect the area (Honneth 1995, Jenkins 1996, Madanipour, Cars et al. 1998). In situations where collective identities are more pluralistic and the systems of signification more fragmented, the task of place management, if it is evident as such at all, becomes a delicate exercise in forging a reflexive consensus (Healey 1997).

In this context, 'institutional capacity' refers to the capacity of urban governance to make a difference in sustaining and transforming the qualities of cities. Our particular interest has been in assessing the potential for building institutional capacity in ways which expand stakeholder involvement and have sufficient power to affect the driving forces affecting life chances, economic opportunities and environmental qualities (Healey 1998b). Such a conception involves going beyond just the formal organisation and technical skills of agencies involved in governance, and encompasses also the more intangible 'governance cultures' of places, the degree of connectedness between the various nodes of business and social life, and the density and quality of the relationships between these. It focuses attention on the webs of relations involved in urban governance that interlink government organisations, those in the private sector and voluntary and community organisations (see the discussion in Chapter 1).

Key to this approach to institutional capacity is the concept of 'institutional capital'. This draws on the various ideas of 'social capital', and encompasses features of social organisation such as trust, norms and networks, inscribed and incorporated in ways of thinking and acting, and produced and used interactively in a governance context (see the preceding Chapters in this book). Building 'institutional capacity' in urban governance means transforming, creating and mobilising the 'institutional capital' of a place in the collective effort of shaping its future.

Drawing on Innes and Booher (1999) in their discussion of consensus-building processes, the concept of 'institutional capital' is used as a conceptual device linking three elements of social interaction. The first is the flow of knowledge of various kinds between stakeholders in a locality, and the learning process that takes place as knowledge is exchanged. These are the *knowledge resources*, the frames of reference, creativity and knowledgeability, the conceptions of place and identity relevant to governance. The second is the nature, reach and quality of the relational networks brought into the governance process by the stakeholders. These constitute the *relational resources*, the resources of trust and co-operation contained in such networks, the nature of the bonding elements in them and their reach. The third element is the ability of stakeholders and their networks to draw resources, rules and ideas into the effort of collective action. This is the *mobilisation capacity*, the capacity of stakeholders to mobilise knowledge and relational resources to act collectively at the level of the city/region/neighbourhood for some common goal.

How does this conceptual framework help us to understand the dynamics of the Grainger Town Partnership? To address a specific instance of governance activity, it is necessary to operationalise the concepts of 'institutional capacity' and 'institutional capital' in ways that allow their evolution and deployment to be observed and analysed. This requires that the three strands of institutional capital should be linked to evaluative criteria, encompassing both output and process dimensions. We summarise how we have done this in Figure 3.2 and explain it further below.

Knowledge Resources

Our concept of 'knowledge resources' avoids treating knowledge as a given, unified object or asset. We use interactive, non-linear formulations of knowledge development and transfer, which focus on the production of knowledge through social interaction (Asheim 1996, Hassink 1997, Innes 1990, Latour 1987). This links social constructivist approaches to the nature of knowledge, which emphasise the range of forms of knowledge, the way what we know inhabits not merely our conscious memory, but our recalling of past events and our routine practices for undertaking tasks (Healey 1997, Connerton 1989). Moreover, as people are embedded in different social relations, mutual learning and knowledge transfer can only happen if the deep cultural frames shaping their ways of thinking and acting are made explicit. Our focus is therefore not only on 'static' formalised knowledge, but also on the interactive production and deployment of tacit knowledge and experiential understanding, all operating at multiple levels, from deep structures to items of information (Schon and Rein 1994).

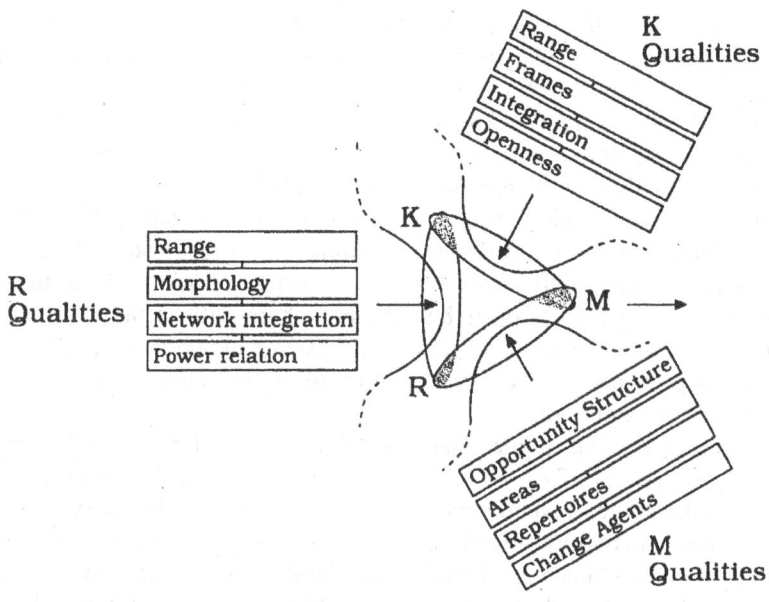

Figure 3.2   **Evaluating the Dimensions of Institutional Capacity-Building Processes**

Drawing on the ideas above, we suggest that the ability of an urban regeneration initiative to build up 'knowledge resources' depends firstly, on access by stakeholders to, and their use of, a rich *range* of knowledge on what to do, why and how (e.g. ideas about place quality, urban 'decay', institutional relations within a partnership initiative, conservation, regeneration and the property development process). Secondly, it depends on the conscious reflection on, and development of, *frames of reference*, that is, the underlying conceptions that shape the meanings and interpretations given to the flow of knowledge. Thirdly, there is the degree of *integration* of the knowledge and frames of reference used by the stakeholders, and the intensity and efficacy of efforts to translate different types of knowledge and frames of reference into one another. Lastly, there is the *openness and learning* capacity of stakeholders to absorb new ideas, to search for new ways of understanding and acting, and to access new sources of information and inspiration.

Relational Resources

For the concept of 'relational resources', we look at the discussion of 'social capital' (see the Introduction to Part 1 and Chapter 2). We draw on concerns with actor networks (Law 1998), the role of trust and reciprocity in business networks (Fukuyama 1995), the role of civic associations in civil society (Putnam 1993) and concepts of the social construction of identities (Berger and Luckmann 1967). Our emphasis is on the embeddedness of governance actors, to varying degrees and in variable ways, in potentially several networks of social relations. Bonds built around relationships of trust and reciprocity tie these networks together. Networks have different reaches, different bonding elements, and different morphologies. Some will focus on a few nodes, others will be more dispersed; some will have clear boundaries, others will be more diffuse. Different morphologies may define how accessible networks are, who are insiders and outsiders, as well as the nature of power relations within and beyond a specific network.

Therefore, we argue that the ability to build up 'relational resources' is linked to four variables: firstly, the *range* of the networks of relations linking the stakeholders, and the nature of the bonding values holding these networks together. Secondly, the *morphology* of the networks, their 'architecture', highlighting the density of interconnections, spatial and temporal reaches, nodal points and key 'switching points' where transfers and connections between networks are possible. Thirdly, the existence of *integration* between the relational webs transecting a place, in terms of common membership, affinity of 'bonding values', density of shared nodes and 'switching points'. Fourth, the nature of the *power relations*, which on the one hand hold and manage the networks and govern access to them (e.g. open, trust-generating versus closed, discouraging), and on the other shape the links which local networks have with national and international centres of economic, legal and ideological power.

Mobilisation Capacity

A broad-based literature on social movements provides the terms for evaluating the stakeholders' 'capacity' to mobilise knowledge and relational resources (Tarrow 1994, Innes and Booher 1999, Harding 1995). All these works are concerned with the processes through which attempts are made to challenge the established practices of governance 'regimes'. Mobilisation is approached from both an 'agency' and a 'structural' perspective. From the former, the emphasis is on technique, on learning processes, on releasing creativity, developing trust and on generating the capacity to act collectively. From the latter, the emphasis is on the capacity to 'read' the institutional dynamics, to identify 'windows of opportunity' in established power structures (Healey 1997), and the right arenas to target mobilisation efforts. Tarrow (1994) brings these elements together in his discussion of the dynamics of social movements. He identifies four key dimensions to such dynamics: a political opportunity structure, the availability of 'symbolic frames' of reference around which people can mobilise, the existence of social networks connecting the leader and the core of a movement to its base, and 'repertoires' of ways of acting to achieve change.

We take Tarrow's approach as the basis to develop our concept of 'mobilisation capacity'. We suggest that the quality of the mobilisation efforts deployed in an urban regeneration initiative is a function of, firstly, the ability of stakeholders to explore *opportunity structures* for collective action, i.e. to identify and lock into structural shifts that create opportunities for change, and to define agendas which can act as magnets for mobilisation. Secondly, it is linked to their ability to identify the *arenas* where key resources and regulatory power lie and where real changes can be made, as well as the most effective access routes to them. Thirdly, it is connected to the availability of a rich *repertoire* of mobilisation techniques, and the stakeholders' ability to select the most effective techniques for each situation. Lastly, it requires the presence of skilled *change agents* to operate at critical 'nodal points' on the routes to resources and regulatory power.

A look at the Grainger Town initiative through the conceptual lenses just described would suggest that there has potentially been access to a rich range of 'knowledge resources', especially given the history of involvement in regeneration initiatives by the core players and sponsors. However, there have been only limited episodes of conscious reflection on the frames of reference that set the project parameters. Ideas and information have been shared among many participants, perhaps 100-200 people drawn in over the lifetime of the actual Partnership so far. But shared understanding is limited to a much smaller group of people active in the Executive, the Board and the various consultative fora and panels, despite considerable efforts by the partnership staff to broaden involvement and awareness. Nor has there been a rich infusion of new ideas, with in contrast, a lot of effort devoted to keeping the whole enterprise on track in terms of compliance to established and accepted practices.

In terms of 'relational resources', the strong networks between the key players at the core of the initiative (see Figure 3.3) have been primarily ones of convenience and mutual interest, especially those between the public and private sector players. They have been characterised by a delicately handled endemic mistrust rather than open co-operation, and they have not been of great breadth or richness. Many of the networks to which the partnership related are hub-like rather than web-like, with a few very powerful controlling nodes. In contrast, many other stakeholders have had an atomised participation, without connection to any networks. Moreover, there have been only limited linkages between 'families' of networks, with the exception of those parts of the business community which are interconnected through the Newcastle Initiative – Chamber of Commerce nexus. Despite the qualities that the Grainger Town partnership has sought to develop, due to the conflicts over control of the initiative, relations between the core players have often been tense, rather than open and trust-generating.

At the supra-local level, there have been some structural opportunities to which stakeholders could target mobilisation efforts, such as the growing policy interest on town centres and sustainable development. However, both the local and the supra-local situation have been too unstable to allow the initiative to flourish, especially since it focuses on what has become an increasingly contested territory (the city centre), and presents challenges to local practices in both the private and the public sector. Moreover, there have been too many arenas where decisions affecting the initiative have been made, with too many 'change agents'. The capacity for collective strategic action has been so far limited. It is possible that new bases for the emergence of a more strategic local governance are now being laid in Newcastle, as the City Council struggles to shift towards more strategic, enabling practices. To some extent, the problem for the Grainger Town Partnership in its first four years lay in its timing in the trajectory of change in governance. By late 2000, the local context was moving in a more favourable direction as far as the Partnership was concerned, with the City Council under pressure from residents in poorer neighbourhoods to adopt more inclusive consultation processes. If such shifts happen, the City Council may wish to maintain the knowledge and relational resources built up through the Partnership.

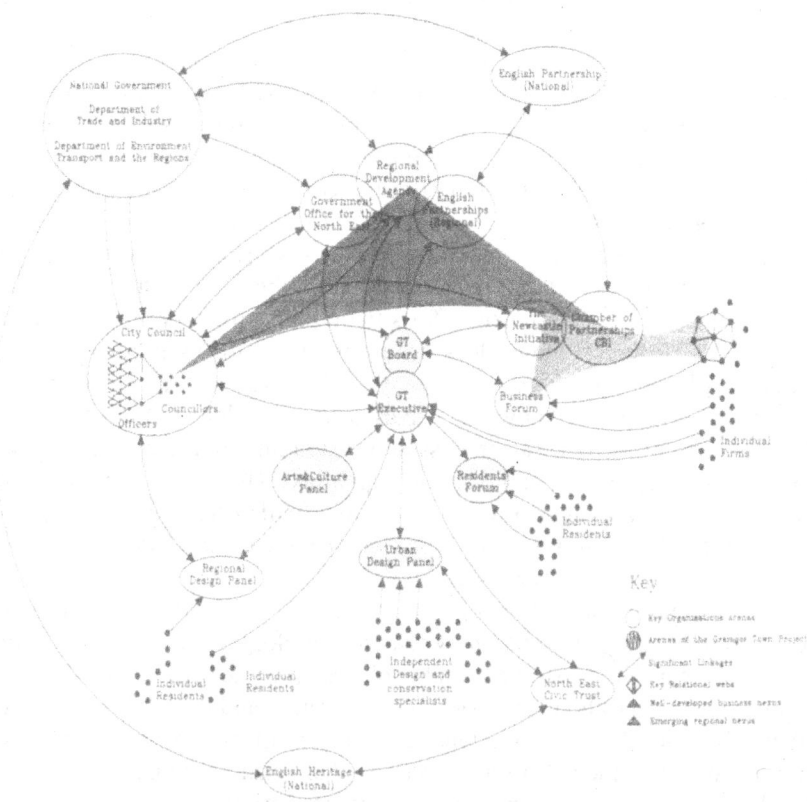

Figure 3.3   Governance Networks and the Grainger Town Partnership

Conclusions

Focusing on the deployment and development of knowledge, relational resources and mobilisation capacity, what can be said about the process of 'institutional capacity building' in the Grainger Town initiative? More specifically, what has been the significance of the density of social interaction, and the extent to which ideas were shared, to the way the initiative has developed? To what extent have new ideas and practices been disseminated and what have been the implications? Since the concern is with the ability to act collectively, how far have the density of social interaction, shared conceptions and dissemination of innovation fostered mobilisation and transformation of the governance processes? And as Grainger Town is not a 'closed system', what has been the impact on it of supra-local policy cultures and practices?

Firstly, the initiative has evolved in a context in which there is a dense array of social networks connecting those with considerable stakes in Newcastle city centre. There is also a common awareness of the 'problem' among a core group of people at the heart of the initiative. There is some agreement on a vision for the future of the Grainger Town area, linked to a specific conception of a 'European City' ambience. This has been built up by development work undertaken before the regeneration partnership was formally constituted and was re-iterated within the work of the partnership and in the City Council's recent efforts to prepare a plan for the City Centre as a whole. However, these ideas were not widely diffused beyond a core group of players and there were many with stakes in the area that were outside this process of knowledge sharing and development. Furthermore, the existence of a shared awareness and vision among the core group was not sufficient to release mobilisation capability. There are strong tensions over ownership and control of the initiative, which have made concerted action difficult. Moreover, the initiative itself has not had an enduring priority for significant key players.

Secondly, the history of the Grainger Town Partnership illustrates how power struggles and network morphologies can inhibit wider collective learning processes. Stakeholders have learned about specific opportunities, and about the priorities, strategies and ways of working of others. But this learning has tended to be an ad hoc, atomised process. Individuals take their learning away, rather than building it into new developments within the initiative or disseminating it widely elsewhere. There has been little involvement in the kind of learning that develops around setting agendas, as the agendas have tended to be pre-set. Stakeholders have used different networks and 'relational routes' to accessing sources of information and power, and involvement in the initiative has not helped them to map out the various arenas where power and influence were exercised. The limits on collective learning processes identified can be linked to the conflicts over control of arenas and over the territory of the city centre, and to the different morphologies of the relational networks which connect stakeholders to the Grainger Town Partnership.

Thirdly, the Grainger Town case highlights the importance of the quality of the connections linking the main players. Although there is a strong nexus of relations between the Council, dominant players in the business community and English Partnerships, there has been mistrust among them. Moreover, and more fundamentally, there have only been limited connections between these players and the array of other groups and individuals with a stake of one kind or another in the City Centre. City Centres as locales have an inherent complexity in their stakeholders. Fostering the confidence and innovative energy of these stakeholders is a necessary part of maintaining the dynamism of these areas in the contemporary context. The partnership staff has put a great deal of effort into widening the linkages with these other stakeholders, but it has been difficult to sustain these when there were conflicts over control at the heart of the partnership and competitive arenas for articulating City Centre networks. Thus, as in the late 1990s, the Grainger Town Partnership lacked a rich inheritance of appropriate networks and was without a sufficiently strong institutional opportunity within which to promote new networks. In this respect, Newcastle in the 1990s may be contrasted with cities such as Manchester (Harding 2000) and Leeds (John and Cole 2000) in the same period, which had a much greater capacity for local collective action.

Lastly, this case shows that local initiatives are shaped as much by local forces as by supra-local ones. Supra-local forces have encouraged the competitive bidding game, which provided the bulk of the resources for the partnership. They have channelled public subsidy into particular pots and agency responsibilities, thus determining to a large extent the nature of the key players and their priorities. They have demanded particular kinds of local practices, including the partnership format and the auditing mechanisms. They have fostered conflicts of responsibilities for the city centre among different Council departments. Moreover, a continual re-organisation of the policy and governance environment at national level has often led to disruption of local relationships and agenda-setting processes. But the effort of place promotion and development has been significantly compromised by local practices as well – the opportunistic way the Council has played the bidding game, the local culture of Council control, the departmental traditions, the competition between initiatives promoted by different groups of stakeholders under different regimes, even competition for ownership of 'visions' and 'strategic ideas'. Thus, the work of the Grainger Town partnership in building wider relations and more shared understanding was continually undermined by this wider context.

It is not appropriate to make broad generalisations in terms of processes of institutional capacity building. Our case suggests that the way knowledge and relational resources are used and developed and how this shapes mobilisation capacity is highly contingent on context- and place-specific factors. However, a few observations of more general character are possible.

The open and fluid nature of the processes influencing institutional capacity building suggests a greater scope for agency than that allowed for by approaches which treat such capacity as a historically-inherited asset. How effectively resources of trust and knowledge are deployed and developed into collective action emerges from our account as a function of inherited resources of knowledge, patterns of trust within social networks and repertoires of mobilisation strategies, but *as they interact with* the ability of stakeholders to re-cast this inheritance to face present challenges. Moreover, the very openness and fluidity of such interaction dispels the idea of institutional capacity as a stock of assets that can be called upon, disposed of or added to as the situation might require. Institutional capacity is better understood as a complex, fluid and evolving 'infrastructure' acting at several levels – from the visible level of organisations and institutional power structures, to the deeper levels of ideas, discourses and identities. Accumulated experience and history certainly count, but their effects are filtered by a continuous, open and multi-level interaction between established practices and understandings and emerging ones, with uncertain outcomes.

However, to temper any excessively optimistic conclusions, our case also suggests that the line separating what enhances from what hinders institutional capacity building is considerably blurred and can be moved either way through the action of local and supra-local forces. If this is so, institutional capacity building is dependent less on the formal shape of new institutional structures of governance than on the qualities of the processes through which knowledge resources, relational resources and mobilisation capacity are developed and used. Understanding *what* is deployed and transformed through these new structures is then the key research task.

Notes

[1] For the full details of this case, see Healey, de Magalhães at al. 2001
[2] This is taken from Healey, de Magalhães et al. 2001.

PART II:
GOVERNANCE IN ACTION IN COMPLEX SOCIAL MILIEUX

PART II

Editorial Introduction: The Challenge of Building New Institutional Capacities

CLAUDIO DE MAGALHÃES

Over recent years, programmes for urban regeneration, community development and regional territorial development have created new kinds of institutional arrangements whose aims have been to overcome the limitations of compartmentalised policy delivery mechanisms, to actively involve private agents and communities in the conception and delivery of policy, and to foster strategies that can respond to a fast changing economic and social environment.

The tradition of policy delivery by vertically constructed State organisations has been questioned through a multiplicity of arrangements often involving the public, private and community sectors, and local, regional, national and supra-national levels of government. The fine-grain and diversity of those with a stake in urban policies has become increasingly apparent and adds to the pressure for institutional frameworks that can consider this diversity. New agendas of sustainability and competitiveness in a globalised economic environment have challenged the traditional ways of managing urban regions and have brought forward the need for new forms of strategic thinking.

In response to these challenges, different institutional arrangements and governance practices have emerged in different contexts as a response to the issues outlined in the previous paragraphs. The contributions in this Part discuss such arrangements and practices, their limits and possibilities. Matthiesen's Chapter presents an account of formal cross-border capacity building initiatives in the German-Polish border and their complex and often conflictual interaction with the informal level of local milieux. Allen and Cars look at the processes of social exclusion in distressed neighbourhoods in Europe, and discuss the need for creating 'micro political processes' that can enhance neighbourhood democracy and counteract the inadequacies, disjointedness and wastefulness of current welfare delivery systems. Taylor analyses UK government strategies for community participation in urban regeneration. She examines the implications of the conceptual apparatus that has been deployed in developing these strategies and how well it deals with the tensions between inclusion, exclusion, and fragmentation. Lambert and Oatley look at the issue of developing a 'collective actor' focussed around the Bristol region and examine the role of the statutory planning system in articulating strategic policies that can deal with the spatial challenges brought by 'post-Fordist' economic growth.

Although these contributions tackle different aspects of governance and move from the local to the international level, there is a common trend running through them. At their respective level of analysis, and in relation to the particular aspects of governance they look at, these contributions cast a light on a number of issues that are at the core of this book.

At one level, all the contributions to identify the nature of the challenges facing urban policy and governance in complex social milieux, to which new institutional arrangements are a response. What are these and how do they impact on the various communities of interest within urban areas? How do they transform the links between the local, the regional and the global? How do they secure long-lasting transformation of those areas?

Allen, Cars and Taylor highlight the emergence of, or the need for, new kinds of governance arrangements to deal with social exclusion and the processes through which it is produced. Allen and Cars locate these processes in the shift away from the Fordist regime that has affected western European economies since the mid-1970s. This shift has resulted in a mismatch between the welfare delivery systems intended to provide universal benefits, and the situation in distressed neighbourhoods. The hierarchical, vertically-organised and specialised structures of welfare delivery add to the problems facing these neighbourhoods. The challenge is to develop forms of democratic governance that can mobilise the preferences and resources of residents, connect the informal and formal networks that focus on the neighbourhood, make sense of the fragmented interaction between residents and the State and also use resources efficiently. Taylor looks at similar issues but with a focus on the development of community involvement initiatives in the UK. In spite of a proven commitment by the UK government towards community participation in urban regeneration manifest in many of the main funding programmes, these initiatives are couched in a discourse that masks many of the real problems in developing partnerships between communities, State and markets. As in the case of city centre regeneration described in Chapter 3, the emphasis on a managerial agenda of demonstrable outputs, on 'best practice' as a repetition of proven solutions, and on strong leadership militate against genuine innovation in welfare delivery mechanisms and the opening up of policy-making to voices from the community. Here, the challenge for governance is to 'find ways of organising at local level that can combine authority with flexibility and entrepreneurialism' and 'bring together what has been learnt from below'.

Matthiesen deals with a different context. His contribution looks at institutions and planning for trans-border co-operation at the margins of the EU, in the German-Polish border city of Guben/Gubin. Successful formal institutions for co-operation are being developed in a context characterised by economic asymmetries between the two sides, the clashes of two different transformation pathways towards market-oriented economics and culture, the existence of processes of economic peripheralisation at a regional and supra-regional level, and long-lasting distrust between cultures. This has lead to a marked contrast between the inclusive formal level of institution building and the informal milieux of the two cities, where exclusionary forces dominate, particularly on the western side. The challenge for new emerging forms of governance is to create closer links between the formal and informal milieux and from this basis to integrate two different societies in common strategies for economic competitiveness, while counteracting ethnic differences and prejudices.

The context for Lambert and Oatley's Chapter is the British statutory planning system and its difficulty in providing adequate responses to strong development pressures in growth areas. The issue here is on the one hand the lack of institutional mechanisms to manage strategic decisions at a regional level, and on the other, the inability to address conflicts between development needs, housing demands and the agendas of environmental protection and sustainable use of resources. The challenges here involve the creation of bottom-up collaborative governance systems at regional level, which can overcome the adversarial culture embedded in the land-use planning system and find ways of reconciling economic competitiveness, social needs and environmental protection.

At another level, the contributions attempt to provide an answer to the question of whether or not emerging institutional arrangements have delivered on the claims being made for them. Have they met the challenges mentioned above in a successful way? Are they transforming established routines and practices of governance, and do they provide the basis for lasting new ones? Which are the issues these emerging institutional arrangements address more successfully, and which ones do they leave aside? The answers are not straightforward, unsurprisingly. In some of the cases discussed, new institutional arrangements are still very incipient as is the case with the regional strategic arenas in England and Wales analysed by Lambert and Oatley. At the same time, as suggested by Taylor, Allen and Cars, State organisations and policy communities formed over the last half century are resistant to change and can easily reconstitute traditional practices and hierarchies of power. As Taylor points out, a real commitment to greater community involvement at government level can be compromised by an agenda that reconstitutes traditional procedures and potentially excludes sectors of the community. It may also be compromised by the nature of operational routines at the lower levels of the public administration. Lambert and Oatley also mention structural resistances to developing a more strategic role for the British planning system. These include institutional fragmentation, the short-termism of politics and the lack of power and resources to deliver development of the intended quality.

In the German-Polish border city analysed by Matthiesen, new institutional arrangements have been put in place to develop economic, social and cultural integration. Moreover, at the level of formal interactions between institutions on both sides of the border, they have proved to be quite successful, and are recognised as such by the European Commission. However, the author highlights the fact that these arrangements largely ignore what goes on in the everyday lives of people. As a result, a mismatch has developed between the formal level of EU and national institutions, the intermediary level of local organisations of civil society in which there are only weak articulations with ambiguous results, and the informal level of local milieux. In the latter, closure processes are in action especially in Germany, fostering distrust and undermining the success of the formal level.

The final common point is that the Chapters assume a definition of the concept of 'institutional capacity building' appropriate for the situations and context they are dealing with. Are these definitions compatible with one another in the sense that there might be common trends underlying them, or are they purely issue-dependent? Which frames of references are shaping these understandings of institutional capacity-building processes and the emerging institutional arrangements and practices?

For Matthiesen, institutional capacity is related to the ability of governance systems to build new institutions and create common discourses and collaboration both at formal and informal levels across the two societies. More importantly, it is also linked to the need to embed formal governance and its associated institutions and discourses into the informal milieux of the everyday life of citizens. The frame of reference used emphasises the informal processes of institution building, their relation with the local milieux and the relationship between these processes and the formal arenas of government and organisations. This goes hand in hand with concerns about the creation of trust, openness and learning-oriented institutions across cultures and different economic dynamics.

This situating of institutional capacity in the convergence of formal governance institutions and informal networks of relationships also underpins Allen and Cars' Chapter. Institutional capacity relates to the creation of 'micro political processes' within neighbourhoods, which can counteract the impacts of wider social and economic processes that cause social exclusion. This is based on a view of social exclusion as the outcome of structural changes in the 'Fordist' economy as they impact on neighbourhoods. It is also based on an understanding of governance that emphasises the creation of 'local collective actors', which can represent local communities to the outside world.

The idea of local level organisations is also present in Taylor's Chapter, as is the convergence and combination of formal and informal networks, and of formal government, markets and civil society. Institutional capacity is associated with the need for a style of policymaking that is not hierarchical, relies on persuasion and encouragement, engages with the different values held by different sectors of the community and allows for mutual learning. Such a style of governance, she argues, should help in meeting the challenge of creating local level organisations that can be actual partners in the task of fighting social exclusion.

A different view of the issue of institutional capacity emerges from Lambert and Oatley's Chapter. The concept is related to the vicissitudes of a particular sector of formal governance institutions. The concern in their Chapter is with the capacity of the planning system to reconcile conflicting interests at the regional level in order to pursue strategic policies, and to build up effective governance at that level. The context for this challenge is the concern with issues of economic development, competitiveness and sustainability at the level of the city-region. Creating the institutional framework that can help local networks and decision-making arenas to transcend artificial geographical boundaries is then the key task.

There are, therefore, differences in the understanding of the challenges facing existing governance arrangements, different assessments of whether emergent alternatives can be effective, and different understandings of what 'institutional capacity' is about. Some of these differences clearly derive from the specific nature of those challenges, the context in which they exist and the details of the governance arrangements in place to deal with them. However, there are also important similarities either in the processes underpinning the emergence of those challenges or in the responses to them. To render these explicit is the main aim of this section. The wider implications of the issues raised are discussed in the concluding Chapter of the book.

4 Transformational Pathways and Institutional Capacity Building: The Case of the German-Polish Twin City Guben/Gubin

ULF MATTHIESEN

Introduction

This chapter discusses the institutional challenges resulting from the eastward enlargement of the European Union. For cities in these areas, enlargement processes are not just about positioning in new geographies. Within these shifting processes, different pathways of modernization and transformation bump into each other, leading to the encounter of different pathways of institutional capacity building. These encounters develop their own styles and pace, strongly depending on the different ways formal institutional capacity building efforts are embedded in their institutional milieux. These can vary from learning-oriented cross-border relations, to cultural closure procedures. In this sense, the German-Polish border zone may be looked at as a crucial testing ground within the preparatory phases of the eastwards enlargement of the EU, where both positive and negative learning experiences of institutional capacity building are evolving.

The laboratory character of this border zone provides the background for an ongoing research project on the evolution of cross-border relations within the German-Polish twin city of Guben/Gubin, straddling across the river Neisse. The research embraces both formal as well as informal institutional capacity building processes. Emphasis is given to the local effects of the interface between the different pathways of transformation and modernisation experienced by the two former socialist societies, and especially the interrelation of institutionalisation processes with embedding border milieux. The delicate border situation confronts the twin city of Guben/Gubin with specific options, hindrances and interaction barriers. This provides a revealing window on the complex processes of the eastern enlargement of the EU. In these transformation processes, the local level plays a crucial but frequently rather ambivalent role. It is at this level that the success or failure of cross-border relations and of transformation processes become evident (Scott and Collins 1997, Srubar 1998, Scott 1999). It is here that new mixtures of formal and informal institution building processes are invented and tested, and it is at this level that new hybrid forms of post-socialist everyday cultures within the respective border milieux mingle with 'Europeanised' institution building processes.

This chapter discusses the laboratory-like situation of this border zone in four parts. Initially, some features of the German-Polish border situation in general are sketched out, concentrating on the two different transformational pathways that bump against each other here. The East German part of the twin city has now been for a decade within the regulatory domain of the EU, whereas the Polish part belongs to the largest and most prosperous candidate for the next round of EU enlargement. The Polish side is preparing itself for this process on the national, regional and local level by way of forced institutional capacity building processes, aiming to fulfil the stringent conditions for an entry into a larger and changing European Union. In a second step, brief information is presented about the specific case of the twin city of Guben/Gubin. Thirdly, the chapter explores a main area of conflict within this twin city and discusses the concept of 'governance paradoxes'. Finally, adopting an evolutionary learning process approach, the chapter suggests an empirical model for resolving and integrating these path-specific and border-specific conflicts and options. The attempt is to integrate them into a learning perspective, in which locally embedded informal institutional capacity building processes can unfold their crucial role.

The underlying argument of this chapter is that studies of post-socialist transformation processes and the eastward extension of the EU, which focus primarily on formal problem solving and institutionalisation processes are not only too narrow but often misleading (Granovetter 1985, Grabher and Stark 1997, Thomas 1999b). Despite lip service to the issue of 'embeddedness', mainstream approaches to governance, policy and modernisation in economics, politics and studies on socio-spatial developments generally tend to dramatically neglect the immense ocean of informal institutional capacity building processes. As sustained in this chapter, this neglect has distorting consequences on our understanding of post-socialist transformation pathways in general. To develop this point, the author draws on conceptions of the lifeworld, re-specifying them within the 'sensitising' research concept of milieux (Matthiesen 1998a). The main argument is that the dynamic stratum of informal structuration processes within the lifeworld has to be taken into systematic account in order to come to grips with the specific options and conflicts that play a crucial role within the process of the eastwards expansion of the EU.

The German-Polish Border Area – Options and Conflicts: An Overview

Within the process of the European integration and the eastwards expansion of the European Union, the German-Polish border region and its specific development trends are of primordial importance (Fassmann 1997, Barjak 1999 and Wysocki and Glante 1999). Since 1989, this border region has played the role of a crucial interface between 'the East' and 'the West'. Besides the growing *functional* interface, this border area has become an important testing ground for *cultural* codification and re-codification processes of the macro concept of 'Europe' itself. Within this functional and cultural enlargement, ingredients of what is 'the West' and what is 'the East' of Europe have changed. In this way the German-Polish border region has become a true testing ground for new trans-border networks as well as new forms of barriers to interaction.

Four main issues characterise this border situation:

- Different *transformation pathways* meet here;
- Multi-dimensional *asymmetries* have developed;
- The immediate border zone is confronted with a marked danger of growing *peripheralisation processes*;
- Last but not least, on the level of everyday interaction processes, both sides of the border are struggling with the ambivalent simultaneity of *formal* processes of European integration and *informal*, disintegrating tendencies of re-ethnicisation.

The following paragraphs discuss the first three points. The final issue will be the main theme of the following sections.

Different Transformation Pathways

The unprecedented encounter of different post-socialist transformation pathways on the eastern border of the present EU offers some interesting lessons to be learned for research on transformation processes in general, for modernisation theories and not the least for policy-oriented institutionalist analysis (Brusis 1999). Post-socialist transformation types have been analytically located between two poles: 'Big Bang' change on the one hand, gradualist transformation on the other. Usually the Polish case is associated with a pronounced 'Big Bang' strategy (von Zon 1999), whereas East Germany is seen as the classical example of a gradualist approach (Fassmann 1997, Mummert 1999, Labrousse 1999). However, a closer look reveals that, instead of a clear-cut dichotomy, we find on both sides interesting differences in the respective mixes of 'Big Bang' and gradualist strategies of transformation.

On the East German side, the three most significant features are, firstly, the transfer of considerable amounts of capital from West Germany to the East in order to modernise the infrastructure and the industrial cores along the Border Rivers Oder and Neisse. Secondly, there is a nearly complete transfer of the 'old' formal institutional structures of Western Germany to the 'Neue Bundesländer' (the new federal states) in the East. Thirdly, with this institutional transfer a far-reaching substitution of regional and partly of local elites has taken place (Neckel 1999).

On the level of mentalities and everyday cultures, this approach to change resulted in a widely-held social sentiment according to which the whole process of German transformation was executed mainly by 'external' governance regimes 'from the West' (the 'colonisation-thesis'). The most frequently mentioned 'evidences' for this thesis are the spatially selective effects of the investment activities of transnational firms – with growing peripheralisation tendencies for some 'unlucky' East German regions, and the enduring location of nearly all head offices of the main investors in the western half of Germany and Europe (Labrousse, 1999).[1] Our own case studies confirm the increasing levels of disenchantment, the complaint about the dissolution of former trust-related networks, the discontent about the 'devaluation' of pre-1989 accomplishments and institutions and a resentful estrangement against western-style individualism – even though consumerist lifestyles and mentalities are quickly spreading within East Germany. Arnold Vaatz, influential East German Christian Democrat, summed up these tendencies with the provocative thesis that a 'humming tone of discontent' is spreading.

On the Polish side, the 'Big Bang' transformation path was labelled 'Balcerowicz-type', after the influential Finance Minister who conceived it. It involved a shock therapy of social change, concentrating on the quick introduction of market mechanisms, the liberalising of legal preconditions for setting up businesses, etc. In many aspects, it indeed comes close to a shock therapy. In others, this description does not fit at all, especially with respect to the politically very sensitive sectors of agriculture (40% of Poles still depend on agriculture-related activities), coal mining and steel production. Nevertheless, stimulated by a quite euphoric modernistic worldview, Poland was the first post-socialist state to get radical transformation politics going (Fassmann 1997). In doing so, it became one of the most successful post-socialist reform states but at the same time it became one of the most contradictory ones, with heavy social frictions and polarisation tendencies between 'proud winners' and 'desperate losers' (Korcelli 1997). There still is majority support for the general strategies behind this Polish way of national and regional institutional capacity building processes, but this majority is diminishing. A more critical look at the social costs of this quick and relentless pace towards modernisation seems to have spread, especially in rural areas and smaller towns (Krätke 1998).

Summing up, in the Polish-German border region two contrasting transformation types meet. They partly mingle, partly bounce against each other and partly react in more or less dramatic forms – ranging from cooperative to repulsive or sclerotised forms of interaction. Often these tendencies overlap Therefore any study of institutional capacity building processes in this border region has to scrupulously take into account these conflictual and overlapping interaction processes *and* their respective embedding forms. This holds true for the study of city management approaches and trans-border cooperation policies, as well as for local and regional institution building and learning processes.

Asymmetric Border Situations

Asymmetries in political and legal ways of governance and regulation have been a major topic of border research in general (Scott and Collins 1997). Nevertheless, the mingling of the two radically different transformation types mentioned above gives these 'regular' border asymmetries an additional twist and additional dynamics.

The developmental prospects of the German-Polish border region in general are inherently dependent on three interconnected processes: the relative strength of the regional economies on both sides, the levels of unemployment and the wage divide. As Krätke (1998) argues, there still is a tendency among Western commentators to underestimate the remarkable proficiency of the Polish type of transformation pathway. Krätke, only slightly overemphasising the facts, comments in this respect:

> Measured by differences in regional and economic strength, the border of affluence lies between West and East Germany, rather than between East Brandenburg and Western Poland ... The real divide in the border region is a clear wage divide (Krätke 1998, p 252).

Another crucial asymmetry that still influences this 'difficult neighbourhood' concerns trust relationships and the concrete interaction structures within the border milieux. Many people who have lived in these areas during the past 50 years came into the region as a result of forced post-war population displacements. On the Polish side, this occurred mostly by way of removal from what are now Russian territories. On the German side too, the number of new inhabitants who came from 'elsewhere' is considerable. Many came from what are now Polish parts of pre-war Germany. This explains at least one layer of the historically deep-rooted insecurities and latent social tensions within the actual border zone. In addition to this, the border is marked by one of the most harsh language barriers in Europe. Especially on the German side, Polish language competence is still extremely rare, to put it mildly.

Local/Regional Peripheralisation Processes

Often euphorically praised as a blossoming interface in trans-European cooperation trajectories, the German-Polish border along the rivers Oder and Neisse is in several respects confronted with the dramatic danger of sliding into a downward dynamic of structural decline. One of the reasons is that the main beneficiaries of the growing trans-European, East-West cooperation networks seem to be not the actual border zones, but industrial and service centres elsewhere and their adjacent metropolitan areas – Berlin on the German side, Szczecin, Poznan and Wroclaw on the Polish side. In addition to this, considerable economic growth can be found in the area of Gorzow Wielkopolski and Zielona Gora, situated within the newly founded, enlarged voivodship (state) of Lubuski and representing the two capital cities of this region (see Figure 4.1). Therefore, the actual border zone is confronted with the real danger that the bulk of economic growth tendencies that should come with the liberalisation process and their trans-European spaces of flow might progressively 'leapfrog' the area. Sure enough, the regional and local actors on both sides of the border were the first to notice this.

The danger of cumulative peripheralisation processes within the border region seems to be even greater for those areas that are located in the interstitial spaces between the transcontinental trajectories of goods and people and communication lines between West and East. These areas are particularly threatened by the changing European economic geography. In the next section, we take a closer look at one of these interstitial areas – which may become one of the new peripheries in the process of EU enlargement.

Figure 4.1   The German-Polish Border Area - and the Twin City of Guben/Gubin

'Laboratory' Guben/Gubin: A German-Polish Twin City on the River Neisse

Scaling down the perspective, the twin city of Gubin/Guben will be the focus of the next stage of the analysis. Both parts of this border city are sufficiently similar in size and in functional impact on the surrounding region that such a comparison seems fruitful (see Figure 4.2).

Guben is one of the oldest cities in the Lausitz region. It grew considerably from the middle of the nineteenth century to become one of the most important textile and hat production centres of Germany. Taking advantage of its central location between eastern and western parts of Europe, major clothing and textile companies settled there. Side by side with the textile industry and respective mechanical engineering plants, commercial trade began to flourish. During the first half of the twentieth century, Guben seemed to be healthily established as one of the major textile locations in Germany.

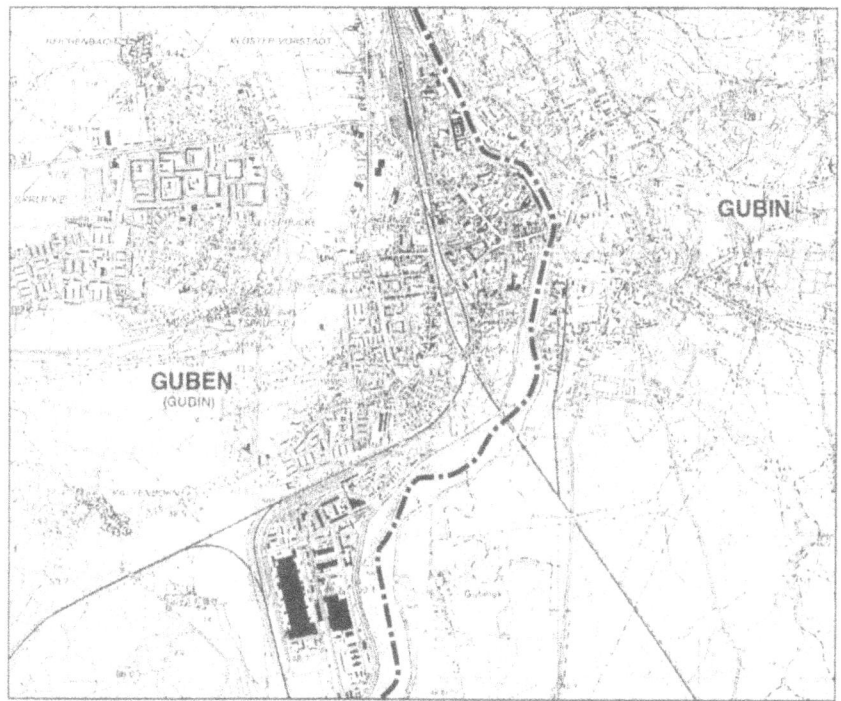

Figure 4.2   The Situation of Guben/Gubin within the Border Zone

Today Guben is hardly known outside the Brandenburg area, except for its baleful image as a town with brutally active right-wing youth groups, who have occasionally hunted foreigners to death. The reasons for this dramatic structural and image decline are manifold. At the end of the Second World War, the city of Guben was completely destroyed and ninety percent of its historic centre went to wreck and rubble. As a result of the Potsdam Treaty, in 1945 the city was divided into a Polish part (Gubin) and a German part (Guben). Since then, two thirds of the former city area, including the historic centre, the Grossner and the Werder suburbs have been part of Poland.

Present-day Guben on the German side grew out of the fragments of the western part of the city, especially the Klostervorstadt quarters, where production sites of the textile and hat industries and most machinery manufacturing plants were located. Before the war, Guben had a population of more then 44,000. Today the German Guben has a population of about 28,000, with substantial decreases over recent years. Gubin, the Polish part of this twin city, has 19,000 inhabitants, also decreasing – though in a more moderate way. The unemployment rates on both sides of the border oscillate at around 25%. Taking the state funded 'second labour market' into consideration, the rate on the German side would be 10 to 15% higher.

After the heavy damages during the last year of the war, the East German socialist state and its Territorial Planning System erected a series of mono-functional industrial structures along their eastern border, mostly on the banks of the rivers Oder and Neisse. In the context of this policy of industrialization, the GDR implanted an important chemical fibre plant in Guben with a 8000-strong workforce (the dominant black structures at the bottom of Figure 4.2). A large housing area made up of industrially-prefabricated monotonous buildings ('Plattenbauten') was developed in functional connection with this plant, but at considerable distance from the old town and the 'Klostervorstadt' (the rectangles in the upper part of Figure 4.2). This chemical fibre plant became one of the pearls of the GDR-chain of industrial structures along the Oder-Neisse Line. After the events of 1989, the now outdated plant was partly modernized through West German investment, but at the cost of a dramatic reduction in the workforce (currently 800 workers).

Up until now, the twin city's settlement structure on both sides of the border is still in a fragmented state, with no city centre on either side, let alone with a centre for the twin city as a whole. Grass and a small market on the Polish side occupy what was once the busy old city centre area. Accentuating the fragmentation of the urban structure, a growing proportion of the large housing area on the German side is unoccupied, as a direct result of the drastic decrease of the city's population. First attempts to demolish these empty housing areas are now under way. Guben recently became notorious for witch-hunts by right-wing youths targeting foreigners, asylum-seekers and refugees, in this way focussing the growing 'humming tone of discontent' in a scapegoat-like manner on members of the very small community of local 'foreigners'. A prolonged court case on the death of a young Algerian reinforced Guben's bad media image as a nucleus for right-wing brutality and its respective culture and mentality.

On the Polish part of the twin city, exiles and refugees from Eastern Europe, the Ukraine, the Baltic States and central parts of Poland moved into Gubin after the second world war. During the first decade, they lived in fear that the Germans might come back across the narrow river Nysa/Neisse. After 1989, in order to increase opportunities in this extremely difficult border situation, many actors within the political arena (state and municipal politicians, economic and policy experts, local and regional institutional actors on both sides of the twin city) have been eager to foster quite successfully *formal* cross-border institution-building processes. In 1990, the two neighbouring cities signed a friendship agreement. Three years later both municipalities joined the recently-founded 'Euroregion' Spree-Neisse-Oder, linked to the EU regional policy objective of promoting cross-border initiatives. The mutual aim was to facilitate a whole set of institution building processes across the river, and both cities participated in the World-EXPO 2000, developing six model projects. The joint topic of these projects runs under the heading 'Euro Town Guben/Gubin', focussing on 'the political will of both towns to bring their own structures gradually closer' (Modellprojekt 1999). One important objective in connection with these projects has been the development of a joint spatial structural concept for the twin city. A co-ordinated plan was agreed upon, focussing on the development of the still-missing town centre of Guben/Gubin. This plan explicitly crosses the border of the 'Schengen' space bridging and connecting the still heavily damaged old city church on the Polish side with the Klostervorstadt area on the German side.[2] In addition to this, both cities have submitted a concept for a common city centre, providing for the mutual development of central city areas on both sides of the river Neisse. The main axis of this project tries to link the two most important downtown areas in function and design. It is hoped that a new commanding landmark on the German side will correspond with the dramatic ruin of the huge old city church in Gubin on the Polish side of the axis (Stadt Guben 1998, IBA 1999). However, up to now no concrete investor is in sight.

Recently, the twin cities have been heavily decorated for their 'formal-institutional' European capacity building and their trans-border accomplishments. The 'Euro-Model Town Guben-Gubin' received several awards for transborder co-operation in different spheres of life: the 1996 Europe-Medal, 1997 Europe-Diploma, 1998 Europe-Flag. In the European Urban and Regional Planning Awards 1997-1998, the joint planning of both city regions and especially the cooperation in spatial planning between a new part of the EU territory (East Germany) and a still external country (Poland) was highly commended. In addition to this, remarkable initiatives in institution building processes and a respectable amount of mostly formal trans-border cooperation between the two Cities are under way. A recent list comprises 45 trans-border projects, ranging from the joint construction of a water treatment plant to multinational gatherings of philatelists. To sum up this concrete local situation, two conflicting processes seem to be under way. On the one hand, there are vigorous and well-regarded formal transborder cooperation initiatives and, on the other hand, there are strong tendencies towards heavy structural/functional peripheralisation processes, accompanied and framed by cultural-mental 'closure procedures'. Taken together, a dramatic mixture of options and conflicts within this twin city is evolving. The image of a dual city still heavily imprinted by the historical disasters of the twentieth century continues to evolve, right in the geographical centre of the 'old Europe'.

Learning Networks and Dislearning Milieux in Guben/Gubin? Interaction Paradoxes at the Local Level within the Overall Project of the Eastwards Expansion of the EU

The conflicting processes sketched above suggest the following question: What is the relationship between the astonishing amount of *formal* cross-border oriented networks on the one side, and on the other the segregating tendencies on the level of *informally* structured border milieux, especially on the German side? To understand these intricate relations, our 'milieu-oriented' approach focuses on embedding milieu structures and their contextualising functions in relation to formal governance structures and cross-border strategies of economic and political actors. In order to detect the logic of these transborder relations within the twin city, it was necessary to mix qualitative and quantitative research methods. The findings can be summarized and visualized in the form of a structural diagram (see Figure 4.3).

In a condensed fashion, this diagram shows three important cross-border action and interaction levels (I: *informal*; II: *intermediary*; III: *formal-institutional*). It also indicates the crucial options and conflict lines within and between these levels and hints at decisive closure procedures and governance paradoxes in relation to transborder interactions.[3]

Firstly, on the formal-institutional level of trans-border politics and strategic networking of economic actors (Interaction Level III), cooperation is going ahead, sometimes weakly, sometimes strongly, often accompanied by flourishing examples of symbolic politics. The twin City Guben/Gubin became especially active on the political level of cross-border interaction and within the domain of symbolic politics, promoting in multiple ways the idea of a 'Euro-Model' city. It was a pioneer in the hazardous process of extending the European unification process quickly eastwards. Many awards and prizes attest to the success of these activities, culminating in the prestigious 'Model Project Eurocity Guben/Gubin' award given by the

European Commission for the twin city's unified overall plan, focussing on the joint development of both parts of the city under a holistic perspective.

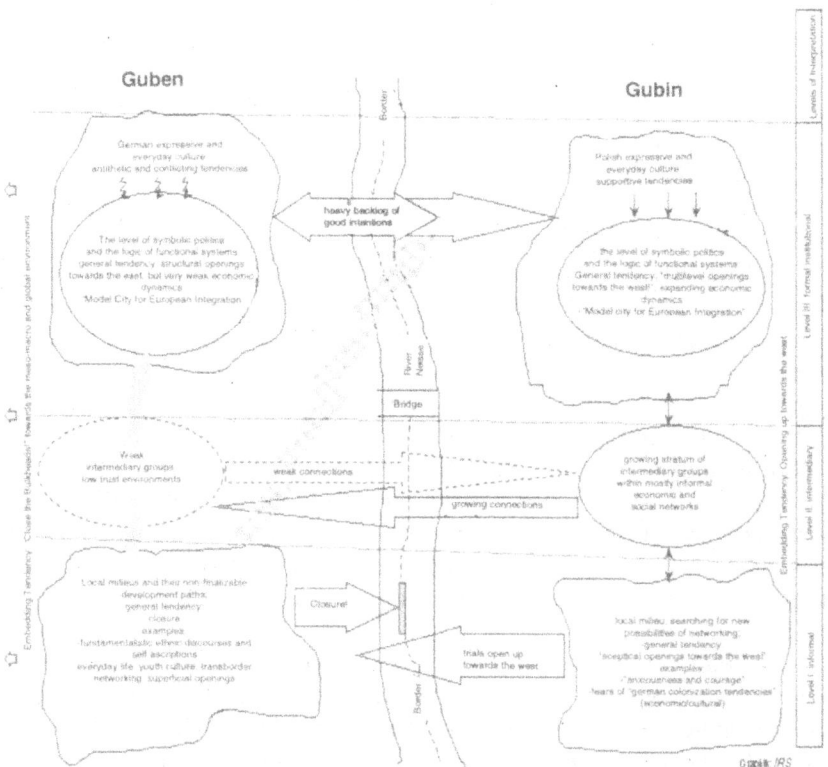

Figure 4.3   Governance Paradoxes and Main Constellations of Conflict

The diagram shows that even on this level of formal, strategic trans-border interaction, one has to take into closer account the embedding processes and forms of embeddedness of these strategic networks within the surrounding everyday cultures (see the small lightning-shaped arrows in Figure 4.3). This may sound trivial, but within the conflictual processes of trans-border institutional-capacity building processes, it is far from that. In the case of this twin city, the issue of 'embedding success' appears to be of utmost importance, not the least because there are marked differences between actual embedding practices on the Polish and the German sides. In Germany, antithetic and conflicting embedding tendencies dominate, whereas in Poland there is a critical consensus and supportive embedding tendencies in respect to the empowerment of strategic cross-border networks and European unification processes. Despite these conflicting and asymmetric embedding tendencies on the level of formal and strategic cross-border networks, an astonishing array of political and planning cooperation is going on – and the highly acclaimed 'European' approach is moving forwards apace.

These joint efforts on the level of symbolic politics are accompanied by an extremely weak economic dynamics, with dramatic shrinking tendencies on the German side and weak growth tendencies on the Polish side. In the latter, informal, sometimes illegal economic networks play a crucial role in the process of 'primary accumulation' under post-socialist conditions.

Secondly, in sharp contrast to these ambiguous tendencies on the level of formal cross-border networks, the networking structures and learning processes on the level of the 'non-finalisable' local milieux (Interaction Level I) are unambiguously antagonistic. Sometimes disastrous 'closure' procedures based on fundamentalist ethnic codification take the lead, implicitly supported by 'normal' everyday cultures (e.g. the witch-hunt of foreigners by right wing youths). This seems especially true on the German side, but there are reports of similar tendencies also on the Polish side. Here the level of embedding milieux plays the decisive role in constituting the locally-dominant relations of daily life in the twin city, generating the life-world structures of shared meanings, of habits, routines and expectations.

Thirdly, on the German side of the twin-city, the level of intermediary groups and associations (Interaction Level II) has not been capable and/or willing to combine the conflicting tendencies between *informal* milieux and the *formal* cross-border relations into proactive forms of local capacity building processes. The following story may illustrate this point. In 1999, intermediary groups started a petition against the mayor of Guben, in an effort to kick him out of his job. In Brandenburg, this procedure is called 'Bürgermeister-Kegeln', i.e. to throw the mayor out of his job, like a pin in a bowling game. This populist attempt was explicitly initiated because of the mayor's clear support for Europe-oriented, cross-border activities and the amount of vested 'symbolic' interests into the eastwards enlargement of the EU. To make matters worse, the mayor had just been awarded a high honour by the Polish government for his accomplishments in improving German-Polish relations in general. This high honour did not do him any good on the political home front, though. On the contrary, it was used as a decisive argument against him. He was labelled 'Polenfreund', 'Friend of Poles', with the implicit assumption that he did not care enough about the interest of his fellow countrymen. Against these 'locked-in' interaction tendencies and interpretation routines within the local border milieux, the intermediary level of civil society-oriented local capacities and groups has been so far very feeble. Sometimes, as in the case of the petition against the mayor, intermediary groups and associations even escalate the conflicts.

Summarising Figure 4.3, we found on the German side of the border a dramatic clash between blossoming formal cross-border relations towards the East on the level of strategic networks and symbolic politics (Interaction Level III), and multiple informal closure processes on the level of social milieux (Interaction Level I). Within the local milieux themselves, locked-in border constructs and low-trust environments are expanding. Consequently, even on the level of strategic cross-border networks (III), irritations and low trust 'loops' are growing. Up until now, the mayor and his local power networks try to stick to their approach of strengthening discursive strategies and not to give in to hostile zero sum games that confront *'them'* to *'us'*. Nevertheless, the option to choose communicative strategies and the respective governance styles within the border situation gets increasingly precarious, influencing the formal institutional capacity building processes. This results in *governance paradoxes*:[4] 'good' institution-building processes tend to produce 'bad' closure effects. The conflicting tendencies between Interaction Levels III and I tend to escalate, insufficiently mediated through intermediary groups of level II. As a result, the danger of structural contradictions between individual expectations and the results of collective trans-border processes is growing fast. Not surprisingly, these interaction asymmetries and governance paradoxes tend to reinforce peripheralisation processes in the 'in-between' border zone as a whole. In this way, a vicious circle is impending over the borderland, combining economic, political, social *and* cultural processes in a downward spiral.

Within this downgrading process, the patterns of network relations have shifted between openness, exclusiveness and closure, between Mafia-style relational structures and learning communities (Hellmer, Friese et al. 1999). Under post-socialist conditions, these network ambiguities seem to have flourished on each side of the border, as well as in cross-border relations. Closed pressure groups and respective 'silent majorities' have evolved, alongside active humanitarian groups and 'good leaders' seeking to develop open, flexible, learning-oriented cross-border relations and institutions.

Amidst many 'negative' episodes, 'good' ones seem to be all the more important: German-Polish schools, associations and clubs involving music groups, ornithologists, anglers, philatelists and politicians. Nevertheless, they all tend to share the ambiguities described above and the problematic relation of 'good' trans-border cooperation plans embedded in 'non-finalisable' milieux developments with strong closure tendencies.[5] Unfortunately, the problematic 'meeting' of two different transformation pathways and their very different economic dynamics aggravate these ambivalences and asymmetries. This 'meeting' often turns ambivalences into contradictions, and asymmetries into governance paradoxes.

In the meantime, each pathway has developed its specific mixtures of formal/informal institutional capacity building, which act as important mediators in structuring closure/opening processes. The Polish 'Balcerowicz-type' transformation pathway impels actors to open up and strive to interconnect with their Western European neighbours on the local, regional and national level. The German 'transfer' type impels local actors to regard possible newcomers from the East as competitors and illegitimate revenue-seekers, competing for the same structural funding. Closure procedures seem to be the appropriate counter-strategy, but as an unintended consequence, they accelerate the local/regional peripheralisation of the whole border region.

The rhetoric of cross-border cooperation, well known in border zones all over the world, seems to be progressively out of contact with the actual 'dialectics' of cross-border relations mediated through local milieux. As a result, it is not only the poor, the jobless, the youngsters without adequate job perspectives who participate in xenophobic/ethnocentric games and in the nourishment of the 'humming tone of discontent' mentioned earlier.

In a more detached analytical mood, the two transformation types that meet in this twin city can be described as two different forms of hybridisation of formal and informal institutional capacity building processes. Their mismatch escalates the normal animosities in border regions leading to self-marginalising tendencies, mostly via closure procedures on the level of the respective everyday cultures. The danger of a 'locked-in' symbolic universe is impending over the twin city, with respective locked-in relevance structures and the consolidation of a low trust environment, with severe political and economic consequences.

Our analysis suggests that the cultural contexts of everyday life, the milieux and their specific forms of hybridisation of the formal with the informal seem to play a decisive role in assessing options and conflicts of institutional capacity building processes in general. This seems especially relevant with respect to capacity building processes within border regions in the eastern parts of Europe. At the same time, and on a more general analytical level, the problems of these post-socialist border regions may help to clarify systematically the structural layers of interaction, which play a decisive role in *all* institutional capacity building processes.

Institutional Capacity Building and Learning Options in Asymmetric Border Contexts – An Empirical Model for Interpretation and Interaction

In this final section, the experience of paradoxical capacity building processes in the Guben/Gubin context will be connected with a proactive learning-oriented model. The aim of the model is to address the intricacies of locally-specific hybrid mixtures of informal and formal institutional capacity building processes. The importance of the informal local/regional rootedness of institutional capacity building processes becomes evident in our analysis of a praised example of the 'Euroregion' initiatives developed on the eastern borders of the EU. The overwhelming empirical evidence is that these initiatives remain superficial and produce feeble results unless they succeed in getting rooted within the local informal/formal-mix of capacity building. Only in this 'rooted' form might they function as springboards for further trans-border cooperation.

The aim of the model, illustrated in Figure 4.4, is to assess the options for developing locally rooted, strategically-open approaches to building cross-border relations and innovation, even in the difficult and problematic cases like the Twin City Guben/Gubin. At the same time the model takes scrupulously into account the interconnected obstacles which have to be overcome to prevent both further entrenchment of self-destructive, low trust environments, as well as the spreading of communication barriers, governance paradoxes, fears of competition ('Angst') and ethno-centred interaction routines.

The analytical perspective of Figure 4.4 may be summarised in four short statements. Firstly, against the current fragmentation of three badly-connected trans-border interaction levels, with their locked-in situations (see Figure 4.3), the model proposes the creation of two highly integrated local systems, comprising both 'soft' as well as 'hard' structures (e.g. production structures, institutional set-up, knowledge structures, mentalities). Despite the epochal changes in the post-socialist period, the 'soft' elements of these structural mixes have proved to be astonishingly stable over time. In this sense, soft structures such as mentalities, expressive cultures and structures of relevance seem to be much harder to transform than hard ones.

Secondly, it is indispensable to take into account the embedding structures of everyday life and the respective expressive cultures, mediated through life styles, consumer demand patterns, etc. Our research shows that where different transformation pathways meet, these embedding structures have to be taken even more seriously on both the analytical level as well as on the level of action strategies. This holds true exactly *because* they are only partly 'finalisable' through planning activities and strategic action.[6]

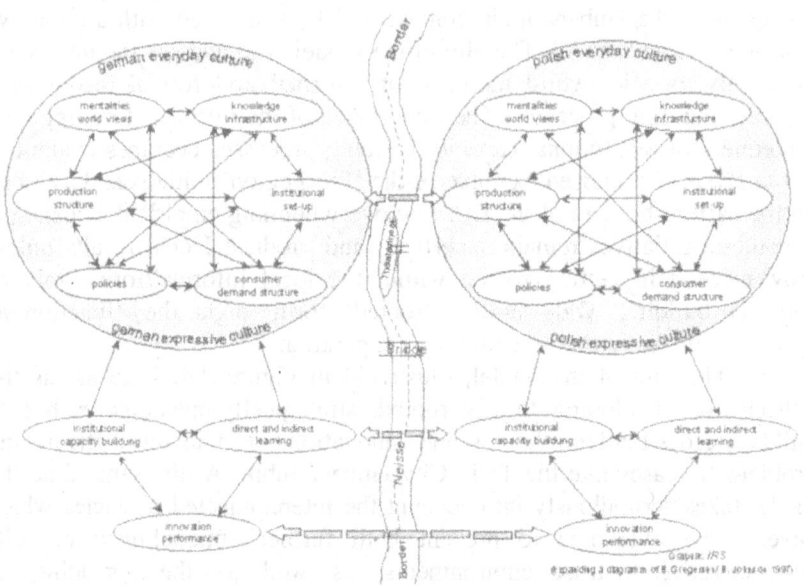

Figure 4.4   Learning Options: Main Factors Affecting Potential Transborder Learning and Capacity Building Processes within the Border Milieux of Guben/Gubin

Thirdly, our research on Guben/Gubin focuses strongly on the case-specific connections between formal and informal institutional capacity building and learning processes. Here we follow recent developments in institutional approaches within the disciplines of planning theory, economics, regional sciences and sociology (see Healey, Cameron et al.1995, Healey 1997, Gregersen and Johnson 1997, Thomas 1999a, Hollingsworth and Boyer 1997, Grabher and Stark 1999), and have tried to extend them into post-socialist transformation analyses. In this perspective, institutions shape the interactive learning processes in politics, economics and urban governance - and they are indispensable in the domain of the socio-cultural lifeworld.[7] In all these domains they also 'fulfil several important roles in relation to innovation activities' (Gregersen and Johnson 1997, p 484).

Finally, Figure 4.4 serves as a reminder that the eastwards extension of the European Union may not be necessarily a humanitarian strategy, bringing lost brothers and sisters into the big turbo boat of western capitalism. In many respects, the contrary seems closer to the truth. European Union policies of eastwards expansion have to be seen within the context of worldwide globalisation processes, combined and hybridised with path-specific transformation. And it is well known by now that both globalisation and transformation comprise a whole set of complementary processes – linking the local in case-specific ways to the global (see Dürrschmidt 1997, Wilson and Dissanayahe 1996, Hannerz 1996, Keim and Matthiesen 1998).

Conclusions

In this chapter, the arduous process of the eastwards expansion of the EU has been looked upon from a micro-perspective, concentrating on local institutional capacity building processes and their embedding practices on the level of milieux.

The focus of the research discussed here was on peripheral regions and communities on the present eastern border of the EU. Even within the EU as it stands today, there is always the risk of rivalries and conflicts between different 'peripheries', and the consequent political reality of fighting among them. The impending eastwards expansion towards the former socialist countries will escalate this problem considerably. Therefore, a closer look at local and regional peripheralisation processes seems indispensable. Especially in areas where different transformation pathways meet, 'traditional' institutional and governance approaches, with their concern mainly if not solely with formal institution building or formal institutional transfers, no longer offer convincing results or realistic policy ideas. This is especially the case in connection with the transformation processes in Eastern Middle Europe and Eastern Europe. The institutional capacity building processes there seem to 'float' on an immense ocean of informality, reaching from the political and economic domains ('shadow economy') through everyday activities, to the transcendences of the social world (Schütz and Luckmann 1972). It is this layer of informality underpinning on-going structuration processes which serves as an indispensable precondition and as a very flexible 'glue' for the well- or mal-functioning of formal institutional capacity building processes in these regions.

Focusing on competitive/cooperative innovation practices in the Twin City of Guben/Gubin, we found indications of an interesting reversal of transborder supremacies between Polish and German local elites, accompanied by a reversal of innovation hierarchies. The young members of the local elites on the Polish side of the twin city expressed profound pride for their own accomplishments in the drastic transformation process their society has gone through. With new self-esteem they look towards their German neighbours, still wealthier and with an incomparably better infrastructure on their side, but with quite pessimistic action orientations and a generalized 'humming tone of discontent'. Indeed, on the German side, some members of the local elite seem to be sinking into a kind of 'structural melancholy', despite the large transfers of capital flowing regularly from West Germany. A good example of this is the long-standing practice on the German side of deriding the Polish economy. However, considering the shock strategy of modernisation implied in the Balcerowicz model mentioned earlier, and the economic effectiveness of the young Polish elites, that practice appears ridiculously outdated. It reveals far more about the minds and relevance structures of those engaged in it and their xenophobic worldviews, than about the practices of the busy Polish actors and their effective levels of informality, which are reaching out for new options 'in the West'.

This leads back to one central problem in the border zone of Guben/Gubin: the conflict around the socially approved 'amounts' of informality within governance processes. The general reluctance of action theorists and policy and planning analysts to take the 'foggy sea of informality' into a more systematic account usually gets justified by three standard arguments: that no precise data is available; that the rate of change is too slow; that it does not exert direct influence on the formal level. As this chapter contends, this objectivistic reasoning quickly loses its strength if applied to current processes of change in Eastern Europe and the impending eastwards expansion of the EU. Without taking the rich level of informality into a systematic account, the analytical expectations connected with far-reaching institutional transfers from western to eastern parts of Europe will stay unrealistic and their political effects will be rather unpredictable: they could work, but they will often fail. This has a further cognitive implication. Underneath the issue of formal and/or informal structuring processes, a very influential 'western' type of policy making and policy analysis seems to be at stake. Against this line of thought and action the case of the twin city Guben/Gubin clearly encourages analytical perspectives which take into closer and more systematic account the embedding procedures of institutions as well as the respective local, regional and national cultural mixes of formal and informal structuring processes.

Notes

1. The cultural effects of the 'gradualist' East German pathway of institutional transformation have been extensively discussed in the literature. For an overview, see e.g. Pollack 1996, Meulemann 1998, Matthiesen 1998b).
2. The Schengen Agreement provided for the removal of passport and customs controls in internal borders within the EU. Conversely, controls on the external borders such as the German-Polish have been reinforced.
3. With respect to the Polish side of the twin city and its relational logics, the far-reaching public administration reforms of January 1999 fostered considerable new efforts in institution building and created new opportunities for Polish municipalities. The local forms of implementing these opportunities are not yet clear. As to the Polish side of the diagram, we suggest a *tentative outline* of the embedding types of formal institutional governance structures within the informal border milieux.
4. The concept of governance paradox designates a type of results from strategic/argumentative interaction, where the intended consequences of action are systematically 'distorted' through the unintended conflicts between formal interaction structures and informal embedding structures (habits and routines, deep codification processes and worldviews, 'trustful' and 'low trust' structures and milieux etc).
5. In contrast to strategic networks and their 'finalised' goal structures, we found that milieux evolved largely by way of context-sensitive, self-regulating developmental processes. Although highly structured internally by intentions, objectives and 'autopoietic' pathways of a peculiar logic ('*Eigenlogik*'), as a whole they are not completely 'finalisable' in the context of strategic planning and governance processes (Matthiesen 1998a).
6. In reinventing a category with a long history in the social sciences, we call these embedding structures 'milieux'. But we de-ontologise the concept of milieu and turn it heuristically into a conceptual device to reconstruct the embedding relations between formal institutions and the surrounding everyday cultures with their trust relations, implicit and explicit knowledge forms and action structures etc. (see Matthiesen 1998a).
7. See the influential conceptualisation of Alfred Schütz and Thomas Luckmann (1973) and Jürgen Habermas (1984). For a critical re-examination see Matthiesen (1985). Similar perspectives combining 'lifeworld' and 'transformation' are fruitfully sketched out by Srubar (1998) from a socio- phenomenological perspective, and by Thomas (1999a) from a neo-institutionalist approach.

5 The Tangled Web – Neighbourhood Governance in a Post-Fordist Era

JUDITH ALLEN AND GÖRAN CARS

The regeneration of 'distressed neighbourhoods' forms the focus for new forms of urban policy approaches across Europe. These approaches derive from wider concerns about urban competitiveness and re-investment in the urban built fabric as well as deeper concerns about the effects of processes of social exclusion within cities. The European Commission sums up the problem in the following way:

> The twin challenge facing European urban policy is therefore one of maintaining its cities at the forefront of an increasingly globalised and competitive economy while addressing the legacy of urban deprivation. These two aspects are complementary (CEC 1997).

This paper reflects on how the problems of 'distressed neighbourhoods' have been produced by uneven structural change, the ways that disjointed economic, political and welfare state structures create the modes of production of everyday life in these neighbourhoods, and the key role of creating democratic neighbourhood governance processes if policies which seek to regenerate these neighbourhoods are to be successful.

Social Exclusion in European Neighbourhoods

The argument in this paper is an attempt to make theoretical sense of the results of a cross-national research project based on detailed studies of social exclusion in ten neighbourhoods in eight countries within the European Union.[1] In doing so, we also highlight some key issues related to developing governance capacity relevant to the situations studied. This section sets out the main findings from this research.

The broad processes of social exclusion were similar across all the ten neighbourhoods:

- *Stigmatisation* of the areas based both on the presence of specific groups within them (minority ethnic groups, migrants and unemployed people) and on the physical signs of neglect.
- Spatial *concentration* of stigmatised groups, whether through private or public sector housing processes.
- Subtle local social processes which *contained* the aspirations and affective focus of everyday life within the neighbourhoods, whether the neighbourhood was in an isolated peripheral position or an enclave within the central urban area.
- The presence of specific groups and conflicts within the neighbourhood which *disrupted* social relationships within it (mental illness and substance abuse, in particular, generated high levels of fear and anxiety).

In all the neighbourhoods, the social bases of conflict were similar: young versus old, minority ethnic versus ethnic nationals, newcomers versus long established residents. These dimensions of conflict tended to overlap and in none of the neighbourhoods was there a pro-active strategy to overcome these divisions.

Disjointed Structural Change

The disjointed processes of structural change since the 1970s create the broad parameters of change which shape the experience of the people living in the neighbourhoods covered by the research. This section of the paper presents a sketch of how the process of change has created the 'disjunctures' within which everyday life is produced within these neighbourhoods. We set our discussion of these processes in the context of accounts of structural change, which identify a transition from Fordist to post-Fordist economic organisation (Lipietz 1998, Amin 1994).

By 1975, the western European economies could be labelled as 'mature Fordist' regimes comprising three strongly interlocked elements: economic systems, welfare state systems, and political systems.

1. The Fordist economic system was characterised by factory-based mass production techniques and a set of labour market institutional structures supporting this method of production (eg mass trades unions, wage differentials and bargaining related to skill levels, male employment,

etc). Within this system, most members of the labour force could look forward to reasonably steady employment and steady increases in material incomes over their lives (see Lipietz 1998). Even in the less industrialised southern states, Fordist systems played a crucial role in urbanised areas.

2. Welfare state systems supported the operation of the economic system. While it is possible to distinguish three or four different ways to structure welfare state systems within western Europe (see Esping-Andersen 1990 for the seminal work typologising systems), three elements in all systems have particular significance for the production of everyday life and the way it is tied to processes of social exclusion:

- Educational systems were designed to meet the skills required by employers from new entrants to the labour force. They also acted as major agents of socialisation, so that the experience of compulsory education provided a 'cultural training' which helped fit children into the roles they would play in adult life.
- General social insurance systems were designed to support workers (and their families) through periods of short term unemployment, illness and old age. Such systems also provided, on a discretionary and needs tested basis, minimal levels of help for those unwilling or unable to enter the labour force.
- Housing systems were designed to ensure that workers were well housed and to provide part of the package of increasing material incomes for those workers who were steadily employed (Harloe 1995).

3. Political systems comprised a set of institutions centred on the nation-state and built on the assumption that their main function was to manage growth and to decide on the allocation of fiscal resources among different functionally-divided programmes of state activity.

From the mid-1970s onwards, global competition and technological development led to rapid changes in the economies of western Europe. In terms of the processes which generate social exclusion, the most important long run-effect was to accelerate increases in the level of service sector employment after 1974.

The growth of the service sector has been associated with increasing demand for flexible labour, that is, labour which is willing to work casually, part time, on piece rates, on temporary contracts, at home and so forth. The skills required are often interpersonal, require attention to detail and the literacy and numeracy associated with mastering new information technologies. At the same time, increased demand for flexible labour has also been accompanied by long run increases in the underlying rate of unemployment.

These structural shifts in the economies of the European Union present significant challenges to the welfare states which had been shaped during the long postwar boom. During this period, they had matured as large, bureaucratically organised institutions, acquiring a life and dynamic of their own, committed to pursuing the programmes and activities allocated to them in the early postwar years and resistant to reforms which would match shifts in the nature of the demand for labour. As a consequence, these institutions were expected to meet demands which they had not been designed for. In parallel, financial crises constrained public finances. Thus, while the needs for services increased, the resources available shrunk.

For a more qualitative assessment of the effects of post-Fordist change, it is necessary to look at how financial crisis and the inability to redesign delivery programmes to reflect the changing economic structure interact at the level of households and neighbourhoods. Examining the evidence from the neighbourhoods in our study showed three kinds of 'adaptive problems' in the welfare state functions:

- The primary and, particularly, the secondary education systems were failing to provide both training in the specific skills necessary to enter service sector jobs and the 'cultural training' necessary to obtain and sustain such jobs. In many cases, this manifested itself in high levels of anti-social behaviour among adolescents. Such problems were also exacerbated by the failure to adapt fully to high levels of immigrant/refugee children entering the schools.
- Means-tested income support systems, designed as temporary help for a minority, were not adapted to intermittent employment patterns. Applying for such support was degrading, undermined the self-confidence of applicants, and contributed to local status hierarchies which further undermined the position of applicants. In addition, the difficulty of adapting rates of payment to local job markets and flexible employment created poverty traps for applicants.
- The operation of social housing systems tended to trap residents in an increasingly residualised stock from which it was difficult to escape.

Ironically, these problems of rigidity in welfare state structures and the ways they contributed to the 'social containment' of residents in the neighbourhoods were most pronounced in those countries with the most extensive and expensive welfare state systems, ie Sweden and Denmark. The precise effects on different groups vary from country to country, reflecting different configurations of specific labour market and welfare state institutions, but the overall effect is one of social exclusion because routes out of the situation are blocked. The underlying cause of this blockage is the increasing disjunction between economic change, which valorises flexible work practices, and a welfare support system designed to complement Fordist work practices.

Policy Responses to Disjointed Structural Change

Responding to the problems of disjointed structural change outlined above requires a strategic view of change as well as the capability to respond strategically. However, not only was economic change affected by globalisation, but the socio-political structures of western Europe were also affected.

While 'ever closer Union' brings with it the promise of enhanced global competitiveness and more secure future economic growth for the Union's citizens, it also creates threats for specific groups. These groups, who are seen as 'left behind' and 'left out' by the processes of economic change and integration, are primarily concentrated in urban areas. In its policy agenda for urban areas, the European Commissioners sum up the effects of disjointed structural change as:

> The starting point for future urban development must be to recognise the role of the cities as motors for regional, national and European economic progress. At the same time, it also has to be taken into account that urban areas, especially the depressed districts of medium-sized and larger cities, have borne many of the social costs of past changes in terms of industrial adjustment and dereliction, inadequate housing, long-term unemployment, crime and social exclusion (CEC 1997).

Thus, the underlying problems which characterise the 'distressed neighbourhoods' which have come to be home for large groups of people at risk of social exclusion in Europe have been created by processes of disjointed structural change. This process of change has unhinged the relationships between the labour market, welfare state and political structures which characterised the Fordist era. In the post-Fordist era, each of these structures has developed along the lines of dynamics established in the Fordist era, which, in turn, create new kinds of problems to be solved if they are to be joined together again in a way which addresses the problems of 'distressed neighbourhoods'. Thus, changes in the labour market imply that post-Fordist welfare arrangements are not effective to meet the needs of today. Realising that the structure and delivery mechanisms of the welfare state need to be rethought inevitably calls for reconsidering the appropriateness of contemporary governance arrangements. The next section of this paper examines the effects of disjointed structural change within neighbourhoods as the basis for developing, in the last section of the paper, a set of ideas for reframing approaches to combating social exclusion.

Disjointed Structural Change and Social Exclusion Within Neighbourhoods

The most useful definition of social exclusion sees it as poverty which is multi-dimensional and persistent (see the work reported in Room 1997). What is 'new' about this kind of poverty is that it is difficult to escape because those trapped within it live their everyday lives within systemic social processes which create barriers to escape (Mingione 1993). In order to understand how these systemic barriers work, it is necessary to sketch out how they operate at the level of everyday life. This section of the paper sets out how the concept of disjointed structural change can be used to analyse the problems of the 'distressed neighbourhoods'.

The concept of disjointed structural change suggests that these barriers can best be understood in terms of a mismatch between welfare delivery systems and the current situation in distressed neighbourhoods. Fordist welfare-benefit delivery systems were designed on the premise that they would help active subjects through the essentially short run vicissitudes of employed life (illness, short spells of cyclical unemployment, etc) and provide a basic income for a period of retirement. These systems assumed that the general welfare of citizens depended primarily on their capacity within the formal labour market and secondarily on their role within informal networks largely based within their families and set within socially homogeneous neighbourhoods. Disjointed structural change has eroded the pillars of this system within neighbourhoods. De-industrialisation removed the Fordist bases of permanent and stable employment. Residents are now primarily dependent on the flexibilised employment practices which characterise (mainly personal) service sector employment.

The effects of these changes in localised employment possibilities and local solidarities are twofold. Firstly, residents lose the capacity to be active subjects because they lose the local relational resources necessary to build their own informal networks across the neighbourhood. Secondly, residents become more strongly dependent on the formal systems of welfare benefit delivery, which begin to determine many aspects of everyday life. In this situation, access to resources 'outside the neighbourhood' becomes very important in sustaining the material conditions of everyday life. This, in turn, enhances the significance of local social professionals, e.g. housing managers, employees in various branches of local government, and those employed in central or regional agencies where their work is associated with 'managing' social relations in the neighbourhood, as gatekeepers or bridges to external resources.

Systemic Barriers: The Paradox of Consensus

One of the more striking findings of the research is that there was a general consensus among residents and social professionals about the most significant material problems facing residents in the neighbourhoods. What needs to be explained, therefore, is why such local consensus leads to so little change in what is done and in how it is done. The general answer to this paradox lies in how the relationship between professionals' knowledge of the area and their action spaces creates stasis in the system. The specific answers lie in the ways that 'normal' professional, organisational and political activities interlock to create a set of barriers to mobilising processes leading to change.

Professional activities are rooted in the social, cultural and educational background of those who deliver services within the areas. Professional roles are based on solving specific types of problems. Each type of professional is trained to see a particular slice through the problems of residents living in the area and sees its own competence as limited to activities within its own area of expertise. The general consequence of professionalisation is that, while the problems of social exclusion are multi-dimensional, responses to these problems tend to be through a set of single dimensional professional activities. The sum of these 'single dimensional' activities does not add up to a coherent multi-dimensional response.

Thus, the paradox associated with professional activities in the neighbourhoods was that, while all the professionals within them might share an 'objective and background' knowledge of the problems within the neighbourhoods, none of them had an 'everyday working knowledge' of the breadth and complexity of place-based stakes and the diversity among residents. Each saw the 'problems' of the area and the rightness and efficacy of their own responses to these problems through the lens of their own specific professional expertise. Nothing in the situation challenged this 'divided and dividing' approach.

Organisational barriers to change arise from the wider formal institutional structures within which professionals work. Although the specific configurations of agencies working in the neighbourhoods varied strongly across the eight countries, they tended to be strongly departmentalised and hierarchical. Resources were distributed to local areas through departmental structures which tended to set localised offices in different neighbourhoods against each other in an internally competitive environment. At the same time, departmental priorities directly reflected the nature of the 'problems' which the departments were meant to solve, meaning that there was no coherent view of the social complexity and intertwined nature of the problems within specific neighbourhoods. These factors reinforced the tendency of professionals to slice up the 'neighbourhood problem'.

Organisational structures also generated other kinds of barriers to change. Firstly, in most cases, departments were free to define the boundaries of their own 'local patches' in ways which would allow them to deploy limited resources most effectively in meeting departmental priorities. In most neighbourhoods, some services were provided from a central town hall while others were provided locally. These problems were even more pronounced where different layers of government were all providing services to residents. Consequently, departmental patches did not match each other. This patchwork quilt pattern reinforced the difficulty of focusing on the multi-dimensional problems of any single spatially-defined group of residents. Thus organisational 'patches' (departmentally defined groups of staff) replaced neighbourhoods (socially defined groups of residents) in thinking about service delivery issues. The consequence for individual residents using a variety of services was that they had to patch the services together for themselves.

Another problem associated with organisational structures is that they reinforce professional divisions. Within modern national governments and welfare states, there are strong connections between central government ministries, localised agencies, local authorities and the 'modern professions'. Thus, professionalism has a strong vertical dimension, in which promotion tends to mean 'up and away' from problems on the ground (Christensen 1999). This tendency exists everywhere although its strength depends greatly on the formal configurations of local government. Two factors seem to be especially important in accounting for the strength of the vertical effect. The first is the extent to which local governments have control of buoyant tax resources or are dependent on central government grants. The second is the extent to which local governments are agencies or partners of central government, which is also related to the nature of formal structures (centralised versus federal systems). Nevertheless, the use of special programme funds by central governments, often awarded on the basis of 'professionally innovative' approaches, reinforces both the vertical orientation of professionals and the 'organisational necessity' of stigmatising the neighbourhood itself in order to gain priority in competing for resources.

Thus, the paradox of the local consensus is that, even with the best will in the world, professionalism combines with vertically-defined organisational structures to constrain the ability of professionals to act on the basis of their consensus.

Political barriers to change interact with professional and organisational barriers. Some of the bases of this interaction have been discussed above. In particular, the political significance of verticality in organisational structures should not be underestimated. Modern European welfare states are embedded in central governmental structures. The four major welfare state functions tend to be administered through separate national ministries. The complexity of these functions means that, even with immense political commitment, it is difficult to change this structure substantially or very quickly, if only because the welfare state affects virtually every citizen in some way. Consequently, the politics of change are simply very complex.

Political barriers also arise from the changing nature of urban politics. Firstly, globalisation has increased competition between cities and regions. In response, cities have frequently developed strategies to improve their attractiveness and competitiveness. These strategies include financial and other investments aimed at improving the image of the city. This competition create its own set of urban political priorities in which the problems of distressed neighbourhoods are seen as secondary. Secondly, the function of the distressed neighbourhoods within urban political-spatial structures has changed. Put most bluntly, they have changed from being dormitory areas for highly skilled, highly valued industrial workers into being reception camps for the reserve army of flexibilised labour. This change in function also changes the relationship between the people living in distressed neighbourhoods and other urban actors, in particular, employers in the fast growing personal service sectors. Consequently, it becomes more difficult for residents in the neighbourhoods to form strategic alliances outside the neighbourhoods and, thus, 'represent themselves' in the complex ecology of urban politics.

By exploring professional, organisational and political barriers separately, it is possible to identify a number of key elements in strategies to combat social exclusion in the distressed neighbourhoods.

- The first priority is to strengthen local solidarities while recognising the ways that increased social diversity affects residents.
- There needs to be a forum which brings together different types of professionals working locally in the neighbourhood. The aim is to generate a commonly held multi-dimensional view of the problems in the neighbourhood. In Chapter 6 the search for a 'third way' to combine authority with flexibility and entrepreneurialism is discussed. The ideas presented, bringing together what can be learnt from below with what is above, are related to our suggestions.
- Politically, it is necessary to create new micro-political structures which are deeply rooted in the complex social relationships within the neighbourhoods, both relationships among residents and relationships between residents and local social professionals.

With these basic points in mind, it is now possible to develop a more grounded discussion of strategies for combating social exclusion in Europe's distressed neighbourhoods.

Democracy, Governance and Neighbourhoods

The paper so far has suggested that the problem of combating social exclusion in distressed neighbourhoods is not a problem of 'objective' knowledge about social exclusion or about the socio-economic characteristics of and problems experienced by residents in these neighbourhoods. Rather the problem is one of thinking about strategies to *combat* social exclusion. If the concept of social exclusion refers to the social processes which create long term, multi-dimensional, inescapable material poverty, then the solution may lie in creating other social processes which combat or alter the operation of these wider social processes.

The remainder of this paper explores a number of ideas about creating 'micro-political processes' within neighbourhoods which may have the potential to alter the impact of wider social processes. It takes its inspiration from Healey's definition of planning as managing a shared existence in space (1997). The overall aim is to identify the major components of a concept of neighbourhood democracy which could guide the creation of micro-political processes.

The analytical framework developed in this paper, suggests that a particular definition of governance is appropriate. Le Galès (1998) identifies two aspects of governance which capture the rationale for designing micro-political structures and processes to combat social exclusion in distressed neighbourhoods. These structures and processes must support residents in gaining:

- The capacity to form a collective actor from diverse local interests, organisations and social groups and with sufficient internal integration to be able to formulate collective goals.
- The ability to represent the 'local collective actor' to other relevant actors within the urban area and various levels of government.

Thus, the key question is to identify how the structures of social relationships in specific neighbourhoods generate barriers to creating the democratic neighbourhood processes which underlie forming a locally-based 'collective actor'.

Micro-Politics, Networks and Webs

Micro-political structures and processes need to be built on existing social relationships within neighbourhoods. Thus, it is important to understand the nature of these relationships in terms of the ways in which they can support or hinder the creation of democratic neighbourhood governance. The notion of networks is useful in this kind of analysis because it is rooted in communication processes.

In all ten neighbourhoods, two different kinds of networks were identified. Informal networks existed among residents, and more formal networks existed among social professionals working in the neighbourhoods. This section of the paper discusses each type of network, and then discusses the relationships between the two types of networks.

In all the neighbourhoods, there was evidence that, for those residents involved in them, informal networks played a significant role in supporting their commitment to living in the neighbourhood. Most of the networks were based on common interests, for example, children/childcare or sports or bingo and old time dancing. Most significantly, both a shared religion as well as other cultural activities were significant in supporting networks among minority ethnic groups. In some cases, extended family relationships were important and, in other cases, friendship networks formed in school persisted for young adults. Where networks did overlap, they were often 'co-extensive', that is, involving the same people in a range of different activities. There was also evidence that many people were not involved in 'locally based' networks, either because they were very marginalised socially or because they were able to use personal strategies which 'distanced' them from the neighbourhood. Some networks were very exclusive and did not welcome newcomers or 'outsiders'.

Formal networks associated with the neighbourhoods tended to be complex because they brought together agencies and/or professionals covering a wide sectoral span. They also brought together actors from different geographically organised services (the 'patching' problem) and different political jurisdictions (neighbourhood, municipality, region). A further complexity in managing these formal networks arose from the extent to which an agency's commitment was a function of the personal commitments and/or ambitions of the individual professionals representing the agency. Most commonly, this problem arose because the local neighbourhood formal networks were seen as peripheral to agencies' main priorities in delivering sectorally and organisationally divided services. Nevertheless, the common objective of the formal networks was to coordinate the variety of services delivered in the neighbourhood. However, these local formal networks tended to languish in the absence of strong leadership and/or a clear local 'project'.

The most striking finding, therefore, was that there was a marked absence of 'webs' connecting formal and informal networks. The main exceptions were threefold: Firstly, in some neighbourhoods, tenants associations and other 'user groups', organised and supported by professionals, were 'brought into' some of the formal networks. Secondly, in three neighbourhoods, relatively independent community workers supported informal networks. In both these two situations the strength of the links was relatively weak. The third exception, however, is very marked. In the Portuguese neighbourhood, as a consequence of a very deep political commitment by the municipality, there was a very strong network of professionals whose main aim was to identify networks among residents in order to relocate the informal networks together in the process of rehousing them from the shanty towns.

In the general case, however, there was no political will to create webs between informal and formal networks as a way of linking residents and professionals. Agencies, stretched for resources, did not see neighbourhood coordinating forums as anything other than peripheral to their main business while residents tended to regard both professionals and formal networks with a mixture of scepticism, cynicism, suspicion, mistrust and incomprehension.

There are two significant consequences of the absence of webs linking formal and informal networks. Firstly, there is no basis for challenging the range and balance of services delivered in the neighbourhood. Some services may receive lots of resources and be well delivered while others have few resources and are inadequate. The absence of strong webs means that there is simply no forum for assessing whether residents could be better served by reallocating resources and services. An additional aspect of this problem is the possibility that some specific groups of residents are indirectly discriminated against, that is, they receive poor quality services across the full range of services. Secondly, initiatives launched within formal networks may disrupt or harm informal networks. Very commonly, such initiatives intensified conflicts between different groups and informal networks.

This review of the ways that informal and formal networks operate and interact (or do not interact) indicates how they contribute to the localised processes of social containment and disruption which characterise how the broader processes of social exclusion affect people living in 'distressed' neighbourhoods. It has four important implications for strategies to create micro-political structures and processes in order to form a 'local collective actor' capable of formulating collective goals and representing the neighbourhood to others.

- Most importantly, these strategies need to be based on a very careful audit to identify existing informal and formal networks and how they operate.
- Locally specific strategies need to be assessed against the ways in which they can contribute to defragmenting informal networks and 'enlivening' formal networks by knitting them into the everyday life of residents in the neighbourhood.
- Locally specific strategies should have the potential to increase the 'effective' resources available to the neighbourhood by valuing the resources of informal networks and avoiding the waste of formal resources devoted to coordination for its own sake.
- Ultimately, they should enable resources to be used more effectively by providing a means of synergising the work of residents and professionals around an agreed local 'project' and priorities.

More generally, this line of reasoning suggests that micro-political structures and processes must be designed in a way which reflects the specific configuration of informal and formal networks in the neighbourhood and which facilitates the evolution of a collective actor. It is particularly important, given the kinds of conflict which are engendered in distressed neighbourhoods, to identify and build on the specific forms of conflict resolution which are used on an everyday basis by residents in the neighbourhood. In short, there is no blueprint for micro-political structures. They must be tailored to the specificities of each neighbourhood.

Conclusions: Practical Problems of Postmodernity

The structure of the argument in this paper means that there are two different types of conclusions to be drawn from it. The first type addresses a set of practical themes which run throughout the analysis. The second type sets the whole analysis in the context of wider views about the nature of change in contemporary European societies.

The key practical issue explored in this paper is the need to create fundamentally new kinds of arenas for communication, negotiation and decision-making in distressed neighbourhoods. Present governance structures are ineffective and wasteful of available resources, both formal and informal. Existing mechanisms for coordination and collaboration between agencies working in the neighbourhoods exclude residents by operating in ways which residents find uninviting and discouraging. As a consequence, the communication and negotiation which takes place in these forums shuts out residents and leads to a 'knowledge deficit' in planning and decision-making aimed at neighbourhood renewal. Those who are shut out of these forums lose their 'voice' and the neighbourhood as a whole loses their knowledge and ideas. In a self-fulfilling manner, professionals working in these 'excluding' forums tend to see the population of the area as homogeneous, all sharing the hardship of living in a distressed neighbourhood and so sharing the same needs, hopes, values and life projects. Thus, at a practical level, it is important to recognise the significance of social diversity, both in terms of the conflicts which it engenders among residents, but also, and more importantly, in the ways in which it represents a resource in terms of accessing a range of different methods of conflict resolution and bases for cooperation. By and large, people living in distressed neighbourhoods do manage to live together within the same space relatively peacefully. However, the means by which they accomplish this on an everyday basis are largely opaque to the professionals who design the 'partnerships' and 'participation' processes associated with neighbourhood regeneration. This Chapter argues that the 'everyday' means of conflict resolution among neighbours are a fundamental resource for designing micro-political structures and processes.

There are four significant practical implications of these observations:

- Output-based models of accountability, based in narrow definitions of organisational efficiency, are inappropriate. An outcome based model which insists that outputs are defined through micro-political structures

and processes built on concepts of neighbourhood democracy is more likely to deliver what residents want and to use resources effectively.
- There is no single model of micro-political processes and structures which will fit every neighbourhood. These processes and structures must be tailored to fit the specificities of each neighbourhood in ways which reflect the preferences and resources of diverse groups of local residents in terms of the forms of communication and negotiation which they find natural and comfortable even if this entails a certain level of 'professional discomfort' among agencies and social professionals associated with the neighbourhood.
- Nevertheless, it is central to create strong and extensive webs which link formal professional networks and informal networks among residents in creating new micro-political structures and processes. By focusing on the creation of these integrating webs, new possibilities for communication, mediation, and negotiation can be identified and used.
- The aim of supporting neighbourhood democracy is much wider than and significantly different from traditional means of promoting 'wide participation'. There is plenty of evidence to suggest that traditional governance mechanisms which only aim at promoting 'wide participation' do not guarantee effective and efficient results. Rather, the concept of neighbourhood democracy is about facilitating dialogue among diverse groups living in the neighbourhood, creating the possibility of mediating conflicts, and thus contributing to collective visions for neighbourhood renewal.

Pursuing the implications of these practical conclusions fully, however, also depends on developing new ways of thinking about change in contemporary European societies. There is a long tradition in sociological theory which analyses modernity in terms of the functional differentiation of societal systems, that is, the separation of economic and political systems from civil society. At the same time, postmodernist commentary stresses tendencies towards the de-differentiation of these social spheres. Most of the analysis which underpins postmodernist commentary has focused on national and urban levels and the de-differentiation of political and economic systems. This paper has focused on the sub-urban or neighbourhood level and the potential for de-differentiation of local social and political administrative systems and neighbourhood civil society. To some extent, it reflects Hirst's fecund metaphor of the 'Ottomanisation' of society, that is, a situation in which it is possible for plural and semi-self-regulating communities to co-exist side by side with very different rules and standards (Hirst 1994). It gives this concept a geographical spin by focusing on neighbourhoods and gives a new twist to Healey's vision of planning by emphasising the problems of managing a shared *co-existence* in space.

Note

[1] *Social Exclusion in European Neighbourhoods: Processes, Experiences and Responses*, European Commission, Targeted Economic and Social Research, Contract No SOE2-CT97-3057. The countries included within the study were: Sweden, Denmark, Germany, United Kingdom, Ireland, Greece, Portugal and Italy.

6 Is Partnership Possible? Searching for a New Institutional Settlement

MARILYN TAYLOR

The prevalence of the language of partnership and community participation in the UK in the 1990s has created significant opportunities for local communities. It seems that a genuine attempt is being made to encourage some of the developments suggested in Chapter 5. In the consultation document for the National Strategy for Neighbourhood Renewal, the Prime Minister states that:

> Unless the community is fully engaged in shaping and delivering regeneration, even the best plans on paper will fail to deliver in practice (Social Exclusion Unit 2000, p 5).

New initiatives, like the New Deal for Communities, a ten-year flagship programme for neighbourhood renewal which is currently underway in 39 neighbourhoods, and Sure Start, a more widespread programme for under 5s and their families, have an inbuilt commitment to 'community-led' partnerships in areas facing social exclusion. The government's National Strategy for Neighbourhood Renewal, based on two years of consultation and development, offers the opportunity to develop new forms of governance at local authority and neighbourhood level which will involve communities alongside other key players. It sees social capital, defined as 'trust and community spirit', as a critical foundation to the reversion of social exclusion:

> It is on this foundation that social stability and a community's ability to help itself is usually built – and its absence is a key factor in decline (Social Exclusion Unit 2000, p 24).

However, the language of community and social capital that is common in government and policy circles masks major tensions that cannot be resolved as easily as the rhetoric suggests. Community participation is nothing new. And the failure of most initiatives to involve communities effectively over some 30 years of regeneration policy is well documented. As the government itself has recognised:

> Too much has been imposed from above, when experience shows that success depends on communities themselves having the power and taking the responsibility to make things better (Social Exclusion Unit 1998, p 7).

In the light of this, some scepticism about the potential shelf-life of this new commitment or its ability to reach the parts that other initiatives have not reached might well be justified (see Stewart's discussion in Chapter 8). Nonetheless, if people in communities are to have access to new forms of urban governance and to the prospect of reversing years of decline and exclusion, it is necessary to move beyond scepticism and criticism of the past to a deeper analysis of the prospects for change and of the persistent faultlines that frustrate the drive for change.

This Chapter approaches this task by discussing some of the language that is associated with the revival of 'community': social capital, civil society and the 'third way'. Then, focusing particularly on the neighbourhood renewal field, it explores some of the dilemmas and paradoxes that lurk behind this language. It then discusses the challenges that need to be met if the proposed shift from government to governance at local level is to produce institutional forms at local and neighbourhood level which can address these dilemmas.

The Language

The fall of communism was seen in some quarters as the end of history (Fukuyama 1992), with claims that fundamental ideological divisions were a thing of the past. But a vision of history that appeared to cede victory to the liberalism of the market was greeted with disquiet among many commentators and politicians, who sought a new range of ideas which could avoid the excesses of either extreme. Concepts of 'communitarianism', 'social capital', the 'third way' and 'civil society'[1] have formed an alternative nexus of ideas, which has driven the rhetoric of a range of institutions from the UK government to the World Bank. But the very flexibility of this language which allows its adoption across significant ideological divides, along with the interchangeable use of the different terms, urges caution. These terms have been invested with a variety of meanings, depending on the perspectives of the people and institutions that have espoused them. So what can they offer to change agents struggling with the realities of social exclusion?

These concepts operate at different levels of analysis and arise out of different theoretical traditions. To analyse each term in detail and the theoretical links between them would occupy far more space than is available here, so this Chapter will explore the ideas that are connected with them in popular use.

Briefly, then, the concept of social capital encompasses the idea that people's 'capital' lies in their networks as well as individual skills and financial assets. It draws attention to the importance of social and associational ties in developing norms, trust and reciprocity within society as well as effective moral frameworks. Putnam's early analysis (1993) links such ties with effective civic engagement, as in a different way do the communitarian analyses associated most famously with Amitai Etzioni and with the ideas of associative democracy (Hirst 1994). Civil society, as popularly used, emphasises the direct collective engagement of citizens and consumers in economic, social and political development. In common usage, it is largely seen as something apart from the state or, nowadays, the market and has been embraced by the voluntary, NGO and non-profit sectors in many parts of the world.[2] In some analyses, civil society is seen as a realm of associative networks (Walzer 1995) and hence closely linked with Putnam's ideas of social capital. The 'third way' (Giddens 2000) seeks to steer a middle course between 'a highly statist brand of social democracy' and a neo-liberal free-market philosophy seeking to combine the strengths of the state and the market, while minimising the disadvantages of depending too much on either.

This is a set of ideas that is frequently associated in the literature with integration and social cohesion, autonomy and plurality and with the potential to negotiate the enormously complex task of 'making sense together while living differently' (Healey 1997, p 50). But it has both advantages and disadvantages. On the one hand, after years of market supremacy, it is encouraging to see attention being paid by policy makers and academics to the need to invest in 'social capital' as well as the individual skills and financial resources that are needed to combat social, economic and political exclusion. It is equally encouraging to see recognition being given to the territory between the state and market that tended to be lost in the ideological battles between right and left. On the other hand, there is growing criticism of the way these terms have been used to spray over the faultlines of a society where global capitalism is creating more and more division and fragmentation.

The positive side of the social capital debate is that it has given life to the idea that wealth and value cannot simply be expressed in monetary terms. Along with financial and human capital it recognises the importance of relationships between people. Even the economy, it has been demonstrated, relies not just on the individual choices of 'rational men', but on relationships and the expectations that they establish about the way transactions are conducted. But a growing number of writers (see, for example, Edwards and Foley 1998) are criticising the normative use to which this term is being put by writers such as Putnam (1993, 2000) and the association he argues between social capital and democracy (see the discussion in the Introduction to Part 1). One negative aspect of the social capital discourse is that, along with communitarianism, it tends to air brush out the exclusion which is the obverse of inclusion, the 'them' that defines the 'us' and which makes exclusion and fragmentation[3] inherent in this terminology. Giddens reminds us that:

> If they become too strong, communities breed identity politics and with it the potential for social division or even disintegration (Giddens 2000, pp 3-4).

Strong communities can also be oppressive to their members as well as to those who are 'beyond the pale' (Taylor and Hoggett 1994).

These issues have been addressed by writers like Granovetter (1973) or most recently in the UK by 6 (1997) who have both made the important distinction between weak and strong ties and who argue that an effective society is made up of overlapping allegiances which pull in different directions and allow different definitions of reality and identity. Weak ties counter the rigidity of strong ties and allow for a dynamic polity. But 6 points out that the interplay between weak and strong ties is complex and may apply differently in different situations. Critics of Putnam have argued that the 'value' of social capital is highly contingent on its specific setting (Edwards and Foley 1998). As I have argued elsewhere (Taylor 2000a), this can make it a difficult concept to apply in areas of social exclusion.

Another set of criticisms focuses on the link Putnam draws between social capital, 'civicness' and hence the health of a democracy. Foweraker and Landman (1997), for example, see the centrality given in this account to small associations, sports clubs and choral societies as simplistic. They argue that the democratic qualities of civil society do not have to do so much with 'civicness' as social mobilisation and political contestation:

> Democracy is not the comfortable result of righteous conduct, but the result of prolonged struggle in often dangerous and difficult circumstances (Foweraker and Landman 1997, p 243).

While the term 'civil society' is perhaps less commonly used in the UK, it has perhaps the strongest global reach, with, to quote Adam Seligman (1992), "its assumed synthesis of private and public 'good' and of individual and social desiderata". It has assumed a particular salience since the fall of the Iron Curtain. Before that, Walzer argues, the term 'rarely served to focus anyone's attention'. The use of the term has been largely 'positive, progressive, emancipating and utopian' (Alexander 1998). But, as Alexander goes on to argue, it is a concept that in popular usage conceals 'intense struggles for legitimacy and legitimation':

> The complex, decoupled nature of the subsystems of contemporary society make archaic any notion of civility as a seamless, overarching principle of social integration and coherence....(It is a) shell behind which privatising and fragmenting institutional processes and interactional practices are played out (Alexander 1998, p 12).

Walzer adds that, left to itself, civil society generates radically unequal power relations. Alexander, too, sees the institutions of civil society as essentially fragile, with a tendency to oligarchy. Excluded citizens, he argues, do not necessarily relate on an equal basis to voluntary organisations. The relationship is often that of patron and client.

Overall, the language is easily exploited by key political actors, who construct particular meanings of terms like community, social capital and civil society for their own ends. It ignores issues of power, both within communities and between them and political elites. In this respect, it is instructive to see how, when communities do get organised, they are dismissed as unrepresentative or as furthering special interests (Anastacio, Gidley et al. 2000). Political actors claim they want to get to the 'real people' and then make their own claims for what those 'real people' want. In fact, as the appeal to community and social capital grows in UK government policy, there is anecdotal evidence that some local authorities are paradoxically cutting funding for the voluntary and community sectors at the same time as they embrace the opportunities provided by the national strategy.

At other times the promotion of community, civil society and social capital can lead societies to rely too much on communities to do the work of the state, leaving them to manage their own deprivation and exclusion:

> the abolition of welfare state policies based on universal benefits and increasing standards of provision. ... is resulting in a hideous increase in levels of pauperisation. It is also marginalising formerly thriving social communities, and transforming inner urban areas into wastelands (Keane 1988, p 10).

An emphasis on community and civil society tends to ignore the role of the state. As such, it either provides a vision of community as an alternative to the state or masks the power of the state.

In summary, then, while ideas of civil society, community and social capital recognise relationships in society that have too long been ignored in political debate, they gloss over their darker characteristics – of exclusion, factionalism and unequal power relationships – minimising the tensions within them and failing to address the relationship between communities and the state. This means that policies fail to understand how the strengths inherent in these ideas can be supported and their weaknesses addressed.

Understanding the Tensions

These criticisms do not constitute an argument to abandon the language of community, civil society and social capital. But they do draw attention to the contested nature of these terms and their complexity. If policy is to build social capital, draw on the strengths of community and civil society and find a genuinely third way, it needs a more sophisticated understanding of how these phenomena operate and the context in which they can flourish. To recover the language of civil society, it must first be reformulated in ways that make it compatible with the recognition of conflict, division and antagonism (Mouffe 1992). This applies equally to concepts of community and social capital, which need to be returned to a normative neutrality in order to be useful.

In addition, this language needs to be reconceptualised in terms of its relationship to the state, rather than seen as an alternative. For it is the state that, in theory, has the capacity to mediate the conflicts and disparities within civil society. In a recent book, Bauman (1999) talks about the loss of spaces in our society that are neither public nor private. He deplores the trend towards individualism and uncertainty that globalisation has caused. He argues for places that can translate private worries into collective levers for change to alleviate private misery and uncertainty. But he dismisses the idea of civil society as a separate zone in antithesis to the state, seeing it instead as a way of describing what he calls the 'great compromise' between state and society which, for him, lies at the heart of any democracy.

In his analysis of the mixed economy of welfare, Evers (1995) has characterised the third sector (or 'social economy', using the European formulation) as a tension field between the state, the market and the personal. This echoes an analysis of civil society as a place that is not distinct from the state or the market but that plays out the tensions between them, and that is characterised by the relationships between different sectors rather than separation. Building on his analysis, the organisations within this tension field constantly risk being sucked into the state or the market. Or they may retreat into the personal and individualistic. On the other hand, without the corners, this territory in the middle would simply collapse in on itself. These are the tensions that have caused some writers to question the whole notion of civil society as an unattainable compromise between the universal and the particular (Tester, 1992). Bauman's 'great compromise' involves the need to juggle multiple accountabilities and disparate values. It means finding an equilibrium between the public interest, the market and the diverse interests of different communities.

Holding and mediating these tensions is likely to require flexibility and new kinds of power relationships between actors across this space. It is likely to require new institutional forms based on dynamic dialogue rather than static control. Partnerships, and the associated emphasis in UK government thinking on 'governance', 'joined-up action' and community involvement, are a response to this, seeking ways to bring new knowledge, new allies and new non-hierarchical ways of working into the making and implementation of public policy. But the ability of 'governance' to work in a radically different way, to shift power relations and to build effective 'social capital' across Evers' triangle, will depend on a clearer understanding of the tensions, the different frames of reference that operate across this territory and the problem to which 'governance' and its partnerships are seen as a solution.

The intention to move from government to governance in the field of neighbourhood renewal, therefore, faces two major challenges. The first is to understand the institutional pressures which unbalance Evers' creative tensions and draw partnerships back into the state or market, in order to understand how these pressures might be overcome. The second, which will remain when and if this undergrowth is swept away, will be to develop the skills and models to work effectively with the conflicts and diversity within this territory.

Where Previous Initiatives Have Fallen Short

This author has discussed elsewhere the extent to which partnership in regeneration has fallen short of the rhetoric and stifled rather than encouraged the growth of social capital, with insufficient time for communities to become involved, divisive and competitive processes for securing funds, and innovation entangled in the mesh of accountability requirements (Taylor 2000a, 2000b and see also the discussion in Chapter 8). Study after study reinforces the finding that community involvement has not ventured far beyond window dressing (Hastings, McArthur et al. 1996, Atkinson and Cope 1997, Hall and Mawson 1999, Anastacio, Gidley et al., 2000).

Critics have questioned the extent of the commitment to partnership at different levels of government. They have demonstrated how the discourse of partnership is couched still in the terms of the state (Atkinson 1999), how institutional inertia and resistance have frustrated past attempts at partnership (Pollitt, Birchall et al. 1998), and how the rules of engagement are constructed according to the cultures of government bodies. Over the years, scholars have shown how policies can be thwarted through the realities of implementation (Barrett and Fudge 1981) and the resistance of 'street level bureaucrats'. Reform has, if anything, led to more sophisticated defences, with communities remaining on the margins of the policy communities which are restructuring to meet new challenges.

There are a number of possible explanations for this. The New Right analysis during the Thatcher era, drawing on public choice theory, blamed the power of the professionals and the producers and sought to redress the balance in favour of the consumer (or more fundamentally the tax payer). A left-wing analysis of power, by contrast, would point to the structural inequalities of capitalism and the role of the state in underpinning the power of international capital. Analysis of the economic development policies of the 1980s would seem to support this analysis with the acknowledged failure of the wealth they generated to 'trickle down' to those most in need. In this analysis, any gesture towards participation could be seen simply as a symbolic gesture to protect the status quo and buy off civil unrest.

A hegemonic analysis, drawing on Gramsci, Lukes and Foucault, would build on these explanations by emphasising the ways in which, even when the need for consultation is conceded, agendas are controlled by the power holders and power is inscribed in the rules of play and the taken-for-granted assumptions on which the institutions of partnership are based. Communities have been invited to the partnership table along with other local players, in an implicit recognition of the need to take account of the different perspectives and bodies of knowledge they bring. But it has been on the terms of government players (Atkinson 1999, Taylor 1997, 2000a and de Magalhães in Chapter 3).[4] The nature of power is such that players do not realise the extent to which their views of what is possible are shaped by dominant interests. As Healey argues (1997), power relations do not just privilege some people over others, but also some ways of discussing and some forms of organising over others. As such power cannot just be seen in terms of a conspiracy or behind-the-scenes manipulation. It is embedded in the thoughtworlds of the powerful. She goes on to describe how policy making and planning has been dominated by an instrumentalist rationalist approach to policy making, which seeks to control not so much through the overt exercise of power but through the application of scientific knowledge, rational planning and management by objectives. But while objectivity is supposed to remove power differentials from the equation, existing power relations have inevitably been inscribed in the technical and managerial processes applied to policy development and evaluation:

> As Fischer argues, there is a pervasive struggle in the terrain of governance at the present time between pluralistic democratic tendencies, which seek to acknowledge a wider range of stakeholders, forms of knowledge and value bases and techno-corporate ones, which seek to keep control over the management of our societies, using the tools of technical analysis and management, or the knowledge and interests of key corporate interests (Healey, 1997, p 241).

As a result, new professions, those of the auditor and accountant in particular, have gained supremacy over the old (Perkin 1999). Partnerships have been disciplined in what Healey (1997) calls the 'politics of meeting targets' with definitions of success and probity generated from central government. This 'audit culture', as Michael Power (1997) has argued, is rarely questioned and institutionalises existing systems and patterns of behaviour. In addition, outputs determined in advance in accordance with a management-by-objectives model preclude risk taking and learning. Nonetheless, Healey argues, following Giddens, that cultures and power structures can be changed. The very messiness of implementation that has allowed professionals and administrators to resist reform also provides the windows of opportunity for reform.

The Potential for Change

It is easy to reach the conclusion that the aims of partnership have in the past been more to pre-empt discontent and bring in the additional resources of players beyond government than to bring in new perspectives. However, the UK *National Strategy for Neighbourhood Renewal* (SEU 2000, 2001) marks a departure from old styles of policy making. Through its 18 policy action teams and extended consultation processes, civil servants from the Social Exclusion Unit and key central government departments engaged with a wide range of stakeholders to find ways of reversing spirals of disadvantage which had remained impervious to earlier regeneration policies. The views of local residents were at a premium, with a growing emphasis on 'developing ways to put deprived communities in the driving seat' of neighbourhood renewal. The emphasis on 'joined-up thinking' in the resulting strategy meanwhile aims to challenge the existing policy making and implementation cultures which have frustrated 'joined-up' action in the past. The concept of local strategic partnerships which is at the centre of the *National Strategy for Neighbourhood Renewal* offers new prospects for working across boundaries in a new institutional settlement, with a clear place for communities. Proposals for neighbourhood management aim to bring the range of services together at neighbourhood level, although the governance mechanisms for this are less clear. The intention to pilot different approaches could, however, allow for genuine institutional innovation.

The centrality of local communities has also been evident in related programmes like the Sure Start programme for under 5s, where the government's intention has been stated by the Chancellor of the Exchequer as follows:

> Instead of the state – local or national – running these programmes, these can be run by volunteers, charities, and community organisations. Indeed, we should be prepared to pass over the responsibility for services in these geographical areas to the voluntary partnership (Brown 2000).

Recent rounds of the government's Single Regeneration Budget have also put more emphasis on community involvement and crucially are allowing for the capacity-building investment that such involvement will need, while communities are set to be 'at the heart of' the 39 New Deal for Communities areas across England.

Many would agree that there has been a watershed in the commitment of some parts of government to work with local communities. In the New Deal for Communities Programmes and Sure Start initiatives around the country, the search is on for new ways of constituting partnerships' which will give communities a new stake, with new patterns of ownership As past regeneration programmes like City Challenge and the early rounds of the Single Regeneration Budget come to an end, the partnerships which were set up primarily to secure funds are now seeking to reconstitute themselves in order to combine the potential to raise money on the private market with the potential to bring mainstream services and their budgets together under a form of governance which combines the major stakeholders, including local communities (Taylor 2000b).

However, while the recent publications of the *National Strategy for Neighbourhood Renewal* (SEU 2000, 2001) suggest that the government is willing to experiment and try different routes into governance, the mix of language and key ideas within these documents between the managerial, the entrepreneurial and the strategic reflects the tensions that still have to be addressed if change is to occur. On the one hand there is the managerialist language of targets; on the other there are ideas of risk and innovation. On the one hand, there is an emphasis on 'best practice' and accredited advisors; on the other a recognition of the need for experimentation and diversity. On the one hand there is an emphasis on individual entrepreneurs and community leaders; on the other there is an emphasis on participation and inclusiveness. These apparent contradictions reflect real tensions to which there are no 'right' answers. But much will depend on how these tensions are addressed.

Accountability and Risk

The managerial agenda of standards and targets will need to be balanced with a willingness to accept risk if the *National Strategy* is to generate genuine innovation and open up policy making to voices from the community.

Ultimately the success of champions within as well as outside government will depend on their ability to circumvent a culture of risk aversion within government which too often catches the sprats who are already trapped in the processes of social exclusion while allowing the sharks who have contributed to that exclusion to go free. While Ministers are arguing for more community control, and the suggestion is that there is a genuine willingness to take risks at the top level, the civil servants back at the ranch are developing the rules, processes, timescales and 'guidelines' that will prevent the development of social capital and continue to exclude those who are most marginalised or based most strongly in local communities. There is a very strong emphasis on targets, carrots and sticks in the National Strategy, which retains much of the new managerialist tradition. This is evident even in the New Deal for Communities Programmes, where the base-line indicators and parameters within which choices could be made and options appraised were set by government. It remains to be seen how far the definitions of success that have come from above will accord with those developed by people living and working in the NDC areas and how much say they will be given in how the programmes are monitored and evaluated.

This is not to argue that targets and auditing processes do not have their place in any strategy. But while targets in the *National Strategy* aim to discipline local authorities who fail to deliver, there is always a danger that champions for change within government and in communities will be caught in their wake. A regulation culture gathers its own momentum.

And, as 6, Leat et al. (2000) argue, a culture where initiatives are 'not allowed to fail' does not allow for learning either.

Best Practice and Diversity

The emphasis on 'evidence-based practice' and 'what works' that has characterised the 1997-2001 Labour government gives the appearance of neutrality. But some would argue that, based as it has been in scientific rationalist understandings of evidence and the new managerialist paradigm, it is likely to continue to exclude significant bodies of knowledge and dialogue as well as conflict, risk and diversity. It is difficult to disagree with consensus-oriented approaches, which define models of 'best practice' from which everyone can learn, but much depends on who is defining 'best' and for whom and what assumptions lie behind this. As Healey argues (1997), all forms of knowledge are socially constructed and context is an important part of this construction. It remains to be seen how far communities are able to question the cultural assumptions which are still visible behind the new policies.

Much also depends on what the achievement of consensus means in practice. Governance requires difference to be aired rather than swept under the carpet, particularly if the interests of the most excluded are to be given voice. Hastings, McArthur et al. (1996) argue that the consensus culture in many partnerships can be extremely disempowering to community participants. Conflict may, as they have argued, be a sign that partnerships are working. Healey (1997) argues that too little attention has been paid in the past to the different cultures which shape people's perceptions of problems and possible solutions. These need to be exposed and understood, both across sectors and within them. This requires an institutional settlement that acknowledges both when it is important to work together but also when it is important to respect difference. It also requires that the diversity within communities is recognised. The politics of identity has been crucial to the struggle for community empowerment. But equally and paradoxically, community empowerment can also become impaled on the politics of identity (Meekosha 1992). As Chantal Mouffe argues:

> For pluralism to be made compatible with the struggle against inequality, one must be able to discriminate between the differences that exist and should not exist, and the differences that do not exist but should exist (Mouffe 1992, p 13).

This is a difficult balancing act to pull off.

If best practice can suppress diversity, it can also suppress learning. Wilkinson and Applebee (1999) are critical of an emphasis on training in neighbourhood renewal strategies. Training implies the transfer of agreed skills and there will clearly be a place for this in the new strategy. But equally important will be opportunities for joint learning between communities and between them and professional bodies. In an arena where the answers are not known, it will be important to maximise opportunities for people to reflect on their learning together, to spread rather than protect knowledge and to challenge the cultural assumptions that lie behind the status quo.

Leadership and Participation

There is a strong emphasis on individual leadership in the *National Strategy*. Neighbourhood management, the framework for joined up services, will have 'someone in charge'. Training and learning strategies are aimed at 'social entrepreneurs and community leaders'. And yet, attractive though the concept of leadership may be to politicians, this too has to be set in context. There are two problems. One is the danger that too much emphasis on leaders will neglect the foundations on which sustainable models for governance will depend. If community involvement becomes too dependent on individual social and civic entrepreneurs, they will be liable to burn-out over time (Anastacio, Gidley et al. 2000, Purdue, Razzaque et al. 2000) or to be pulled away from their community base into the culture of their partners. The second danger is that community representatives can be set up to fail, accepted when they fit in, rejected as being unrepresentative when they do not, or criticised for not being able to speak with a single voice.

Community leaders need the resources to ensure that they can be informed by and accountable to their communities. Equally, the communities which they lead need to develop the organisational capacity and the depth of knowledge and understanding in communities, which will allow them to hold leaders accountable and ensure the succession. Milofsky (1987) calls this organisational intelligence, Healey, drawing on Innes, Gruber et al. (1994), refers to 'social and intellectual capital', Fordham (1995) calls it organisational and institutional capacity (see the discussion in Chapters 1 and 2).

Opening systems up to influence is a major aspiration for many who are involved in current regeneration and neighbourhood management initiatives. Many people are writing now about the knowledge economy and the need to spread knowledge rather than contain it. There are many examples on the ground of mechanisms to try and spread participation, including participatory appraisal exercises which draw on experience from developing countries, 'planning for real' exercises, power mapping, legislative theatre and so on. These involve residents alongside policy makers and practitioners (front-line staff also have important 'tacit knowledge' that needs to be tapped) in understanding the environment in which they are operating, assessing need and mapping assets. But it is important that involvement does not stop here. These approaches also have the potential to involve a wide range of stakeholders both in making policy and evaluating its effectiveness. Without institutionalising this sustained involvement, it is likely that policies to counter exclusion will exhaust the limited supply of leaders and continue to founder both on institutional resistance and inertia from above and disillusion from below.

Constituting Partnerships

Ultimately the ways in which these balancing acts are negotiated will depend on two things. They will depend on the pressures from above that are imposed by a central government which does not wish to see this initiative fail. These pressures have already been discussed above. But the ability of a 'governance' approach to tackle these tensions creatively will also depend on the institutional form that neighbourhood renewal partnerships take. How will these local partnerships address the tensions discussed above?

Organisational theorists usually distinguish between three main principles of organisation: hierarchies, markets and networks (Thompson, Frances et al. 1991).

- Hierarchies are based on clear rules and have a clear leadership In the case of neighbourhood renewal, an overarching parent body would assess needs and decide on strategy. It would then delegate the delivery of that strategy to subsidiaries. A hierarchical set-up would probably employ a neighbourhood manager with delegated authority over local agencies to ensure that the plan is delivered or with staff seconded from partner agencies. In this model, all the roles of neighbourhood renewal may be contained within one organisation. Conversely, the organisation would need to tie in, and have delegated authority over, all the participating organisations.
- Markets are based on contracts. An overarching governance body might agree a neighbourhood plan and would then act as a purchaser, specifying services and projects to be put out to competitive tender.

But delivery would be done by independent organisations through contracts with targets attached.
- Networks are based on trust and reciprocity. A neighbourhood renewal model based on the network principle would rely on informal opportunities for co-operation and joint ventures emerging from informal alliances. In this model, informal networks would be developed to facilitate processes for needs assessment and priority making, and to develop connections and project teams around these priorities (Wilcox and Mackie 2000). In time, local organisations may federate to develop a facilitative umbrella body which can provide support services and long-term maintenance as well as ensuring that their interests are represented. In this model, co-ordination would be driven from below.

In the past, hierarchical models have been in the ascendant. More recently, market models have been preferred, underpinned by the authority of the statutory purchaser. But many now find the alternative of networks an attractive way forward in a territory that is uncertain and complex and where solutions are not known.

Current constitutional forms in the UK seem ill-adapted to this agenda. There has been a surge of interest recently in mutual forms of organisation (Leadbeater and Christie 1999), but experience in other countries and in the housing sector suggests that there are drawbacks to the mutual form, which has little capacity for differentiating between different stakeholders and whose mutuality tends to be eroded once the organisation grows. The company limited by guarantee seems the preferred form. However, a growing number of consultants and writers, faced with the evidence that formal structures have not worked in the past, argue for process, rather than for procedures and structures, and for informality rather than the formality which favours existing patterns of power. Formally-constituted partnerships are easily captured by existing systems. Even when they bring in a new set of players, they can easily ossify and succumb to Michels' iron law of oligarchy, creating a new substratum of powerholders rather than pushing power out into communities and other stakeholders (Michels 1958). Informality allows partnerships to operate nimbly across boundaries rather than creating new boundaries of their own. Informal systems are also infinitely more accessible.

However, there are drawbacks. Pratt, Gordon et al. (1999) argue that co-operation and co-ordination, where participating organisations maintain their boundaries and separate identities, may be the most appropriate strategies for known and predictable goals. But, where goals are difficult to predict, they argue that partners need to be bound in closely and risk needs to be shared. Otherwise there is a danger that partners will opt in and out. Informal structures can still be dominated by powerful partners, with their informality rendering their power less visible and accountable. They can exclude those who do not know the ropes and the ways in. They can be vulnerable to take-over if membership is too open, or to being used as the forum for perpetual conflict between different community or political factions. There is potential for considerable role confusion and conflict of interest as the different hats people are wearing become mixed up They are difficult to hold to account and depend on the integrity of key players. How can a new institutional settlement hold the virtues of both approaches without succumbing to their inherent weaknesses?

The institutional settlement required of governance does not all have to be contained within the one body. It is also possible to combine the strengths of different models within one overarching structure:

> The most effective programs have had systems of 'nested' organisations that start from a base-level group or association..... Small organisations by themselves may be beautiful, but their impact will be limited if they are not joined in some larger enterprise. Any programme that aims to produce widespread benefits must address the question of how to organise a hierarchical structure that is animated from below rather than above (Uphoff, Esman et al. 1998, pp 66-67).

Articulated and interlocking systems are likely to be the most productive and flexible, but they can be extremely complex and time-consuming to administer. Wilcox and Mackie (2000) argue that in some places where partnership has been introduced, the complexity of working arrangements and community involvement makes it almost impossible to produce results. Institutional forms need to be designed which demonstrate a clear understanding of the different roles that need to be performed and how they link with one another, but which allow for dynamism and flexibility.

Whatever the institutional design it will need to be underpinned by robust processes which recognise the value of difference. Several commentators (Pratt, Gordon et al. 1999, Stewart, Goss et al. 1999, Wilkinson and Applebee 1999) argue for a co-evolutionary 'whole systems' approach. Healey (1997) proposes a form of 'inclusionary argumentation' which is built on a greater understanding of how people come to have the ways of thinking and ways of valuing that they do, and how policy development and policy implementation processes can be made interactive. Such collaborative discussion, she argues (p 33) would build up a store of mutual understanding – the 'social and intellectual capital' referred to earlier (Innes, Gruber et al. 1994) which could be drawn on when dealing with subsequent issues. It would also help to build up, across the diversity of ways of living and ways of thinking, the institutional capacity to collaborate and co-ordinate (see also Milofsky 1987, Gilchrist and Taylor 1992).

This is a dynamic model. Partnerships are too often entered into at speed and repented at leisure. Partnership design needs to allow for change and flexibility at different stages of involvement. It may take time for partners to learn to work in new ways. It may equally take time for residents to gain the skills, confidence and organisational capacity to make a full contribution. Conversely, involvement may taper if the renewal strategy changes the quality of life locally. The anger and frustration with local conditions and services that can lead to high levels of involvement at the outset does not necessarily last. If things improve, the majority of residents may be more willing to leave it to others:

> The groups go in cycles – when you're meeting to form decisions at the beginning you get more people interested than when it gets to implementation and contracts – people aren't that interested.[5]

Lowndes and Skelcher (1998) have suggested that the Single Regeneration Budget and City Challenge partnerships tended go through several stages, acting like networks in the initial stages, more formal as the partnership was established and got going, like markets as the work was specified and contracts or service level agreement let; like networks again as the special initiative on which they were based came to an end.

Conclusions

The current interest in community, social capital and civil society is part of the search for a 'third way' which seeks to avoid the extremes of either state or market. But a simplistic view of these three ideas is not likely to yield policies which will tackle exclusion in the way this government seeks to do. These are complex and contested ideas, masking major tensions between inclusion, exclusion and fragmentation. Involving communities in partnerships with the state addresses some of these tensions. Thus Keane defines the state as a device for:

> containing inevitable conflicts between particular interests within well-defined legal limits, and preventing civil society from falling victim to new forms of inequality and tyranny (Keane 1988, p 15).

But, while partnerships offer opportunities to pool resources and knowledge, they are themselves fraught with tensions, operating in a space between market, state and the personal. These tensions are manifest in new policies for neighbourhood renewal, which seek to promote risk, diversity and participation, but contain this within a more conventional new managerialist language of targets and best practice, as well as a strong emphasis on individual leadership, which could enshrine centralist and 'top down' definitions of effectiveness, unless its assumptions are open to challenge. The author's own research has suggested that power holders are rarely aware of the way in which their assumptions shape partnership agendas and the extent to which they are experienced by less powerful actors as imposed rather than shared (see, for example, Stewart and Taylor 1995).

Healey (1997, p 49) poses the question: how can governance draw upon the richness of knowledge and understanding available to people in their different cultural worlds without oppressively limiting that richness through the dominance of particular ideas and power relations? The inclusionary argumentation approach which Healey (1997) proposes seeks to address the kinds of tension outlined here, by acknowledging the very different cultural frames which participants bring to partnership and by seeking to develop a social learning process which makes the invisible assumptions which have structured partnerships in the past visible. Table 6.1 summarises the differences that this might involve.

Table 6.1   Contrasting Styles of Policy Making

Rational policy making	New styles of policy making
Hierarchy or market	Network
Strong tools – carrots and sticks[6]	Weak tools – persuasion and encouragement
Value free	Engaging with values
Training	Learning
Centralised	Decentralised

Healey's approach has something in common with other new ideas for policy development, the 'whole systems' approach of Pratt, Gordon et al., and approaches drawn from chaos and complexity theory (see, for example, Haynes 1999, Gilchrist 2000). All acknowledge the uncertainty and complexity facing the policy maker and the impossibility of providing blueprints. But there is still a major institutional challenge to find ways of organising at local level that can combine authority with flexibility and entrepreneurialism and to find ways that can bring together what has been learnt from below rather than from above.

Notes

1. Or 'civic society' – the preferred term of the UK's Chancellor of the Exchequer, Gordon Brown (Brown 2000).
2. In the UK, the former Centre for Voluntary Organisation at the London School of Economics and Political Science, whose Director, Antony Giddens is the architect of the third way, has renamed itself the Centre for Civil Society.
3. Cohen and Rogers refer to this as the 'mischief of factions' (Cohen and Rogers 1992).
4. Private sector players, however, may find themselves as favoured players if they are able to argue that they can bring significant investment into an area and able to bend the rules to their advantage (Anastacio, Gidley et al. 2000).
5. From an interview for the evaluation of the Brighton URBAN Project by the author and colleagues.
6. Leat et al. (2000) The reference to strong tools (of regulation, pooled budgets, inspection and sanctions) and weak tools (persuasion, informative, learning systems, training, building networks and changing culture) is taken from Leat et al. (2000).

7 Governance, Institutional Capacity and Planning for Growth

CHRISTINE LAMBERT AND NICK OATLEY

Introduction

In this Chapter, we discuss the issues of governance and institutional capacity as they apply to the planning system in the UK. The Chapter draws empirically on research carried out in the South West region of England, and the Bristol area in particular.[1] We outline some of the main challenges facing planning, especially those which revolve around the issue of planning for growth in the most economically dynamic parts of the country. However, the process of planning and managing urban growth in a number of the areas where growth pressures are strongest is characterised by significant weaknesses and biases. Spatial planning in some of these localities seems deficient in capacity to address conflicts around land-use and development, negotiate appropriate trade-offs and reach and implement decisions that can deliver economically and environmentally sustainable development. In conclusion, we discuss some of the ways in which institutional capacity in planning for growth might be enhanced, in particular the extent to which new organisations linked to the developing 'regional governance' agenda are potential vehicles for consensus building in the longer term.

Planning in the UK is currently facing considerable challenges. The pressures it faces reflect firstly, changes in the spatial logic of the economy, generating strong development pressures in parts of the country where environmental concerns are especially powerful. Secondly, changes in households are generating significant additional housing demands, with the highest demands occurring in the most successful areas economically. Thirdly, environmental protection and the pursuit of sustainable development has assumed great significance in the planning system, but this often seems to be irreconcilable with the accommodation of the development requirements of contemporary economic and social development. As a result, planning in the UK is an increasingly contested policy terrain. It is also a terrain where the shift from government to governance raises complex challenges.

Governance and Institutional Capacity

As discussed in Chapter 1, one meaning of the term governance encapsulates a shift in modes of policy making and implementation, away from the dominance of formal state power organised through bureaucratic hierarchies, towards more open networks of cross-sectoral coalitions and partnerships, characterised by shared power (Jessop 1997, Goodwin and Painter 1996, Peck and Tickell 1994, Rhodes 1997, Stoker 2000a).

The factors that underlie this shift from 'government' to 'governance' have also been discussed in detail (Jessop 1995b, Stoker and Mossberger 1995). The reasons include: restrictions on state finance and powers necessitating partnership with quasi-public and private interests who can access resources; recognition of the complexity of contemporary social and economic problems, requiring more flexible and fluid responses; growing competition between localities for investment; and central government requirements that policy making and implementation processes be opened up to involvement from business and community interests. All of these factors are driving the trend towards increased co-operation between governmental and non-governmental interests.

As a result of this shift to governance, action is said to flow from the co-operative efforts of a range of interests and agencies. Government itself has only 'imperfect control' (Rhodes 1997, p 8) and its capacity to govern depends on 'the effective co-ordination of interdependent forces within and beyond the state' (Jessop 1997, p 96). Organisations, including state and non-state, come to co-operate by recognising mutual dependency in objectives, resources, power or authority in order to achieve any substantive policy outcome (Bryson and Crosby 1992).

Recognising the new conditions of governance, the editors of this volume identify increased academic and policy interest in the concept of institutional capacity, and how it can be created or enhanced. Elsewhere, Healey (1998b) defines institutional capacity as the 'capacity of organisations to create new relationships for engaging in purposeful, collective action'. She goes on to discuss how the conditions affecting capacity may vary between different localities:

> A key element of such capacity lies in the quality of local political cultures some are well-integrated, well connected, well informed and can mobilise readily to capture opportunities and enhance local conditions.

Others are fragmented, lack the connections to sources of power and knowledge and the mobilisation capacity to organise to make a difference (Healey 1998b, p 1531).

Pointing to the failure of individual, centrally-imposed regeneration initiatives to generate sustained improvement, in terms of both institutional relationships and social and economic conditions, Healey identifies a more crucial issue as creating and maintaining a new form of (strategic) governance, removed from the specific conflicts and negotiations that surround project implementation:

> This new form of governance and planning involves building up collaborative relationships with 'stakeholders' in territories, to generate not merely specific programmes but governance cultures through which territorial political communities can collectively address their conflicts and maximise their chances to shape their places .... (Healey 1998b, p 1535).

The key qualities that are sought in the institutional relations and qualities of new governance include:

- Broadening 'stakeholder' involvement, in order to;
- Facilitate the flow of knowledge and help build up intellectual capital;
- Build relations of trust and help to establish consensus;
- Enhance capacity to act through opening up access to resources and sources of power (Healey 1998b, p 1541).

It seems to us that the creation of strategic capacity is a particularly important issue in relation to strategic, sub-regional spatial planning in areas under growth pressure, where there is often intense controversy about urban growth and its accommodation. Recent debates in the South East of England are perhaps the highest profile example of such a controversy (Panel Report 1999). In this case it is argued that locally-based anti-development sentiment has taken precedence over strategic responses to the development challenges of economic and social change in the region. Similar disputes are occurring in other regions, including the South West and Eastern regions of England.

In many cases, localities (defined as regions or sub-regions) are unable themselves to develop a 'strategic line' that is acceptable to all stakeholders in the process. Central government, which retains an important role in the planning system, is drawn into these disputes, sometimes imposing a 'strategic line'. Top-down imposed solutions may, however, continue to face obstacles as implementation processes take over. But where governance at a regional or local level is seen to be failing, more traditional hierarchical arrangements take over. For these reasons, Cowell and Murdoch (1999) claim that land-use planning has proved rather immune to the wider shift to governance apparent in other policy areas.

In a number of ways, which we go on to discuss, spatial planning at a local level displays a variety of specific problems in its institutional arrangements. However, there are a number of broader, more structural features of the way that planning regulates the development process, which in turn affect the nature and quality of relationships between key interests. In the UK, the practices of the planning system tend towards an adversarial culture. This is encouraged by the quasi-judicial nature of aspects of the planning process, notably the inquiry procedures for Regional Planning Guidance and development plans (McAuslan 1980). Development and property markets tend to be volatile and highly susceptible to external influence. This in turn tends to increase risk and reduce predictability, which may impact on levels of trust between participants. In general, the public distrust the development industry to deliver on commitments, and this can rebound in terms of public attitudes towards planning professionals (McCarthy and Harrison 1995). Finally, despite the importance of planning as a form of regulatory intervention in economic development, debates about planning and development issues at inquiries and other consultative forums tend to be dominated by a well-defined policy community. Planning processes are by no means exclusive, with a number of opportunities for interested parties to comment and statutory rights of objection, but public debates tend to have the flavour of an introverted discussion between the 'usual suspects'. Planning professionals, development industry representatives and certain environmental pressure groups are the key participants, engaging in mainly technical debate about demographic and economic forecasts and environmental constraints (Hull 1997, Cowell and Murdoch 1999, Wenban-Smith in Chapter 10).

Planning is, however, a policy area where there have been significant changes in the powers available to steer patterns of development, in administrative arrangements and procedures for policy making and mechanisms of implementation. In addition planning has to respond to environmental and political challenges, such that past assumptions about aims and objectives are increasingly questioned (Evans and Rydin 1997, Blowers and Evans 1997). This questioning of aims applies also in other contexts, seen, for example, in debates about urban growth controls in the US (US Dept of Housing and Urban Development 1999) and in the European context (Committee for Spatial Development 1999).

Planning: 'Old' and 'New' Governance

In the UK, a national commitment to 'urban containment' is a long-standing and well-documented feature of the planning system (Hall, Thomas et al. 1973). While there was some loosening of controls and selective attempts to de-regulate urban growth in the 1980s, the planning system escaped any fundamental reform (Bramley and Lambert 1998). Green Belts and other statutory, protective designations have in the past and continue to powerfully constrain urban expansion.

On the other hand, features of the system promoted nationally also facilitated a process of managed urban growth. Comprehensive and pro-active regional policy was one aspect of national policy, dealing with inter and intra-regional dimensions of urban and regional development. Historically, new towns and town expansions were a key tool in accommodating growth, with substantial resources available to manage and steer development. Traditional regional policy was in serious decline by the 1970s, though 'regionalism' has experienced something of a renaissance more recently. New towns have also fallen out of favour in recent years, though the legacy of this particular policy tool is long-lasting, with former new towns continuing to experience high levels of population and employment growth (Begg, Moore et al. 2000).

Another important tool in recent years has been the use of demographic household projections to establish targets at regional and local level for land release for housing and related purposes (Bramley, Bartlett et al. 1995). Taken together with housing land availability targets and monitoring arrangements, these could be seen as a tool of central direction to ensure at least a minimum supply of development land at local level (Murdoch, Abram et al. 2000).

The demise of traditional regional policy and the new towns programme, coupled with more generalised cut-backs in public expenditure, have substantially reduced the role of the public sector in promoting development and providing key elements of urban infrastructure. Public subsidy is increasingly targeted to small area 'urban policy' initiatives in areas where the market is demonstrably failing. Planning agreements or obligations have partly taken the place of public investment in relation to infrastructure investment. However, the use of planning agreements is very unevenly developed, reflecting a mix of legal and policy uncertainty and highly variable market contexts affecting the economics of development and the scope for 'planning gain' (Healey, Purdue et al. 1993).

In administrative terms, there have been a number of changes to local government structures and boundaries, with important implications for planning. Successive rounds of local government re-organisation in the mid-1980s and mid-1990s removed metropolitan level government in most urban areas, and metropolitan-wide strategic planning tends to have been a victim of these reforms. Joint arrangements of various kinds have instead developed in most of the affected areas, which seem to operate more or less effectively in different city-regions (Dowding, Dunleavy et al. 2000, Kumar and Paddison 2000, and see Chapters 9 and 10 in this book). The history of institutional relations and the political culture of different cities and their hinterlands may go some way to explaining variations in contemporary practice.

Regional planning experienced a revival during the 1990s, with Regional Planning Guidance prepared by central government following advice from standing conferences of local authorities. Criticisms have been made of the effectiveness of this system, in particular the emphasis on bottom-up decision-making processes and the bland and minimalist policy outcomes that tend to result (Breheny 1991). The status of Regional Planning Guidance has been enhanced more recently, along with the development of a more consultative, partnership model for its preparation (DETR 2000g). As a result transparency and openness in the preparation of Regional Planning Guidance is enhanced. However, the critique of bottom-up decision making processes and bland policy outcomes arguably still stands. The developing regional agenda has also led to the establishment of new institutions, the Regional Development Agencies (RDAs) in place since 1999. RDAs have an explicit remit to promote regional economic competitiveness and social cohesion, preparing regional economic strategies in parallel with the preparation of planning guidance. Regional Assemblies, acting as an arena for politicians, have also been established, taking on a more significant consultative and decision-making role, though this falls some way short of a democratically-elected regional tier of government.

In more substantive policy terms, national planning policy is generally tending to reinforce urban containment and consolidation. Planning Policy Guidance Notes,[2] the Rogers Report (Urban Task Force 1999), and numerous ministerial statements emphasise the benefits of urban renaissance and recycling of brownfield land as a way of minimising the environmental impact of new development and restraining car use. These policy shifts reflect one side in a contested debate about the environmental benefits of planning for 'compact cities' (Jenks, Burton et al. 1996, Breheny 1992). Current government guidance on planning for housing (DETR 2000f) is advocating a new approach to establishing the need for new house building and land release, so-called 'plan, manage and monitor', involving the adoption of somewhat shorter term planning horizons. This implies a move away from top-down prescription of household forecasts. Sequential release of housing sites to reinforce urban containment is advocated, and previous requirements that local planning authorities maintain a minimum five-year supply of housing land have been dropped. These changes potentially reduce the scope for central direction and expand the scope for regional and local discretion in planning decision-making.

An important point about these national policy changes is that there is some tendency for selective application. Virtually all of the discussion and policy innovation applies to housing development. There is much less national policy prescription in relation to employment development or other land uses. We return to this point and its implications for urban development later in the Chapter.

The Challenges Facing Planning in Growth Regions

The challenges facing planning in growth regions essentially revolve around the difficulties of reconciling economic competitiveness, social need and environmental protection.

Divergent regional economic performance was an issue that attracted a great deal of policy attention in the 1980s (Fothergill and Gudgin 1982, Keeble 1980, Martin and Rowthorn 1986, Massey and Allen 1988). More recent evidence suggests that this long-standing north-south divide in growth rates remains firmly entrenched. This reflects the manufacturing-service shift in the economy, the key role of London and the South East region in financial and business services, R&D and technologically advanced manufacturing, and the environmental attractions of the south to a more mobile and affluent population (Breheny 1999, Simmie 1998). As a result, national economic competitiveness is increasingly seen as tied to economic success in those regions in the south of the country where the 'new knowledge economy' is concentrated. Coupled with this, there are strong processes of decentralisation of employment (Breheny 1999, Turok and Edge 1999), away from the largest cities to suburban and fringe areas and smaller towns. The fastest growing areas in employment terms during the 1990s tend to be accessible small and medium-sized towns in the greater South East, with particular pressures in selected growth corridors on the national motorway network.

One specific manifestation of the new geography of employment is the development of 'edge cities', areas of mainly low density, mixed, mainly business uses (including commercial, leisure, retailing and warehousing), typically developed around motorway intersections. In some cities (Bristol is an example), these zones have grown to the extent that they seriously rival the traditional CBD as employment centres. Edge cities, and decentralisation trends more generally, begin to change conventional views about the structure of urban regions. Reflecting these shifts in the spatial organisation of the economy, there is increased debate about the emergence of urban networks and polycentric urban regions, replacing traditional notions of mono-centric cities, coupled with debate about the extent to which policy should recognise these shifts (Committee for Spatial Development 1999, Cooke, Davies et al. 2000).

The role of planning in 'managing' regional economic development was an issue debated at some length at the recent enquiry into Regional Planning Guidance in the South East. The Panel Report (1999) of the enquiry argued in a robust manner that planning should accommodate market-driven processes, essentially because the scope to do otherwise is now quite limited.

> It was suggested to us on a number of occasions that 'regional imbalance' should be tackled by preventing the 'economic magnetism' of the 'overheated' South East from 'draining away (economic) vitality and population' from other UK regions. This view, with its manifest overtones of post-war Barlow-based industrial development policy, we were advised was not current Government thinking. Rather, it was a question of the economy being encouraged 'to go ahead at full speed on all engines'. In our view it is high time that the ghost of Barlow (his report, that is) be finally exorcised from regional strategy. Whereas in the 1940s and for some time thereafter, it may have been quite reasonable to consider the UK as the principal unit for economic planning, this is manifestly not the situation at the present time. Economic activity and investment discouraged from settling in the South East of England will not now find alternative landing places in other UK regions; they are just as likely to go to other parts of the EU (Panel Report 1999 para 4.9).

The subsequent government response accepted the panel report's significant recommendation for the promotion of major town-expansion schemes, apparently agreeing with the need for a positive accommodation of economic development and related development implications in the South East. However, in a somewhat contradictory fashion central government is down-playing the need for long-term planning for growing housing requirements in the region.

Differential trends in demographic and household change rates tend to match those of employment change, with the highest projected household growth in three southern regions (the South East, South West and Eastern) (DETR 1998b). Overlaying these trends is a continuing urban-rural shift of population (Champion, Atkins et al. 1998), seemingly expressive of strong preferences for suburban and rural as opposed to urban living.

Over the last decade or so, the spatial planning system has taken on a new role to promote environmental goals, encapsulated under the term 'sustainable development'. This role derives in part from international policy influences and commitments linked to global climate change. Sustainability, as a key guiding principle or set of principles, is increasingly reflected in national planning guidance, official policy statements and regional and development plans. The concept of 'sustainable development' itself is very broad, encompassing economic and social, as well as environmental dimensions. However, in planning, particular aspects tend to have been emphasised, notably the transport impacts of land-use decisions and the need to minimise the use of undeveloped land for new housing development.

The emphasis on sustainability poses major challenges and difficulties in implementation. Planning policy stances and particular decisions and developments in themselves may have only a small impact on economic and social behaviour and environmental outcomes, even if they are consistently applied. It is frequently argued, for example, that economic instruments may be a more effective form of intervention than the rather crude regulatory mechanisms available through planning (Pearce, Markandya et al. 1989). Sustainability is also a very long-term goal, but the time horizons of policy makers, and especially political actors in the planning system, tends to be much shorter term.

The general trends in economic and demographic development described above also pose dilemmas. 'Edge city' type business developments present particular challenges for a planning system committed to reducing car use, as such developments typically rely very substantially on car-based access, and are inherently difficult to serve by public transport. Differential regional trends in household growth and counter-urbanisation trends also provide something of a dilemma for planning policy that is increasingly seeking to promote higher levels of new housing development within towns and cities. Urban areas in the south have much lower stocks of vacant and derelict land, and consequently much lower capacity for development within urban areas, than towns and cities in the north of England (NLUD 2000).

Biases and Weaknesses in the Planning System

In this section we discuss a number of operational features of planning that seem to characterise current practice. These issues are of significance because they tend to undermine the development of strategic responses to the kinds of challenges faced in regions with high growth pressures. The issues include: selective restraint, between areas and development sectors; fragmented institutions and inappropriate local government boundaries; short-termism/opportunism; and limited powers and resources to intervene positively in the development process.

Selective Restraint

Planning at a local level in those parts of southern England which are experiencing the greatest growth pressures is frequently dominated by an approach that seeks to resist development. The evidence for this can be seen in well-publicised recent debates in the South East of England (Panel Report 1999), and also neighbouring areas facing similar growth pressures (SWRPC 1999). This aspect seems to reflect a wider, more structural feature of planning, giving rise to systematic variations in planning policy stance, more restrictive in affluent and growing areas and more permissive in poorer, declining areas (Bramley and Lambert 1998, Bramley 1999). The former, that is, the growth areas, are likely to be attractive, with residents who value environmental qualities more highly, who are likely to be owner occupiers with a stake in local residential property values and who have the capacity to organise in order to protect their environments. The residents of the latter areas and their political representatives may be more concerned with promoting economic development, jobs and housing-led regeneration.

Moreover, restraint seems to be applied rather selectively to housing as opposed to economic development. Motivation to support employment development might be expected to be most powerful in areas which have experienced economic decline and high unemployment, but it is suggested that this attitude has become prevalent in most areas, including prosperous parts of the country (Bramley 1999). This is consistent with a view that cities and regions are increasingly in competition with one another for economic growth. The amount of land allocated for employment typically exceeds likely requirements in the short to medium term. Housing development targets and land supply are in contrast more likely to be held down, reflecting a view that the impact of housing development is largely negative and a threat to local environmental quality.

These general features can be illustrated more specifically by planning policy developments in the Bristol area. After a period of relatively permissive planning policy in the 1970s and 1980s, developed in a context of greater uncertainty about the impact of manufacturing decline on the local economy, planning policy in the Bristol area has undergone a significant shift. Growth restriction sentiments generally are relatively strong, but anti-housing development views are becoming particularly powerful. While there is localised resistance to further employment growth in parts of the city-region which have grown fastest in recent years, there are wider aspirations to sustain economic growth in general terms and significant, yet-to-be developed employment land allocations in highly marketable locations. One impact of this selective policy stance is for employment growth to outstrip population growth, and a tendency for housing growth pressures to spill over into less politically-sensitive, less constrained neighbouring areas, lengthening journeys to work. Balanced development of housing alongside employment, one of the key objectives of 'sustainable development', is therefore not achieved.

The difficult politics of planning-for-housing is nothing new in the planning literature, though previous research tends to find that local anti-growth sentiments are generally overridden by central intervention (Short, Fleming et al. 1986, Murdoch, Abram et al. 2000). However, national planning policy changes are currently tending to reinforce local policy stances. The down-grading of statistical projections, increasing brownfield targets and sequential testing apply selectively to new housing development. There is extensive discussion of the environmental impacts of new housing development, but very little discussion of the use of land for non-housing development, despite the fact that this is quantitatively almost as important (DETR 1998b, Urban Task Force 1999). This may be because of a heightening national political sensitivity to these issues.

Institutional and Geographical Fragmentation

As we have already discussed, the last twenty years have seen a retreat from strategic planning at regional and sub-regional levels. The institutional structures that are in place, such as the standing conferences of local authorities producing Regional Planning Guidance and joint arrangements in larger cities, are more informal collaborative arrangements that rely on consensus emerging from the constituent authorities. In the Bristol area, for example, a joint committee representing the four unitary authorities has been created following the abolition of Avon County in 1996, supported by a small technical unit, and charged with the task of preparing a structure plan for the former county area. Wenban-Smith argues in Chapter 10 that the more informal collaborative arrangements replacing the former strategic metropolitan authorities can be more effective, because of a stronger sense of ownership of the processes.

However, our impression, based on observations of planning policy processes in the South West region and Bristol area, is that these more informal arrangements, dominated by bottom-up processes and consensual modes of decision-making, tend to militate against bold strategy or strongly pro-active planning decisions. Consensus is generally maintained by avoiding difficult decisions. One example is the general vagueness of both Regional Planning Guidance and the joint Structure Plan when it comes to specifying locations for growth and new development. Another is a strong political imperative to challenge forecasts of housing requirements and reduce levels of provision, in spite of strong evidence that housing demands are likely to materialise, given the general economic buoyancy of some parts of the region and county. Central government intervention may ultimately overcome these 'short-comings'. For Wenban-Smith, this is an unfortunate aspect of the governance of planning, encouraging local fatalism and buck-passing (see Chapter 10). For others, it represents the safeguarding of national policy priorities and fundamental rights that people should have access to housing.

Inappropriate geographical boundaries of administrative jurisdictions have also tended to militate against strategic sub-regional planning. Where cities within urban regions are tightly bounded in their administrative areas (as is the case in Bristol), they lack control over development and development opportunities in their hinterlands. The impact of this may vary somewhat with the wider context in economic and political terms. On the one hand, edge-of-city jurisdictions may strive to achieve more status and independence and plan to capture more central place functions such as employment or retailing. There is some evidence of this happening in the Bristol area in the 1980s. A different response, possibly more typical of growing, prosperous suburban areas, is for edge-of-city jurisdictions to oppose development. This is now the case in the Bristol area. In spite of strong functional linkages across a larger area, political attitudes in the suburban authorities around Bristol tend to be insular and oriented largely to resisting further urban encroachment. In other words, the current institutional arrangements and administrative boundaries for strategic planning are not well-equipped when it comes to issues of territorial inter-dependence. This relates to a more fundamental tension, highlighted in the debates on local government reorganisation, in Bristol and elsewhere, in the mid-1990s. This is a long-standing antipathy between urban and rural areas and populations, assertion of distinct urban and rural identities, and suburban resistance to incorporation within urban boundaries. These differences are often reinforced by concerns over issues such as local taxation and politics (Stewart 1999). The case for city-region government and administration in England, while strong in functional and intellectual terms, has yet to establish sufficient credibility to be seriously considered.

Short-Termism

Since 1991, development decisions in England are in theory 'plan-led' (Tewdwr-Jones 1996). Plan-led development provides some potential for more coherent and predictable patterns of urban development. It should also check the tendency for central government to intervene and over-ride local decision-making, as happened extensively in the 1980s. However, in practice decisions may still be driven by more short-term or opportunistic motivations. For example, unanticipated opportunities to capture some major piece of inward investment may result in established policy being put on one side. Extended review timetables for development plans also mean that many areas lack plan coverage, or that current plans run out in the near future. This is the case in Bristol, where current plans run to 2001, but replacement plans are mired down in central-local conflict over housing development targets.

Short-term perspectives are reinforced by the local politics of planning, with, in the UK system, local elected councillors having a key role. In growth areas, local politicians may be reluctant to face the opposition likely to be generated by an explicit long-term vision of how growth might be accommodated. It has been argued that these difficulties reflect a set of wider tensions in the British planning system, between technical rationality and local politics (Cowell and Murdoch 1999). Technical rationality, manifested in terms of demographic forecasting, is by its nature long-term and future-oriented. While the dominance of such techniques is increasingly questioned (Wenban-Smith 1999), technical questions continue to dominate the policy process, the debate at public inquiries and much of the professional literature. Local political processes, on the other hand, are driven by a different rationality. Political time-scales, driven by the electoral cycle, are relatively short-term, and responsiveness to local electoral pressures in many areas under growth pressures translates into concerns with protecting the existing environmental qualities of areas. The turnover of local politicians can also undermine processes of building knowledge and 'intellectual capital'. A sometimes obsessive focus on issues of housing development means that more integrated understandings of local economic and social development and potential are neglected.

Powers and Resources

The key point here relates to our earlier comments about public expenditure constraints in general and the abandonment of many of the mechanisms of what might be called 'positive planning'. A significant weakness of contemporary planning practice is that there is only limited capacity to ensure the delivery of the kind and quality of new development that meets collective concerns with issues such as transport and social infrastructure. These concerns are heightened in contexts where relatively large-scale urban extensions are being considered.

In the past, new town development corporations or local authorities as part of town expansion schemes were able, as major landowners, to exert considerable control over the overall development process. Public land ownership also provided the means by which some of the returns on development could be re-invested in key elements of social and community infrastructure. In this way a local consensus for growth could be sustained (Boddy, Lambert et al. 1997). The urban development process in most growth areas is now much more firmly market-driven. One consequence of this is that supporting infrastructure either fails to appear or lags well behind the commercial aspects of development.

The inadequacies of infrastructure in the burgeoning 'edge-city' developments in the Bristol sub-region – the road network, public transport provision, health, education and other forms of social provision, underlie much of the local resistance to growth discussed already. Planning agreements and obligations have been exploited to some extent, and generally there is scope in areas like this for more exploitation of such mechanisms. However regulatory planning powers, supplemented by planning agreements negotiated with developers of specific sites, have not delivered coherent and integrated forms of urban expansion. It is possible that failures in the foresight and skills/expertise of planning authorities, overwhelmed by unanticipated development pressures, have also contributed to this. However, this fuels local political and popular perceptions that further growth is inevitably negative in its consequences and delivers few local benefits. Institutional fragmentation contributes where major infrastructure investment requires cross-boundary collaboration and possibly cross-subsidy. Possibly the biggest planning issue facing the Bristol area is how to rationalise and connect the new 'edge-city' employment and retail developments with the traditional city centre in transport terms.

Conclusions

Why is the governance of planning ineffective in the kinds of contexts we describe? This analysis points to the impact of certain contextual features of the planning-development process in the UK which we identified earlier: an adversarial culture; risk and unpredictability undermining trust; and a policy process that leans towards exclusivity rather than inclusiveness. In addition, there are a number of institutional biases that further undermine the capacity of the system to develop strategic responses to the environmental and development challenges that derive from economic and social change in growth regions. Selective responses to pressures for economic development and housing is reinforced by current national policy development. Institutional fragmentation contributes to difficulties in developing an 'integrated imagination' of place (Healey 1998b). Inter-authority collaboration has not developed a way of dealing with the difficult politics of territorial inter-dependence and short-term perspectives driven by local electoral pressures reinforce the problems of making long-term strategy explicit. The Bristol example points to inconsistency in policy stances, as perceptions of risk, vulnerability and strength in the local economy and environment change over time. Finally, the limited capacity of the public sector to intervene positively in the development process reinforces local political perceptions that growth inevitably brings negative consequences.

There is now an active debate about 'regionalism' in England (Mawson 1997) and some discussion about the territorial politics of city-regions. Metropolitan *governance*, if not *government*, is seen as the 'missing middle' in English territorial administration (Roberts 1999, Robson, Peck et al. 2000). Regional institutions are evolving quite rapidly in England with the setting up of the Regional Development Agencies. In the South West, developing regional capacity is somewhat hampered by the 'unease' of the region (Stewart 1999) characterised by significant east-west and rural-urban differences in culture, politics and economic circumstances. The RDA has limited powers and resources, relying on partnership and persuasion of other agencies to invest in line with their priorities. To date, there has been a strong emphasis on consensual relations with the local authorities in relation to Regional Planning Guidance, and no overt questioning of what could be seen as a reluctance of planning to face up to the consequences of economic dynamism in the Bristol sub-region. The RDA is also providing some impetus to sub-regional groupings of interests, which in the Bristol area have developed out of previous inter-authority and inter-sectoral initiatives designed to promote economic development and capture inward investment. To the extent that these new institutions (at regional and sub-regional levels) comprise different professional interests, different elected politicians, business leaders and economic development agencies, they may be expected to change the parameters of the debate about growth and its management, and possibly develop different priorities. As yet, the new institutions are at an early stage in development.

One recent analysis of planning (Cowell and Murdoch 1999) suggests that questions of land-use and its regulation, characterised by strongly divergent priorities and conflicts, makes it particularly difficult to implement governance-type solutions. 'New institutional frameworks...do not necessarily provide a neutral space for conflict-resolution, but rather another site where conflict can take place' (Cowell and Murdoch 1999, p 667). In some ways, institutional innovation and the proliferation of partnership at different levels also adds to complexity and the opacity of planning processes. On the other hand, these new organisations may provide vehicles for consensus building in the longer term.

In other contexts there are some signs that inter-authority and inter-sectoral networks are developing with the capacity to establish more consensus about how economic growth and sustainability politics may be reconciled (Cooke, Davies et al. 2000). In this case, it is suggested that partnerships between neighbouring authorities in highly pressured and economically-significant locations in the South East of England are facilitating the accommodation of growth in locally-decentralised forms. Significantly, economic development partnerships seem to be the key locus of new collaborative capacity in these areas, rather than planning. Recent research in the Glasgow area (Kumar and Paddison 2000) also provides a somewhat more optimistic evaluation of the operation of joint working in relation to strategic planning than is suggested by our evaluation of the Bristol case (see also Chapter 10). Here a key feature of the institutional arrangements is an elaborate set of overlapping organisational networks bringing in a wide range of interests from the sub-region and beyond. Through frequent dialogue and interaction, these promote trust and reinforce collaboration. What may be different here, however, is the scope to build consensus around the issue of economic regeneration in a region that has experienced significant economic decline, leaving a substantial legacy of vacant urban land for redevelopment.

In the Bristol area, drawing in other stakeholders, from the region and sectors that traditionally have been distanced from planning debates, may be an important way in which apparently limited institutional capacity can be addressed. A benefit of wider stakeholder involvement may be to move planning debates away from the narrow issue of the 'housing numbers' and the impact of new housing development, to a more balanced discussion of sustainable urban futures. It also seems necessary to set up arenas in which debate and exchange can disseminate a better understanding of territorial inter-dependence across the city-region and beyond in order to overcome the 'drawbridge mentality' that infects planning debates. Finally, there is the crucial issue of building trust between constituent authorities in the city region. One legacy of the debates surrounding the mid-1990s reorganisation of local government in the Bristol area is a distrust of the territorial ambitions of the core city authority by suburban districts.³ Moving beyond this is perhaps only possible with sustained contact over time. The narrow focus of the joint arrangements on the production of a new structure plan is unhelpful here, as once the plan is completed, the impetus for the continuation of joint arrangements begins to decline. This is another reason for expanding the agenda to encompass a wider debate on the future of the city-region. In other words, we conclude that a more strategic and focused development of networking and of debate about futures might help to build more robust institutional capacity to enable the city and the sub-region in a growth area such as Bristol to act as an effective collective actor.

Notes

[1] This research is part of the ESRC funded Cities, Competitiveness and Social Cohesion Research Programme- Bristol Integrated City Study, grant number L13030100116.

[2] These have been produced by central government since 1988 on a range of topics, revised periodically.

[3] During the debate leading up to reorganisation of local government in the Avon area in the mid-1990s, Bristol City Council, supported by business interests in the city region, argued for an enlargement of its boundaries, incorporating in particular parts of the suburban hinterland where new economic developments were concentrated. These efforts to enlarge the territorial control of the city were successfully resisted by surrounding suburban and rural jurisdictions.

PART III:
BUILDING NEW INSTITUTIONAL CAPACITIES

Editorial Introduction: Creating Milieux for Collective Action

GÖRAN CARS

In this Part, issues concerning institutional capacity as policy and practice are addressed. Ultimately the aim is to analyse and discuss what the conceptual development reported in the rest of the book mean for policy and what policy can focus on. A realisation among the authors contributing to this Part is that 'traditional' governance arrangements are not adequate for handling problems in contemporary urban development. Running like a 'red thread' though the contributions is a concern about how existing governance structures and governance mechanisms can be developed to meet the challenges of urban development in the contemporary era. Fragmentation of policies, high transaction costs and lack of co-ordinated action are arguments put forward in favour of change.

The three Chapters included in this Part provide inputs to highlight these concerns. The contributing authors have a close relation to practice, as either consultants in, or as employees of, local and regional authorities. The authors chose different arenas when addressing these issues. Two themes are stressed, neighbourhood regeneration (i.e. efforts to upgrade disadvantaged areas or neighbourhoods within the urban agglomeration) and urban development and comprehensive planning (i.e. efforts to improve the attractiveness and competitiveness of cities and regions). Despite these differences in scope, the governance issues and governance problems addressed are similar.

A first concern is about governance structures and arrangements. The need to revitalise 'traditional' governance arrangements is addressed by all of the contributors. The stories told by the authors contributing in this Part coincide with what seems to be a shared experience in Europe. The role of the state has been to some degree hollowed out from above (international interdependencies), sideways (e.g. by agencies) and from below (e.g. by local and regional actors). This development has resulted in a greater need for co-ordinative structures, while at the same time the capacities to co-ordinate have been reduced (Pierre 2000). As Mayntz argues, the issue of ungovernability is related to the lack of acceptance of political leadership and decreasing levels of compliance (Mayntz 1993). These crises have given rise to demands for the re-thinking of present governance arrangements. In this Part, efforts to create new governance arrangements are presented. It is claimed that present modes of governance must be reconsidered, as they have a number inherent problems. The division of roles and responsibilities between the various actors and interests must therefore be rethought.

A second theme addressed by the authors in this Part concerns issues of collective action. The stories told confirm that cities and sub-regions are facing substantial problems in their ambitions to become collective actors. The problems referred to are in the same vein as those described in more general terms in Chapter one in this book. One problem lies in how to organise collective actions. For example, the shortcomings of 'traditional' organisational approaches for urban development are addressed. Also, the performance of partnerships is debated. It is claimed that work within a partnership is often associated with substantial transaction costs. Another problem highlighted is that partners are seldom equal in terms of power. Some 'formal' and 'established' partners have a dominant role while others have weak and vague roles. Finally, it is claimed that partnerships are often based on alliances of like-minded actors, incapable of incorporating conflicting interests that are common in this type of development situation. The issues addressed coincide with concerns expressed in the wider debate (Peters 2000, Pierre 1998). Another problem addressed in this Part is how to identify the obstacles that inhibit the formation and effectiveness of locally-based collective actors. Goodstadt, Buchan and Wenban-Smith all address how to form a collective actor from diverse local interests, and how far such actors have the ability to represent the 'local collective actor'.

The first contribution in this Part (Chapter 8) by Murray Stewart is written from the perspective of a policy consultant and critic, working closely with 'New Labour' national policies on urban issues. Stewart's starting point is recent attempts to revitalise local government by decentralising power, engaging local communities and promoting 'joined-up' working. These efforts have in many respects not been as successful as hoped for. Problems of vertical and horizontal integration are obvious. Stewart agues that, in order to improve effectiveness and bring about integrated governance, issues concerning cultural, organisational and administrative mechanisms have to be addressed. In his contribution, Stewart recognises, using a similar conception to that presented by Marilyn Taylor in Chapter 6, that there are different modes of governance (market, hierarchies and networks). The argument put forward is that these modes are not mutually exclusive. Instead, they co-exist as modes of governance.

This lack of a single culture of governance gives rise to transaction costs. This leads Stewart to advocate a need for a single culture of governance, in order to achieve integration and improve effectiveness. Further, he argues that the significant role of 'social capital' is not fully recognised. The quality of the stock of social capital is vital in building more effective institutional and inter-institutional capacity. Stewart claims that the concept 'social capital' must be given a wider focus. It must be realised that social capital can create synergies binding state and civil society together. However, materialising these synergies presupposes an increased focus on issues of trust and risk taking.

When comparing the assessments and conclusions made by the contributors in this book, a varied picture emerges. While many of the contributors in previous Chapters see major obstacles in creating governance arrangements that allow for 'joined up' action and integration, Goodstadt and Buchan (Chapter 9), and to some extent also Wenban-Smith (Chapter 10), are more positive about the possibilities for collaborative efforts, providing examples of how governance milieux can be promoted which develop a considerable store of embedded resources for strategic urban management and development.

In Chapter 9, Vincent Goodstadt and Grahame Buchan, working at the Glasgow and Clyde Valley Structure Plan Joint Committee, present experience from comprehensive planning in the region. Their contribution addresses the issue of governance and strategic urban planning. The authors note that strategic planning has been fragmented in recent decades, due to the transfer of functions to a variety of public bodies, reinforced by the privatisation of local government functions. In the Glasgow and Clyde Valley Structure Plan Joint Committee, a new approach has been adopted to rebuild institutional capacity to undertake strategic planning. The approach, still under development, is based on two primary considerations; a new way of defining the role of the planning system and the planner, and a more structured approach to networking. As for the first of these considerations, the problems of fragmentation and the risk of planning being marginalized is counteracted by widening the focus of planning to include also economic regeneration, social inclusion, environmental quality and integrated transport systems. In terms of networking, the approach adopted requires a 'new' type of partnership, which has a longer-term perspective and includes potential 'competitors' with diverse objectives. In summary, it is claimed that the approach developed opens up ways to achieve collective and collaborative action in strategic planning.

In Chapter 10, Alan Wenban-Smith, a consultant in urban and regional policy, with experience of local government at the strategic level, focuses on the issue of institutional capacity and urban planning. The crucial message of this Chapter is that the existence (or lack of) institutional capacity is not an enduring condition. Rather, institutional capacity is varying and shifting over time. Furthermore, this capacity is not only dependent on 'outside forces'. To a large extent, institutional capacity is dependent on efforts to develop appropriate local governance arrangements and a milieux which encourages 'joined-up action'. The author suggests that, unless active steps are taken, institutional capacity will decline. The West Midlands in the UK is used as the laboratory to examine these assumptions. The Chapter reveals the story of how governance arrangements and planning have developed over the last two decades. The development is illustrated in terms of processes, 'virtuous' and 'vicious' cycles. Features of the virtuous cycle are engagement of a wide range of stakeholders in collaborative endeavours. Building institutional capital implies consciously developing the institutional heritage. It presupposes internal support (promoting shared intellectual, social and political capital) and external support (rewarding 'joined-up' thinking). In this way, Wenban-Smith shows not only how institutional capacity may be generated, sustained and destroyed. He also shows how these processes may in turn shape the social milieux in which they are undertaken.

8 Compliance and Collaboration in Urban Governance

MURRAY STEWART

Introduction

Improvement in local democratic government has been a major plank of the UK Labour Government's programme in the last years of the 1990s. A range of measures, many now given formal statutory basis, espouse a revitalised local governance. The aspiration is to decentralise power, reinvigorate democracy, engage local communities, and encourage integrated (joined-up) working. The Government's programme includes a local government modernisation programme addressing, amongst other things, representative democracy, best value, and the establishment of strong mayoral or cabinet leadership (DETR 1998a). An anti-exclusionary drive, involving the Social Exclusion Unit and 18 Policy Action Teams, together with a rash of experimental area-based pilot 'zone' initiatives across a range of policy areas, invite local actors to engage in innovative forms of planning and delivery. Community Planning and Local Strategic Partnerships have emerged as vehicles to carry the new policies forward. Central to the whole governance endeavour, however, is the drive for more integration, for more willingness and capacity of institutions to depart from the 'silo'-mentality ascribed to them and to engage in joined-up government.

Despite the work of the *Joining It Up Locally Policy Action Team* (DETR 2000d), the currency of debate on joined-up working is becoming debased. Too much rhetoric and exhortation has been expended; too little exploration undertaken of the obstacles to integration; too little recourse made to the powerful evidence-base of decades of disjointed working. This fragmentation of the planning and delivery systems, so accentuated in the 1980s by the institutional proliferation of the Thatcher governments, weakens both the local capacity to deliver integrated services and the ability of the centre to control. What emerges is an implementation gap between intention and outcome. Failure to integrate and to close this gap allows and often encourages individual planning and providing agencies, central and local, to follow their own priorities. A complex battle of organisational politics occurs with everyone pursuing single and selfish goals. Well-used methods for controlling implementation begin to break down and compliance with policy intention is less rarely observed. In such a situation the centre attempts to retain or regain control, whilst localities attempt to gain autonomy.

There now exists a multiplicity of government and non-government agencies accountable to different government departments for different targets, each with different professional cultures and theoretical frameworks, with different systems of accountability, different financial regimes and all with considerable operational autonomy. It is difficult to overstate the organisational complexity that results, since while there are a number of important organisational actors involved in the policy process, there are also different combinations of actors involved in the delivery process at local and neighbourhood levels, giving rise to problems of both vertical and horizontal integration.

The inbuilt momentum of departmentalism and sectional interest is enormous; joined-up talking is easy, joined-up working apparently intractable. The government's aspirations to integration, together with its widespread experimentation with new local initiatives, inevitably poses questions about the effectiveness of the cultural, organisational, and administrative mechanisms which are in place to bring about the necessary new capacity building for integrated governance.

This Chapter explores these issues drawing on recent research on 'joined-up' working – or more accurately its absence – and, by reference to parts of the social capital literature, draws attention to the contradictions inherent in the Government's attempts to bring about greater integration within the systems of central and local governance. The essential argument is that there are different modes of system control open to governments, with markets, hierarchies and networks being a convenient and now well-known characterisation of what is available. All of these modes when applied to urban governance involve high transaction costs of market clearance and market regulation, of administrative rule and programme management, and of network building, trust creation, and information exchange. Under all three modes, however, a stock of social capital, defined in terms of a set of social relationships, can oil the wheels of the more formal business of urban governance and assist in building a more effective institutional and inter-institutional capacity.

The assertion of this Chapter is that central government has been unaware of, or is uncaring about, the level of transaction costs involved in the implementation of a number of its current initiatives. The consequence is the co-existence of two alternative paradigms for system management. On the one hand, there is a tight control and compliance model which emphasises compliance and the imposition, if necessary, of mandated co-ordination (Webb 1991) as the mechanism through which integration may be achieved. On the other hand, a looser model is promoted based on trust and tolerance and relying on voluntary collaboration as the driver of integration. Both strategies impose high transaction costs. These are on the one hand the costs of establishing and maintaining the systems of monitoring and control which co-ordination implies and without which fragmentation and disintegration occur, and on the other hand the equally high costs of building voluntary agreement and participation in the many partnerships which now characterise English public administration.

The second section of this Chapter sets out some of the current evidence about the capacity or otherwise of government to address cross-cutting issues in a joined-up manner. The third section points to the importance of defining governance as a 'whole system' and of recognising the several drivers which reinforce or weaken cultures of integrated 'whole-system' working. But whole systems must be driven from somewhere. This section concludes with a reminder of the three well-established paradigms of governance – markets, hierarchies and networks – together with discussion of the extent and nature of their common feature transaction costs.

The fourth section of the Chapter argues that effective capacity building for urban governance must seek to remove the inconsistencies inherent in current system management, and to reduce the level of transaction costs inherent in the system. Establishing a stock of social capital is one route towards this aim, but the accusation of the Chapter is that central government has been confused about the nature and function of 'social capital'. It has thus failed on three counts. It has imposed multiple sets of transaction cost, it has failed to recognise the need to embed governance in a set of social relations, and it is has failed to accept that central government itself must participate in those social relations. A final section reflects on the role of social capital in each of these paradigms and draws out the implications for urban governance.

Disconnected Government

The Historical Evidence

The absence of 'joined-up working' raises long-standing issues about the impermeability of organisational interests and the internal circuits of organisational power. British public administration has little territorial tradition. It has been organised on vertical functional lines since the outcome of the Haldane report (1918) and local government has in general mirrored central government in establishing functional departments as the basis of organisation. This has often been recognised to work against integrated policy development. In the 1970s, the Heath government initiated attempts to foster integration. At the national level, larger departments (notably the then Department of the Environment) reflected the intention to achieve integration by internalising conflicts within large Ministerial responsibilities, whilst the Central Policy Review Staff was intended to foster cross-cutting working. The Joint Approach to Social Policy in the 1970s (CPRS 1975) addressed many of the same issues of integrated social policy as does the Social Exclusion Unit, and came up against what appear to be many of the same difficulties - Ministerial ambition, departmental survival, rigid boundaries, public expenditure inflexibility (Blackstone and Plowden 1988, Challis, Fuller et al. 1988). Comprehensive Community Programmes (CCPs) and Area Management were tested and found wanting in the 1970s (Spencer 1982, Webster 1982).

Later, reflections on urban regeneration programmes, such as City Challenge (Russell, Dawson et al. 1996) and the Single Regeneration Budget (SRB) (de Groot 1992, Brennan, Rhodes et al. 1998), together with fuller understanding of partnerships (Mackintosh 1992) had a positive impact on joint working. At the same time, however, and echoing widespread complaints about over bureaucratisation from local delivery organisations, the evaluation of SRB warned that closer co-ordination between different strands of policy and programmes, was highly desirable. Problems have arisen in the timing and scheduling of systems and public sector programmes (Brennan, Rhodes et al. 1998).

The absence of integrated working is thus 'long-standing, culturally embedded, historically impervious, obvious to all concerned and deeply entrenched in central and local government' (Stewart, M. 2000, p 27). There has been a dominance of special funding and area-based initiatives at the expense both of policies and programmes directed at the most vulnerable groups and of main programme bending. The absence of integrated joined-up working has been a consistent theme. From the 'traditional' Urban Programme, CCPs and Area Management, through the Inner Cities policy of the late 1970s, and eventually into City Challenge and SRB, the inability of government – central and local – to work in an integrated manner has been widely acknowledged. Successive waves of policy have reflected the ideology and values of particular governments. Each wave brings on the one hand novelty in institutional form and on the other hand continuity in terms of a long-standing tension between area-based and people-based programmes.[1] Nor have the problems been peculiarly British. Rittel and Webber (1973) recognised the vertical intractability of government when they invented the 'wicked issue' a quarter of a century ago.

The Current Evidence

The most recent evidence is that the leopard has not changed its spots. Research on *Cross-Cutting Issues* for the Department of the Environment, Transport and the Regions (Stewart, Goss et al. 1999) examined the interaction of Whitehall, regional and local governance in relation to five such 'cross-cutting' issues – sustainable development, community safety, disaffected youth, social exclusion, and regeneration, all issues which are argued to demand the removal of the departmental 'silos', which inhibit collaborative working.

The findings of this work can be briefly summarised. In none of the cross-cutting issues was there an unambiguously specified central government definition either of the 'problem' or the desired outcomes. There was little agreement about cause and effect and therefore about 'what works', and in particular what preventive measures may be effective, or what the balance should be between alleviation of current symptoms and longer term measures. At local level a wide range of innovative stakeholder involvement had been established, and there were creative multi-lateral initiatives building sustained dialogue with communities, and engaging with previously 'unheard' groups, such as young people. Consultation by the centre had been widespread, but was seen as too rushed, and there were few listening and feedback loops allowing central or regional government to learn alongside local government. Rigid structures - protected geographical, professional, or departmental boundaries, inhibited effective inter-organisational or inter-departmental working and made cross-cutting initiatives hard work. Departmental compartmentalisation remained strong in Whitehall, whilst inside local authorities strong departments claimed most resources for mainstream and statutory responsibilities, driving cross-cutting issues to the margin. Government Offices for the Regions could have offered a more integrated regional policy focus. Systems and procedures dominated and new initiatives were often defined in process terms, with valuable resources often expended in setting up partnerships or project teams, in establishing working procedures, in writing bids or delivery plans. Where local capacity was weak, explicit central guidance assisted these processes. But in local areas where experience of integrated working was growing and capacity was stronger, excessive system management was seen as being inflexible, unhelpful and inhibiting to joint working.

In terms of organisation at local level, new flatter management systems, horizontal working groups, and interagency projects had begun to cut across conventional structures in innovative ways. However, the pressure of mainstream departmental priorities meant that responsibility and accountability for cross-cutting issues was often weaker than for conventional service delivery. Traditional bureaucratic practice, proliferation of meetings and duplication of work, maintained a hold especially at middle management level. Policy delivery was heavily influenced by organisational culture which varied between a compliance, survival, 'can-do' activism, and strategic implementation. New skills and capacities were essential, particularly strategic capacities, and skills in listening, negotiation, leadership through influence, partnership working, performance management and evaluation. In terms of motivation, central government incentives and rewards tended to drive system compliance. Often completion of process (submission of delivery plan) dominated, with no additional reward or recognition for achieving real results. There were disincentives to radical thinking and action. Finally evaluation remained fragile with more emphasis on monitoring or formula driven approaches to output assessment than long-term outcome evaluation. Short termism remained dominant in monitoring, and evaluation for the long term (e.g. longitudinal tracking of populations, comparison of area baselines with long-term impacts) was rare.

Nowhere has the fragmentation of government been so heavily criticised as in the experience of *area-based initiatives*. In pursuit of experimentation, innovation, a targeted approach to countering exclusion, and the aim of integrating services to disadvantaged communities, the Government has initiated a range of 'zone' or area-based initiatives (ABIs) Each individual initiative has objectives relating to unemployment, health, education, community safety, urban regeneration and wider social well-being (DETR 2000b). All demand a partnership structure and a collaborative, multi-agency approach and are to be evaluated nationally and/or locally.[2]

In practice there are different types of initiative, with different implications for evaluation. There are 'exploratory' initiatives – pathfinders, pioneers, trailblazers – concerned with finding new ways to approach social inclusion, to challenge existing procedures, to innovate, and to try out new ways of integrated working. As a variation there are 'experimental' initiatives which aim to test new approaches and measure the extent to which changes in approach, resources, responsibilities, and accountabilities bring about measurable change in outcomes. There are 'targeted' initiatives which are designed to focus resources onto the worst areas, to support the most disadvantaged and thus to achieve positive and measurable outcomes against a number of ever more tightly-drawn targets. There are 'pilot' initiatives which are designed to lead other organisations along a safe route, and to assess issues of transferability prior to the replication of initiatives elsewhere and eventually perhaps to their application across all localities. Exploration, experimentation, targeting and piloting are often complementary, but can be mutually exclusive and there is widespread uncertainty in localities about precisely what government policies entail and therefore what kinds of evaluation might be appropriate.

The picture presented from preliminary research on area-based initiatives (DETR 2000c) mirrors that from research on cross-cutting issues. Vertical initiative-specific structures co-exist with horizontal integrative mechanisms. In general, the former dominate and most local structures are designed to deliver the specific targets of the initiative. Whilst there now exist a range of forums, groups, and partnerships which are beginning to take an overview of the ways in which local initiatives complement one another, these structures as yet lack the authority to impose a locally-generated agenda in the face of vertical structures required by central government.

Many of the complaints expressed at local level about the proliferation of initiatives relate to the systems and procedures associated with implementation. There are complaints about inflexibilities in the system, centering around issues of financial management in general and flexibility and virement in particular. Differing time scales create problems both in respect of the time to prepare and submit bids and programmes, but also in relation to time horizons. The fact that some zones have to focus on quick wins while others can take a longer term view on phasing and time to deliver, inhibits joined-up working. The volume of planning activities (there are reportedly thirty nine separate planning systems in local government), together with differing timetables for the different planning systems mean that planning cycles and deadlines seldom coincide. Systems could be better integrated and brought into line one with another. Project appraisal procedures vary widely between the tight SRB procedures and the much looser HAZ procedures, for example, but confusion arises when jointly-funded projects have to pass two appraisal systems. It is clear that power is unevenly distributed amongst stakeholders, and that a set of central government, civil service values drives the initiatives (see Chapter 6). This stems from the vertically-driven nature of the agenda and from the strongly-felt central ownership of many of the initiatives. For several departments the initiatives are, if not flagship projects, certainly highly visible, demanding tangible political returns. It is not surprising, therefore, that the initiatives are not rooted in a real appreciation of the importance of local variety, do not strongly reflect the realities of community experience, and fail to give sufficient time for the shifting of long-held stereotypes.

Above all there remains a lack of trust between central and local levels. Central government is not of course homogeneous and there are cultural differences between departments. But none of the central departments involved was exempt from the criticism that the centralised top-down culture is pervasive. It would be wrong to suggest that the most introspective cultures are to be found only at central level. Indeed many local authorities remain fragmented with both officers and members hanging onto an established political or professional power base. Even in those localities where super-directorates have drawn together a range of different divisions or departments, there remain strong (some say reinforced) sectional interests with the new directorates labelled as 'super silos'. Finally it is evident in some policy areas – education is a widely quoted example – that stakeholders from centre and locality with a common interest combine to create barriers against what they perceive as ill-informed and unwarranted interference by others. The 'silos' stretch from centre to region, to locality and even to neighbourhood, immuring actors from all levels within their walls.

There are also, of course, cultural differences within departments, and at both central government and local authority level there is tension between initiatives on the one hand, and main programmes as drivers of change (or protectors of no change) on the other. The culture of an initiative is determined importantly by the place of its management unit within the Whitehall structure, a point well-illustrated by the nature of Sure Start (a joint DfEE/DoH initiative but established as a separate unit outside normal civil service structures). Initiative culture is also influenced by the route by which individual area-based initiatives make their bid and are chosen, or, in most cases, win their competition. The competitive bidding culture has a lasting impact on initiatives in terms of a special status and an impetus to implementation which main programmes can rarely achieve. This separate status seems to be a function of the number and visibility of the winners. New Deal for Communities pathfinders, of which there were initially seventeen, have high visibility (and high expectations attached to them) as compared to SRB winners, of which there are now almost eight hundred. In a locality without previous winners, however, even an SRB 5 or 6 win created a new success and released the new initiative culture. To oversimplify, initiatives are seen, especially by those who wrote the winning bid and have responsibility for delivering the programmes, as exciting, drawing in more resources, reflecting a local 'win'. Conversely those who manage the much larger main programmes tend to view initiatives as marginal and devote the bulk of departmental resources and energy to managing the main programme. To this group, initiatives are at best a distraction, at worst an irrelevance, to the business of managing main programme budgets or on a larger scale, confronting the modernisation of local government.

Within the web of vertical and horizontal connections discussed throughout this section, the evidence is that the top-down influence is critical. A lack of integration between central departments creates problems over conflicting objectives, unintended consequences, and contradictory incentives which contribute strongly to the fragmentation and separation of initiatives. In addition hierarchical control through contracts and/or bureaucratic management creates a framework which can limit the discretion available to local implementing agencies. The systems and procedures demanded by the centre inhibit flexibility and innovation at the local level.

Nevertheless local implementing agencies can themselves feed off, and indeed sometimes intensify, the tendencies to compartmentalisation which central practices create. Thus the absence of joined-up working at central levels is mirrored by a similar lack of joined-up working regionally and locally, with the consequence that the silos are shared. Again, as we argued in research on area-based initiatives, professional alliances which bridge central-local levels reinforce fragmentation in policy development, as central and local stakeholders conspire to resist the pressures for greater intra- and inter-organisational integration (DETR 2000c). The failure of central government to joint it up is crucial, therefore, and represents a symbolic as well as a practical barrier to co-ordinated action on area-based initiatives. It is quite wrong, however, to lay all the blame for the absence of integration at central government's door and it is essential to recognise the mutually reinforcing tendencies to fragmentation that exist at all levels – central, regional, locality and neighbourhood. Creation of the capacity to counter the forces of vertical and horizontal disintegration is perhaps the most challenging institutional challenge confronting the new urban governance.

This diagnosis of the nature and extent of disjointed working in Whitehall and Town Hall, is reinforced by concurrent analysis from the Government's own policy initiatives. The Government's Policy Action Team 17 established in the wake of the Social Exclusion Unit's report on *Bringing Britain Together* (SEU 1998) reported on the issues surrounding *Joining It Up Locally* (DETR 2000d). That report, *Reaching Out*, points to the continuing failure of government departments to join up The Cabinet Office's subsequent 'Reaching Out' analysis pointed to the weakness of the role of government in the region (Cabinet Office 2000a) demonstrating a vacuum around the operation of the Government Offices in the Regions. It was matched by a further work on 'Wiring Up' which looked more closely at the ways in which government in Whitehall[3] fails to make the connections necessary for holistic government (Cabinet Office 2000b). The establishment of the Regional Co-ordination Unit (RCU 2000) together with implementation of the modernisation agenda all reflect recognition of the need for improvement in integrated working. The proposals for Community Strategies embodied in the Local Government Act 2000, together with the establishment of Local Strategic Partnerships (DETR 2001), give concrete expression to these long held concerns about the fragmentation of policy and practice.

Managing the Governance System

'Whole-Systems'

Countering the tendencies to fragmentation and disconnectedness requires significant shifts not only in the vertical relationships between centre, region, locality and neighbourhood, but also in the horizontal linkages between organisations at all levels of the governance system. There is increasing advocacy of 'whole system' approaches (Stewart, Goss et al. 1999, Appelbee and Wilkinson 1999, Pratt, Gordon et al. 1999, 6, Leat et al. 1999, Stewart, Gillanders et al. 2000). Whole systems approaches are useful in offering an alternative way to understand and plan intervention within a complex set of interactions. They are based on the premise that complex systems need to be understood in terms of the interactions between parts of the system and its environment. These interactions involve feedback loops, whereby elements in the systems feed influence and information to each other over time. Outcomes are the result of the interaction of a large number of organisations and agents each of which is attempting to respond to a changing environment, by adapting behaviour and by shaping the environment itself. The system is 'open' in the sense that there is constant interaction between each organisation or agent and all the other agencies that make up the environment they find themselves in.

In the context of the implementation of policy on cross-cutting issues and joined-up working, the 'system' cannot simply be seen as local government, or as government agencies operating at local level. It must be thought of as the totality of players, including private and voluntary sectors and citisens. Effective policy implementation requires effectiveness within each component of the system and effective links between them. If one element in the system is not working well, this can have adverse consequences for other elements in the system, negative reinforcement or a vicious circle. Conversely virtuous circles can be set up in which effective working in one domain reinforces effective working in others.

What is also crucial are the dominant drivers, since, whilst a whole systems approach implies interdependence between system elements, it also implies a number of key drivers. It is clearly important not to underestimate the influence that central actors have on the system of governance.

> national government and civil servants can never see themselves as 'outside' the system, or as observers, monitors or controllers, since their actions are crucially important in influencing other players. The signals, systems and rewards developed by national government and by civil servants are as important in driving or inhibiting success as the actions of local players (Stewart, Goss et al. 1999 p 47).

Modes of Governance

Whole systems models are useful in recognising the interdependence of parts of the system of governance, but are less helpful in deciding precisely where to intervene. Systems models are inherently liable to failure as disequilibrium sets in. Holism is desirable in principle, difficult to achieve in practice. In effect, as argued above, all systems have particular drivers which maintain the system in motion and mediate the relationship between the parts and the whole. One of these drivers is the stance taken by central government towards system management and control. Equilibrium is achieved, or at least sought, through the imposition by government of a dominant administrative paradigm which imposes itself on the institutions, norms and practices of governance and establishes common system rules of operation.

In discussing the implications of neighbourhood renewal for institutional form in Chapter 6, Taylor reminds us of the distinction between markets, hierarchy and network. In recent years these three paradigms have struggled for supremacy. There is a long literature deriving from Williamson (1975) which distinguishes markets and hierarchy. To these have been added a third paradigm, that of network governance. The network paradigm as applied to urban governance derives in part from a political science literature on policy networks (Marsh and Rhodes 1992, Klijn, Koppenjaan et al. 1995, Dowding 1995, Rhodes 1996, Marsh and Smith 2000) and in part from an economic geography literature (Cooke and Morgan 1993, Collinge and Srjblanin 2001). Networks of governance are multi-sectoral across public, private, voluntary and community sectors. Individual relationships, interpersonal association and voluntary motivation dominate. Membership is defined largely by self-selection. Networks are characterised by indistinct boundaries, fluid composition, and low formality. Partnership by contrast is the normal imposed organisational form of urban governance and is defined by formal agreement, clear boundaries, stable composition, and high levels of formality. This distinction is not always helpful. Networks do possess structure, have members and where regular interaction between network members is concerned may well adopt formal mechanisms, for meetings, or for the sharing of information for example.

Regeneration partnerships in part reflect the network mode, but they have also been formed out of the market paradigm since they have been a required form for competing for resources and delivering outputs under a contract regime. Partnerships are also characterised by hierarchy as authority is exercised through the DETR/Government Office of the Regions/Regional Development Agency structures. Thus bidding regimes reflect a competitive mode of governance, and in practice the systems of urban governance are also strongly hierarchical, at least in terms of system regulation. Procedural considerations dominate with contract compliance a key feature of system operation. Here we see targets (often set in contracts based on delivery as with SRB), and a governmental system designed to monitor conformance rather than performance.

Transaction Costs

The three paradigms of governance are not however mutually exclusive. Networks, hierarchies and markets co-exist as modes of governance (Skelcher, McCabe et al. 1997), with organisational form changing according to the salience of one or other mode in any particular policy area. Common to all modes, however, are transaction costs. Under a market mode of urban governance come the costs of establishing bidding agencies (often partnerships), identifying the bid opportunity, preparing bids, and engaging in selling it to government (including perhaps long drawn out processes of political and professional lobbying). These costs have been incurred in relation to internal competition (for City Challenge, for SRB, for Millennium projects, for a number of the area initiatives identified above), but also in relation to external competition – European City of Culture, the Commonwealth Games, Expo – and there is extensive evidence that there are large opportunity costs to local actors in preparing bids, especially where, as with European funding opportunities, the rules of the competition are complex and ever changing (Griffiths 1998a, 1998b).

In urban governance, however, the transaction costs of bidding are exaggerated by the costs involved in conforming to the demands of a subsequent hierarchical regime. Enforced by a contract system more legalistic than the French 'contrat de villes' (Hall and Mawson 1999, Le Galès and Mawson 1995), and incorporating firm targets and performance measures, regeneration has been dominated by procedural concerns. Management by contract became the dominant culture of government regional offices, with contract management one of their major functional responsibilities, as illustrated by a Government Office for Yorkshire and Humberside study of government contracting in Sheffield which identified over a hundred contracts to be managed by the Government Office in a single year (DETR 2000b). Outputs rather than outcomes became the currency of performance with quarterly monitoring (under SRB) inhibiting the achievement of almost anything other than the return of the monitoring forms. Project appraisal requirements demanded extensive staff and external consultant time and resources. It is interesting to note that whilst the rhetoric of government with respect to the New Deal for Communities programme is about experimentation and flexibility, its appraisal requirements are more demanding than those of SRB (DETR 2000e).

Social Capital

Recognition that economic or administrative actions are embedded in social relations (Granovetter 1985) draws out the observation that the burden of transaction costs under any mode of governance can be lightened if the parties know, like and trust each other. The existence of such a social capital is key to understanding the possibilities of institutional capacity building in urban governance (see Part 1 of this book). But this interpretation of social capital is not the one which is central to the government's attack on disadvantaged neighbourhoods. The National Strategy argues that social capital is 'the contact, trust and solidarity that enables residents to help rather than fear each other' (SEU 2000, p8). Under this interpretation social capital reflects the extent of neighbouring, of mutual caring and sharing, of reciprocity in resource use, and of civic engagement as expressed by the formation of, and participation in, community organisations. It is an interpretation grounded in a view of social capital as reflecting the strong ties of family, kin, and neighbours (Granovetter 1973). It derives from the social network analysis of Mitchell (1969), Bott (1971) and Barnes (1969), and suggests the 'return' to the 'gemeinschaft' of traditional community in order to rebuild a social cohesion which may or may not ever have existed. We should remember that there are numerous reminders in contemporary society of the darker networks of drugs and crime which dominate many local communities and demand a reciprocity which is less morally founded and less mutually beneficial (Hoggett 1997). Taylor recognises the 'strong ties' interpretation of social capital but helpfully also points to the fact that what is needed for capacity building is exploration of the space between state and civil society, between levels of political power and decision making and the networks of everyday life (Taylor 2000a).

In this sense, she echoes the distinction between organisational integrity, the capacity of the institutions of the state to work in an ethical and coherent manner, and synergy, the capacity of the state to establish collaborative relationships between state and civil society (Woolcock 1998). This recognition of the complementarity of both formal and informal connections between the stakeholders of governance echoes the stress laid by Granovetter (1985) on the role of social relationships in mediating organisational behaviour. He argues, in a critique of Williamson (1975), that action, whether economic or administrative, is embedded in sets of concrete social relations, that these substitute for the rules which hierarchy demands, the contracts which markets demand, and the interaction which networks demand. Granovetter points up a range of situations where trust and mistrust, probity and cheating (malfeasance), rewards and punishments, incentives and disincentives, hopes and fears are governed by social as well as technical considerations.

> It is well known that many firms, small and large, are linked by interlocking directorates so that relationships among directors of firms are many and densely knit (Granovetter 1985, p 495).

It would be hard to deny the analogy with the multiple membership of many regeneration partnerships. It is equally well known in the administrative hierarchy of regeneration that the bidding, delivery and monitoring requirements of SRB working give rise, if not to cheating, certainly to the provision of imaginative output returns. Central to the operation of systems of governance are issues of trust.

Trust is the key concept raised in all discussions about the attributes of a good partnership, and it is a concept about which there is a huge literature (Kramer and Tyler 1996, Coulson 1998, Hardy, Phillips et al. 1998, Vangen and Huxham 2000). But it is less clear whether trust is a necessary input to partnership or is an output from it. That is, can trust be assumed or does it have to be built, earned, won, or given. There are different definitions of trust. For some (Hardy, Phillips et al. 1998) trust is a proxy for predictability. The greater the degree of trust the more likely is it that actions will be predictable. In this sense trust underpins economic transactions, endorses the principal/agent relationship and reduces the need for binding legal and costly contracts. Vangen and Huxham observe that trust needs to be both formed and fulfilled to generate bilateral trust. They also point out that trust can both be rooted in expectations (that something predictable will occur) and in experience (that something has occurred). Granovetter reinforces this view in commenting that trust does not arise 'when the transactors are previously unacquainted, where they are unlikely to transact again, and where information about the activities of either is unlikely to reach others with whom they might transact' (Granovetter 1985, p 496). Trust is therefore generated by reputation. Trust also lies at the heart of two other features of partnership working, risk and power. In situations where no one partner has the will, resources, or capacity to carry through some task on his or her own, then trust in others minimises risk-taking since the possibilities of failure or resource wastage are spread. Trust ensures that risks are genuinely shared as opposed to being off-loaded in the case of failure. Furthermore trust reduces the risks arising from domination, exploitation or other abuse of power. Partnership relationships are seldom equal in terms of power. The traditional partners dominate whilst others, often the voluntary/community sector, are relegated to junior partner status. But trusting relationships go some way to reducing the importance of differential power holdings and in any instance are essential to the development of reliable, quick and consistent joint action.

Implications for Urban Governance

Three broad conclusions come from this Chapter, therefore. The first is the need for agreement over, and adherence, to a single culture of governance, whether this be a culture of competition, compliance or collaboration, and to a set of conventions of political, administrative and social behaviour which reinforce that culture through the nurturing of trusting relations. At present there appear to be two competing paradigms at work in shaping urban governance. On the one hand, there is tight control, heavy inspection, the policing of demanding targets, with resources going to those who perform in delivering outputs which work, and naming, blaming and shaming of those who fail to deliver. On the other hand, there is a commitment to local autonomy, local democracy and the renewal of values of reciprocity and trust: civil society is being recreated; citisenship and civic obligations reappear; mutual benefit from partnership is reinforced. Espoused policy currently seems to favour the latter interpretation in advocating the withdrawal of the nanny state, together with governmental emphasis on the role of civil society.

In practice, the Government has remained willing to incur high levels of transaction cost as the price for ensuring that ambitious reform and modernisation targets are complied with. Risk avoidance through procedural control is preferred to risk-taking. Thus modernisation in general, and the struggle against exclusion in particular, are hedged around with costly mechanisms of inspection, control and compliance. But effective cross-sectoral integration (joined-up working) is dependent *either* on strong administrative control through structures which assure compliance, the mode widely adopted by the Government, *or* on the moral control exercised through relationships, reciprocity and trust to be fostered through networks and partnership Joined-up working does not, however, require both.

My own preference is for a system of networks rather than one of hierarchy. For such a strategy the premium must be on enhancing social relations. The second major conclusion, therefore, is that social capital must be built and a wider definition of social capital adopted. Taylor (2000a) and Woolcock (1998) show the way: more space for creating constructive discourse in the space between state and civil society; more emphasis on weak ties between community and government; more emphasis on participative democracy rather then reliance on representative democracy; less procedural dominance in the affairs of partnership; more humility in the heart of the government. Current rhetoric supports such a shift which, whilst in part reinforced by the increased engagement of both community and voluntary sectors in the partnership machinery of urban governance, is also simultaneously offset by the absence of trust. The government's interpretation of social capital is too narrow a one, focussing as it does on the intra-community social capital of strong ties, community integration and local networks. There is little recognition of the social capital which creates the synergy to bind state and civil society closer together. There needs to be the investment in social capital which will legitimise and sustain values of trust and risk taking.

Lastly, however, such values must be shared by all parties, central and local government, private sector, voluntary and community sectors. In particular the centre, Whitehall and Government in the Regions, must become more engaged with local governance and must develop shared understandings and values. More emphasis should be laid on networks, trust, informal relations and mediation as the basis for joined-up working. It is clear from observation about the historical and to a large extent current state of joint working that trust based on experience is fragile. The task then is to build trust around shared expectations, and to generate for future partnership or other forms of joint working new relationships which admit the failings of past efforts at joint working and begin to build a new capacity for urban governance. Government must thus itself engage with the creation of urban capacity. If the latter is dependent on the establishment of the social relations which cut transaction costs and construct social capital, then the priority must be to provide those responsible for the strategic management of the system with more contact with those operating it. Civil servants must engage with the world of local stakeholders, through secondments, making visits, establishing informal as well as formal contacts (Stewart, Gillanders et al. 2000). Other forms of building social relationships might be developed – common educational or training experiences, recognition that capacity building is needed in government rather than in communities, more action learning, greater presence of central government on Common Purpose[4] programmes. There is also scope for improving inter-organisational behaviour and for clarifying the terms of engagement between organisations: more explicit encouragement of risk taking for example, more flexible systems, use of mediation between local interests where conflict may arise.

It is clear that some lessons have been learned at national government level. The need for greater coherence between local stakeholders is inherent in the philosophy of Community Planning as required by the Local Government Act 2000. The preparation of the Community Strategy will undoubtedly bring together a range of interests whose mutual interdependence will be reinforced by the consultative processes required to produce that strategy. The Local Strategic Partnerships needed to draw up both Community Strategies and to endorse Neighbourhood Renewal Strategies (DETR 2001) will need to build on interpersonal linkages and socially-embedded relationships if they are to be effective. Furthermore a key aim of the Local Strategic Partnership is co-ordination and rationalisation, simplification and reduction in the number of partnerships, and establishment of straight forward structures. Finally, in recognition of the fact that joint working in partnership is exhausting and that burn-out is an increasingly evident phenomenon in community organisations, the Community Empowerment Fund will support capacity building in order to ensure that the transaction costs imposed on communities by involvement in partnership working are offset at least in part by the provision of resources.

Thus with funding to support involvement, and rationalisation to reduce the burden of engagement, central government clearly aspires to a smoother running system of community planning and neighbourhood management. The assumption is that common interest and mutual advantage can be extracted from multi-stakeholder interaction and that effective urban governance will emerge from the relationships built through new strategic partnerships. A 'new institutional settlement' of the kind implied by Woolcock and set out by Taylor in Chapter 6 is clearly possible. Taylor reminds us, however, of the contradictions implicit in government thinking, in the 'new policies for neighbourhood renewal which seek to promote risk, diversity and participation, but contain this within a more conventional new managerialist language of targets and best practice'.

The language of control and inspection remains. The Government's Regional Co-ordination Unit has begun to exercise a strong influence on relationships between departments, on the functioning of government offices and on the establishment of new area-based initiatives. Co-ordination rather than collaboration is inherent in much government thinking. Above all, the new machinery of local partnership is to be strongly performance driven. Contributions to public service targets in education, crime, employment, health and housing will be demanded of Local Strategic Partnerships. Such targets essentially reflect a quasi-contractual relationship between Government Offices and Local Strategic Partnerships. Above all the new partnerships will need to show their effectiveness in order to be 'accredited' by Government Offices for receipt of Neighbourhood Renewal funding. Whilst this may focus the thinking of LSPs and push them towards a more robust management structure, it may do less to strengthen the linkages between Government Offices and LSPs or to forge the central/local relationships which are needed to support the capacity for new urban governance. If such governance is to continue to be multi-sectoral, multi-facetted and co-ordinated through institutions of partnership, coalition and alliance, then the reliability of inter-sectoral, interorganisational, and inter-personal relations becomes even more crucial. Transaction costs must be minimised. A new social capital is demanded.

Notes

[1] For a fuller historical review of past efforts at Joined-up Government, see Stewart, M. (2000).

[2] Education Action Zones typically cover two or three secondary schools and their feeder primary schools in areas of under-achievement or disadvantage. Employment Zones cater for long term unemployed people over the age of 25. Health Action Zones involve the development and implementation of local health strategies to deliver measurable improvements in public health. New Deal for Communities tackles multiple-deprivation and social exclusion in the most disadvantaged (and typically very small) areas. New Start aims to re-engage 14-17 year olds who have dropped out of learning or are at risk of doing so. The Single Regeneration Budget provides support for local partnerships schemes which address a range of social, economic and environmental aspects of regeneration. Sure Start works with parents and children to promote the physical, emotional, intellectual and social development of pre-school children. Community Legal Service Partnerships aim to co-ordinate the planning and funding of legal advice services. The Government's Crime Reduction Programme

contributes to reversing the long term growth rate in crime by targeting resources onto innovative and high impact projects at local level.
3   Whitehall refers to the national government executive and its London offices.
4   Common Purpose is a not-for-profit organisation based in the UK which runs training programmes for middle managers in organisations across a city and region, to promote mutual understanding of strategic issues.

9 A Strategic Approach to Community Planning: Repositioning the Statutory Development Plan

VINCENT GOODSTADT AND GRAHAME BUCHAN

Introduction

One of the hallmarks of the Scottish planning system has been its sustained commitment to strategic or regional planning for over fifty years. The form and process by which this has been achieved has varied greatly, reflecting the changes in the institutional context of planning. The system has been able, however, to produce seminal planning strategies that have guided the settlement strategy for the long-term development of regions and sub-regions. In 1946, the Clyde Valley Plan laid the basis for major urban expansion including three new towns (Abercrombie and Matthew 1949). In the 1970s, the need for new strategic directions focused upon urban regeneration and on arresting the historic trends of urban expansion. These were set out in the advisory West Central Scotland Plan (West Central Scotland Plan Steering Committee 1974) and given statutory force through the Strathclyde Structure Plan[1] (1979). By 1996, the Strathclyde Structure Plan had become a major driver of urban renewal, resulting in 70% of all new housing being built on recycled land within the preceding fifteen year period which, in effect, was equivalent to building a new town within the established urban fabric (Glasgow and Clyde Valley Structure Plan Joint Committee (GCVJSPC) 1998, p 19).

This capacity for metropolitan planning was put at risk by the abolition of the Scottish regional councils in 1996. Not only did this restructuring of local government result in the fragmentation of the then strategic planning authority, Strathclyde Regional Council, into 12 smaller unitary councils; it was also associated with the transfer of significant strategic services to external, non-elected or private sector agencies. These included water services, economic development, public transport, strategic roads, and environmental protection. This fragmentation has been accompanied by a drastic reduction in the scale of available resources and radical changes in the approach to the provision of such key services as education and housing.

There has, however, been a collective political will in the metropolitan west of Scotland (referred to as the Glasgow and Clyde Valley Structure Plan area) to avoid the potentially damaging effects of these changes in governance upon the long term planning of the area. As a result, a joint statutory strategic planning Committee has been established for the metropolitan area of Glasgow and the Clyde Valley. This was done, not with the intention merely of sustaining the inheritance of the previous system, but with a desire to establish a fundamentally new approach to strategic planning.

The need for a new approach was related to the changing nature of local government, to the separation of power and responsibility which characterises most, if not all, strategic governance in the United Kingdom and to the new agenda of socio-economic and environmental issues that the spatial planning system is now expected to balance. The new system has sought to reintegrate the strategic planning process through a series of strategic alliances and collaborative mechanisms based upon a structured approach to 'network development'. This has been complemented by sustaining and developing new technical competences to ensure that the development of partnerships is to be based upon informed debate, and not governed by the lowest common denominator.

This process of creating 'institutional capacity' is closely linked to the wider Community Planning initiative that has been promoted throughout Scotland by the Scottish Executive.[2] Community Plans are joint policy documents that are required to be prepared by all Councils, setting out a common vision and 'corporate' agenda for their area. These have been prepared with all key public sector agencies and relevant bodies, including trades unions and voluntary sector. It needs to be recognised, however, that the local authority area does not always form a practical area for preparing such plans since very often the community of interest is wider. The structure plan, therefore, provides a mechanism for these wider cross-boundary considerations to be assessed and resolved. At this level, the structure plan and its wider strategic umbrella can make a fundamental contribution to the community planning process.

The following sections provide an overview of this process[3] in terms of:

- The strategic planning challenges.
- The technical capability.

170 *Urban Governance, Institutional Capacity and Social Milieux*

- The institutional competence.
- The inclusive processes.
- The implications for national planning.

The Strategic Planning Challenges

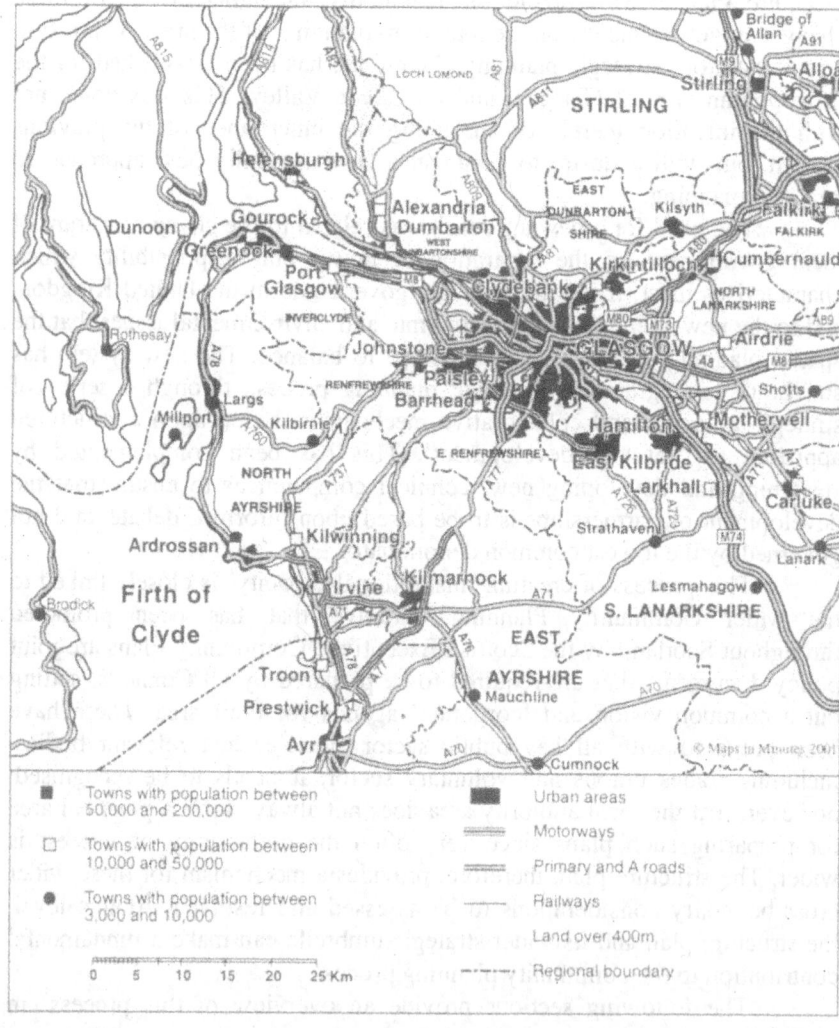

Figure 9.1   The Glasgow and Clyde Valley Subregion

The Glasgow and Clyde Valley Structure Plan area represents the natural region of the river Clyde, and metropolitan region of approximately 1.8 million people and its 800,000 workforce (see Figure 9.1). Despite major economic decline, it still remains the main focus of the export industries of Scotland, particularly the electronics and food sectors. There are, however, major threats to the quality of life of its people (GCVJSPC 1998), in particular, the following:

- Despite the presumption in favour of economic development projects in the Plan's development strategy, relative economic decline is still forecast to occur over the next five years, albeit at a lower rate, with continued levels of 'real' unemployment of 9.3% (SLiMS 1999, p 22), out- migration of 3700 persons per year (GRO(S) 1999) and income and expenditure levels of around 90% of the national average.
- Despite the overriding priority to the recycling of urban land (referred to as brownfield development), there will be continued high levels of vacant and derelict urban land. Greenfield developments are forecast, on the basis of current trends, to provide a significant proportion of future development opportunities, 34% of housing sites and 60% of the quality industrial and business sites.
- Despite the priority given to the support of established town centres through retail, office and transport planning policies, there is a continuing growth in 'out-of-centre' commercial locations, particularly business and retail parks.
- Despite the high level of support for public transport, there will be significant growth in car usage and decline in public transport patronage, with constraints upon the implementation of required new network development.
- Despite a strong green belt policy and substantial development capacity within the urban area, there will be continuing pressure for greenfield locations to allow urban expansion, because of the high speculative development values that can be achieved.

Two key issues need to be tackled which threaten the effectiveness to undertake planning generally. First, the statutory planning system has been seen as increasingly marginal to the key issues in our society, yet expected to make a major contribution to them. The planning system must therefore redefine its function. Thus, for example, it can introduce a much-needed spatial dimension to the social inclusion agenda by addressing the increased polarisation that is emerging in the distribution of health, wealth and living conditions. Similarly, proactive development plans prepared within the framework of planning legislation need to be recognised as the only available accountable mechanism to demonstrate, and not merely to assert, the linkages between land use and transport, or between economic development and environmental improvements (Minister for Transport and the Environment, 1999) This requires, however, the limitations of existing techniques for evaluating these relationships to be acknowledged.

Secondly, there has been a 'dumbing down' of the presentation of public policy whereby there is a reduced emphasis upon reasoned debate and a preoccupation with 'sound bite' rhetoric, for example, in the preoccupation with the length of plans (The Scottish Office 1999, p 3).

There is similarly a rhetoric and a fashion for partnership which is producing 'consultation overload' and yet does not necessarily deliver additionality in terms of sustained commitment and resources from 'potential' partners. Joint working tends to focus on what can be agreed rather than tackling the core dilemmas that require hard decisions. This is compounded by ever reducing resources and a lack of any real commitment to investment priorities beyond the short term. These issues therefore represent major constraints upon the institutional capacity to deliver strategic planning.

The central questions that determine the capacity of the institutional structures to undertake effective, efficient and equitable strategic planning can therefore be considered in terms of:

- Technical capability to take informed decisions.
- Institutional competence to take effective decisions.
- Inclusive processes to take deliverable decisions.
- Implications for national planning.

The following sections elaborate the approach of the Glasgow and Clyde Valley Structure Plan Joint Committee to the above issues. This experience provides a model of the inclusive strategic approach that is required by the new framework for the sub-national governance of Britain. More importantly, it is also suggested that this strategic approach to Community Planning could make a contribution to the required radical overhaul of the planning system.

Technical Capacity to Take Informed Decisions

The technical capability for plan making is critical to the effectiveness of any institutional arrangements for planning. The Glasgow and Clyde Valley Joint Committee has therefore given priority to maintaining two basic technical requirements which underpin the process of formulation, review and monitoring of the strategy and policy content of the strategic planning process, namely, analytical methodologies and related data bases.

Whilst the development strategy and policy have to be cross-cutting (inter-linking economic, social and environmental issues within a framework of sustainability principles), technical studies tend to be issue-specific or thematic. In effect, this can be viewed as a check-list of technical steps which seek to provide solid foundations, analytical rigour, and defensibility to the strategy and its policies in the face of a multiplicity of competing views and interests from political lobby interests, development sectors or single-issue groups.

This check-list has three basic parameters:

- Demand and supply assessments.
- Analytical techniques.
- Monitoring techniques - both contextual and strategy specific.

The key aspects of these analytical methodologies are now discussed.

In addition to the traditional and not-so-traditional demand assessments, strategic planning needs to develop the capacity for developing scenarios for long-term future development (including 'blue-sky' approaches)[4] looking at the impacts of economic cycles, events and globalisation trends, information and communications technology (ICT) developments and governmental action.

This type of forecasting, as compared to hard, quantitative projections (see below) is the process by which joint strategic planning evaluates the long-term futures that will frame the planning strategy and which the strategy must address. Inevitably, with time horizons in the 10 to 20 year frame, much is unknown and can only be analysed in scenario terms. There is therefore an issue of the technical process of scenario building, both in demand terms and in associated supply terms, which needs to be 'rediscovered' in strategic planning work.

The effective analysis of demand and supply, and of origin and destination relationships, requires the definition of functional inter-relationships within the metropolitan area, that is, the catchments and market areas which define the basic analytical planning and policy geography. Without these geographies which provide the frame for the overall planning strategy, it is not possible to take coherent decisions.

The most integrative analysis in the process is transportation modelling. This analyses the linkage between land-use and transportation and the capability of the transportation networks to support spatial development strategies. In this sense, such modelling is a tool, both for the formulation of strategy, but also for the appraisal of spatial strategy against declared objectives, supporting targets and indicators guiding that strategy. In the Glasgow and the Clyde Valley case, such modelling utilises both a four-stage network-based model and a three-stage non-network policy model. The former is used to analyse, in detail, the implications of preferred development scenarios for the capacity of the networks over the period of the strategy. The latter is used to analyse the supporting policy measures which may be required to address network congestion and capacity issues which may result from the preferred land use strategy. In combination, such modelling provides the basis for strategic network investment requirements and network demand management programmes.

Monitoring techniques support a number of functions in the strategic planning process. These are:

- Assessing the effectiveness of the planning strategy.
- Establishing any signs of 'strategic drift' from the aims of the strategy.
- Providing the basis for strategy, programme and project review.
- Ensuring the currency of data-bases.
- Scanning the macro-environment for new strategic influences and issues.

At the core of these objectives is the need to maintain up-to-date spatial data-bases. This is accomplished via a series of surveys. Some, predominantly on the supply-side of the equation, are being conducted on an annual basis. Others, more extensive (and expensive) on the demand-side, are conducted on a four-to-five year cycle. From these data-base efforts, the nature of development and contextual environmental change can be directly related to strategic indicators and targets, as well as to the basic strategy, market areas, catchment areas, etc.

Institutional Competence to Take Effective Decisions

The Inter-Metrex Benchmarking Report (METREX 1999) on metropolitan planning in Europe raises some key questions about the tests that should be applied to the competences of the institutional arrangements to undertake metropolitan spatial planning. These include the following:

- the *coherence* of the area as a spatial planning unit in terms of social, economic and environmental integrity;
- the *legal powers* to prepare and enforce the plan through the control of new development proposals; and
- the *linkage* to Plan implementation programmes and policies.

Coherence of the Area?

The 'coherence' of the planning area can be measured by the extent to which decisions, other than by national governmental, about the future development of the metropolitan area are internalised within the structure plan area, or whether decisions could be taken in an adjoining area which will critically affect the ability of the plan to make effective choices. The more self-contained the plan area, in terms of these measures, the more coherent, and therefore competent, it will be in making effective choices about how the area is developed. This is an aspect of *subsidiarity*. The opposite also applies – namely, that the less self-contained an area, then the less competence that planning authorities have to prepare an effective plan.

The following question is therefore posited: How does the structure plan area relate to the following measures?

- The Labour Market and Journey-to-work Areas – that is the area within which people search for jobs and travel to work.
- The Housing Market – that is the area within which people search for new homes (this is related to, but is not the same, as the labour market).
- The Retail Catchment Areas of the city centre and major towns – that is the area within which people shop.
- The Public Transport Network – the area which is served by the core transport system, in particular fixed rail.
- The Natural Region in terms of water catchments or watersheds – that is the area within which there is dynamic and functional ecological interdependence.
- The Property Market – that is the area within which property investors make decisions about investing in new developments.

These measures have been assessed in the Glasgow and Clyde Valley Area through the analysis of the 1991 national census and more recent specific surveys, including:

- an analysis of all housing sales by origin of purchaser, 1987-96;
- a survey of all new industrial and business developments, 1991-96;
- a sample survey of all industrial and business premises, 1996;
- a sample survey of the household shopping habits in the structure plan area, 1998;
- a survey of all mineral operations, 1997.

Despite the large size of the individual local authorities in the Glasgow and Clyde Valley area, their administrative boundaries are essentially arbitrary and do not relate to any real geographically coherent units, as might be defined, for example, in terms of the areas over which people search for jobs or houses, or within which they shop. The typical level of interdependence that exists between the eight authorities can be illustrated by a number of critical exemplars. Over 70% of all journey-to-work trips are cross boundary, over 40% of all house moves are cross-boundary and over 35% of all comparison retail trips are cross-boundary in nature.

By considering the eight council areas as a single planning unit, it can be seen that the overall structure plan area is very self-contained. Development choices, in terms of shopping, house-buying or journey to work are internalised. This applies also to other sectors of the economy including the business sector. For example, 79% of all new industrial and business development is occupied by firms, as either start-ups or relocating from existing premises within the structure plan area. The remaining 21% may be classed as 'inward investment', that is, from international sources or from other areas of the UK. Similarly, 89% of aggregate mineral extraction (e.g. for use in the building industry) is mined and used within the structure plan area.

In terms of the Glasgow and Clyde Valley area, the above surveys confirm that the structure plan relates to a region within which over 90% of all decisions are taken, whether this applies to where people work, live or shop. The coherence of the area is reinforced in terms of environmental and transportation factors since it covers the major part of the suburban electric rail system, and forms the whole of the natural region of the river Clyde water catchment.

Most planning decisions therefore are internalised and cannot be transferred to 'someone else's backyard'. Therefore, the structure plan has the capacity to make strategic decisions for most land uses. It also therefore has a strong sense of identity, which is important in reinforcing the willingness to collaborate locally. Those decisions which have to be taken in a wider spatial context (such as inward investment policy) are related to national policy issues. This raises the question of the effectiveness of national planning policy guidance, which is considered later.

Legal Powers?

In terms of legal powers, however, there is a clear legal framework which enables and requires structure planning to take place. In addition, the government sets out, through a statutory instrument (The Scottish Office 1995) that councils must work together to produce a joint structure plan. This joint working has been established formally, and as a result, all eight

Councils that cover the Glasgow and Clyde Valley area are preparing a single structure plan under the auspices of a Joint Committee established under the provisions of the Town and Country Planning (Scotland) Act 1972,[5] and a legal Minute of Agreement. If a local council cannot agree with the content of the proposed Joint Structure Plan when it is about to be submitted for approval to the Ministers of the Scottish Parliament, then the 'alternative' proposals of that council will be submitted at the same time to the Ministers so that they can arbitrate between the majority view and the alternative view. The legal powers therefore clearly require a single strategic plan for the metropolitan area.

Linkage to Implementation?

The competence to undertake strategic planning relates to the extent that 'power' and 'responsibility' are integrated. Before 1996, Strathclyde Regional Council, with its responsibility for the preparation of the structure plan, also had powers for implementing that plan in terms of roads, public transport, education, water supplies and sewerage facilities, and to link the development strategy to the economic and social strategy for the whole metropolitan area, including European policy.

Following the reorganisation of local government in Scotland in 1996, this integration of 'power' and 'responsibility' has changed and these implementation functions have been fragmented, with all strategic functions formerly undertaken by the regional council being transferred to central government or to separate boards. This process of change was reinforced by the privatisation of other local government functions; a process which is still underway (see Table 9.1).

Table 9.1   Fragmentation of Former Local Government Powers

Function	*Transferred to*
Strategic Roads	Scottish Executive
Water Services	Board
Police	Board
Fire	Board
Public Transport	Board/Privatised
Housing	Public/Private
Education	Public/Private
Economic Development	(Reduced resources)
Strategic Planning	Joint Committee of Local Authorities

The one exception to this has been the retention of strategic land-use planning within local government which, in most cases, is implemented through some form of joint arrangement as described earlier. As a result, the power to 'prepare the plan' has been separated from the power to 'implement the plan'. In effect, therefore, there is a split in the distribution of power and responsibility for strategic planning. This is expressed in Figure 9.2. The Joint Committee has therefore pursued a very deliberate course of action to create new networks and thereby rebuild the institutional capacity' for metropolitan planning. These matters are dealt with in the following section.

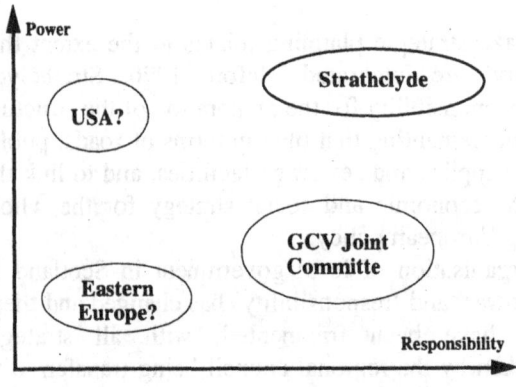

Figure 9.2   The Power-Responsibility Matrix

Inclusive Processes to Take Deliverable Decisions

In view of the need to reintegrate the strategic planning process in the Glasgow and Clyde Valley area, it has been necessary to establish additional processes to increase the efficiency and effectiveness of the Metropolitan Plan. These include the following:

- The creation of networks.
- A participatory planning process with public sector key agencies.
- Complementary policy reports.
- A participatory planning process with key private sector agencies.

Creation of Networks

The local planning authorities have set up a number of formal networks of organisations to facilitate the plan preparation process in addition to their own statutory Structure Plan Joint Committee. The interrelationships between the various components of the plan preparation network are set out in Figures 9.3 and 9.4.

The networking groups and fora are as follows:

- *Technical Topic Groups* for Housing, Industry/Business, Transport, the Environment, Retailing and Vacant and Derelict Land. These include representatives of each council and, where appropriate, other bodies (e.g. Scottish Homes) and adjoining authorities with the remit of maintaining up-to-date data systems for the respective topics. These groups ensure that the technical capability to deliver the plan in ways that all councils, in the shape of their in-house, technical advisers, feel 'ownership' of the core data and assumptions of the plan. This is critical to the subsequent political acceptance of the plan itself.
- *Scottish Enterprise Liaison Group*, involving the four local enterprise companies and the national economic development agencies[6] with the remit of linking physical development policies with economic programmes and policies;
- A *Regional Transport Forum* has been required to integrate the views of the separate transportation agencies. This started as an 'ad hoc' transport topic group but may now become a formal requirement of the Scottish Parliament. Reflecting both this national perspective and the need for a transportation strategy to complement the land-use strategy of the structure plan, a decision has been agreed to prepare a Joint Transportation Strategy through joint working between the area's strategic planning teams and their transportation counterparts, to form the context for local transport strategies.
- The *Strategic Futures Group* involving nine other agencies with statutory responsibility for the development of long-term sectoral strategies for the development of the area. It also includes the two main universities which have research departments in planning and urban studies (see Table 9.2). This group has had responsibility for testing the assumptions of the plan, identifying development scenarios and advising on the targets and implementation of the plan.
- A *Consultative Forum* involving a wide range of interested groups from the private, public, voluntary and community sectors of the area. The groups involved in this forum all have a remit which is wider than any individual authority.

180 *Urban Governance, Institutional Capacity and Social Milieux*

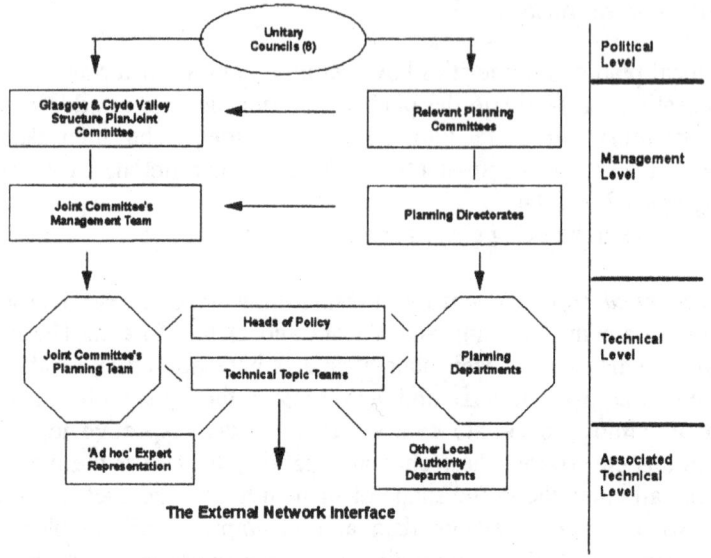

Figure 9.3   The Plan Preparation Network – Internal

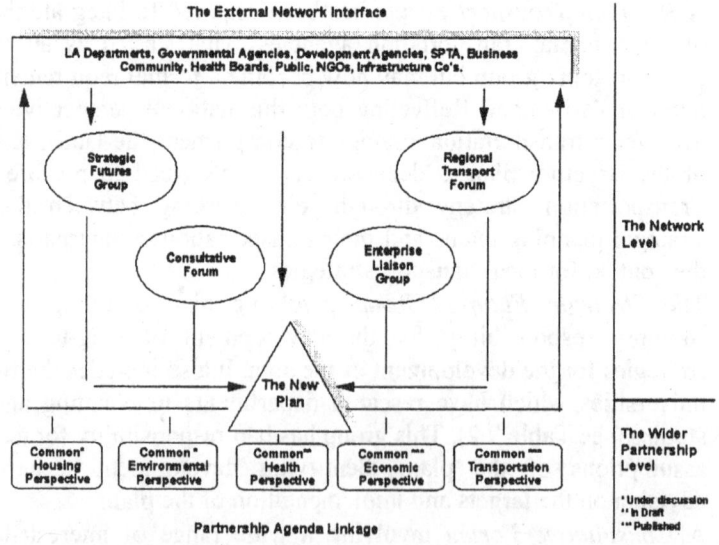

Figure 9.4   The Plan Preparation Network – External

Table 9.2 Membership of the Strategic Futures Group

Strategic Futures Group –Membership
Scottish Enterprise / LEC Network
Scottish Homes
Scottish Natural Heritage
Scottish Environment Protection Agency
Strathclyde Passenger Transport
Glasgow University
Structure Plan Joint Committee
Strathclyde European Partnership
Scottish Executive (observers)
Strathclyde University
Health Boards
West of Scotland Water

These arrangements try to address a central dilemma in the British planning process, namely, the confusion between 'participation' and 'consultation'. The current system places the emphasis on the formal legal consultative processes. These are essential to protect the rights and interests of individuals and organisations, if necessary through challenges in the courts. But they do not replace the powers or responsibilities of any individual organisation. This would create confusion and ambiguity about the decisions that need to be taken. Each partner in the plan-making process retains the right to object to the plan when it is placed on formal deposit for public consultation. These new networks, however, seek to create a sense of 'ownership' by as many parties as wish to be involved through both the process by which the plan is prepared and the content of it. Clearly it is unrealistic to expect all parties to be in total agreement. It is hoped however that, where there is disagreement, there is at least an understanding of the how the decisions have been made by the Joint Committee. As a result of these arrangements, it is hoped to reduce the confrontational nature of the process at the formal consultation stage, and increase the willingness to compromise. The adoption of this 'participatory' approach links to the drive in local government towards wider community participation, community planning and 'joined-up government' in response to the policies of the Labour government of the day.

182 Urban Governance, Institutional Capacity and Social Milieux

Participatory Planning Process with key Public Sector Agencies

The involvement of key partners through the Strategic Futures Group has been a critical part of the process. Without this involvement, a mechanism would not exist whereby each is made aware collectively of the individual approaches to the issues which are also being pursued through the plan. It is also evident that most agencies do not have a spatial vision for the delivery of their services. The plan provides a vehicle for them to be made aware of these linkages.

The key areas of joint working have been to undertake the following exercises:

- Testing the assumptions of the plan: a key initial stage has been to get agreement on what assumptions should be used in the plan, in principle (i.e. not in detail). This stage involved undertaking a broad 'strengths weaknesses opportunities threats' (SWOT) analysis, using the *European Spatial Development Perspective* framework (CSD 1999), and was built into the *Strategic Issues Report* (GCVJSPC 1998). It also helped to identify those factors over which the plan had little or limited control but which were important to its success.
- Identifying development scenarios: workshops were held to explore the collective understanding of the potential development scenarios that the area faces, in terms of the relationship between urban form (i.e. the spatial strategy) and such matters as social inclusion, sustainability and economic growth. This allowed the identification of 'risk' scenarios which were built into the *Strategic Issues Report* (GCVJSPC 1998).
- Advising on the targets for the plan: it has been seen as important, not only to set new directions for the development of the area, but also to identify the scale of change to which the plan should aspire during the plan period, that is, to set targets. These have to be shared and agreed with key partners.
- Advising on the approach to linking the plan to the respective implementation programmes of each agency: a particular issue that has arisen is the extent to which the plan (and its targets) should be related to action which is feasible within existing resources and mechanisms or to identify potential development programmes which could be achieved by changes in the scale of resources provided for the mechanisms by which they are to be implemented. A typical example is the policy for the treatment of derelict and degraded or contaminated land. In the structure plan area, a 30% increase in the rate of treatment is required.

As with other aspects of the work of the Joint Committee, it is too early to assess the strengths and failings of the Strategic Futures Group It is however possible to make three observations at this early stage. Firstly, the people who need to be involved in the Group are, of their very nature, 'busy' (a typical British understatement). It has therefore been important to minimise the time commitment expected of all players, by pre-planning and clear 'task' definition. Second, as with all situations that involve group dynamics, the personal interrelationship between partners is important. Thirdly, the participation of partners may reflect a vacuum in the strategic policy under which they operate and therefore a recognition that the development plan process may fill part of that vacuum. It is possible also to view their participation as a reaction to the same government urgings regarding 'joined-up government' which are central to the community planning process.

In addition to the work through the Strategic Futures Group, special consideration has been given the integration of the structure plan with economic policies. The Scottish Enterprise Liaison Group has been used to undertake joint technical studies (e.g. on the marketability of development opportunities and evaluation of renewal priorities) and joint policy studies (including the submission of a special expedited alteration of the plan for the development of inward investment sites). This latter project provided a vehicle for developing mutual confidence in the joint working process with the development agencies, in advance of the main structure plan review process. The Structure Plan Joint Committee has also worked as a member of the plan team on the Strathclyde European Partnership in which the structure plans (including Ayrshire) have provided the agreed 'spatial planning perspective' in support of the new Single Programme Document for EU funding.

Complementary Policy Reports

The experience in the Glasgow and Clyde Valley area is that increasing attention is required to the preparation of complementary documents. These include technical reports which are listed on the Joint Committtee's Web Site.[7] These in effect summarise the data and analyses that have been undertaken jointly by the Topic Groups, referred to above. In addition, there has been an attempt to prepare a series of complementary '*Common Perspectives*' with key partners on such matters as Economic Development, Transportation, Health and the Environment. Further *Perspectives* are being considered on such matters as Housing.

These *Common Perspectives* are prepared and published jointly with partner agencies in order to:

- set out formally the common SWOT analysis for their particular field of action;
- provide a spatial interpretation of the policies of the agencies in question;
- set the structure plan's polices within a wider context of joint action; for example, to demonstrate that the need for economic development requires not only new development sites but also linkage to job training programmes;
- define key areas of joint action required to implement the strategy.

In essence, these *Perspectives* are intended to demonstrate 'joined-up thinking' and to give a common basis for meaningful partnership and 'joined-up action'. In so doing, they provide further practical linkage between the development planning system and the community planning process.

To date, the more critical issue of integrating the plan's policies with the programmes of the implementation agencies has not been addressed. This is particularly difficult in view of the short term nature of their programmes (3-5 years) and the lack of transparency in the approval process by the Scottish Executive. The standard approach that is pursued in development plans is to list programme commitments of partners. The development of the new partnership will hopefully allow an agreed statement in the plan on resource requirements. In effect, the aim is to use the plan as 'bidding' document, where there is a debate, not about 'whether' resources for implementing the plan will be made available, but 'when' they will be.

In the long term, the linkage between the development plans and the implementation agencies could change more fundamentally as is emerging through European programmes. In this situation, alignment of spending programmes with the development plan would not be merely a 'brownie point'[8] but a 'condition of entry' to funding. This is potentially possible with the powers that are now vested in the Scottish Executive and Parliament and the fact that the structure plan is approved by Scottish Ministers and not the authorities themselves. It would require a change, however, in the culture of government and ownership of the plan. It could no longer be seen merely as the product of local councils, but as a governmental instrument in which its agencies had some control. This would probably require changes in the regulations governing the plan preparation process so as to institutionalise the role of the implementation agencies in the process of plan preparation.

This emerging requirement of 'partnership' and 'joined-up' action is mirrored closely in the community planning process. Evidence is emerging that community plans may fail unless each partner feels an equal obligation to add value to the current arrangements by a more formalised linkage between plan-making and plan-implementation, particularly between public sector authorities and agencies.

Participatory Planning Process with Key Private Sector Agencies

The investment decisions of the private sector are critical to the implementation of the development strategy. Although public sector resources are necessary to the provision of long term infrastructure and the 'steering' of development decisions, private sector finance will be the main source of funding. This is illustrated by a consideration of the level of urban renewal that has been achieved through the impact of planning policies in the West of Scotland. It has been estimated that, during the 1980s, the level of development that was effectively redirected from suburban expansion areas to inner urban locations was in the order of £2 billion in value. In view of the sustained level of urban renewal over that period, it could be expected that the structure plan and related local plans have therefore harnessed over £4 billion of investment in urban renewal by the private sector.

In this context, it has been of particular concern to engage in a constructive dialogue with key private sector development interests. The means by which this has been achieved has varied, depending upon the 'willingness to commit' of the various interests involved. It would be inappropriate to specify particular organisations but the following factors have determined the ability of industrial sector groupings to engage in the strategic planning process:

- organisational arrangements: not all industries have an 'umbrella' organisation which provides a collective view of the long term development needs and aspirations of their industry,
- organisational resources: most industrial groupings have very limited resources to undertake liaison. This limits the time available and the technical work that they are able to support,
- conflicts of commercial interests: all groupings, where they exist, pose problems for individual companies in terms of the extent to which they are able to share information. In many cases they are in direct competition with the other members of their industrial association,
- conflict of private and public sector interests: there is an endemic issue that is posed by the role of the planning system in arbitrating between the private gains and community costs of development proposals. This tends to mean that private sector representatives enter into dialogue as a

process of 'negotiation' rather than 'partnership'. In consequence, whilst industrial associations are well placed to 'react' to planning proposals and policies, there is great difficulty in their ability to express, for example, a collective long-term view of supply and demand, which is at the heart of most planning assessments.

The Joint Committee has tried to compensate for these endemic difficulties of the private sector in engaging in the planning process by a range of initiatives, including the following:

- Market research: for example, a survey of the development needs and motivational choices has been undertaken of all industrial and business developments 1991-1996.
- Market testing: for example, regular tripartite sessions have been undertaken to audit the 'effectiveness' of the housing and industrial land supply.
- Market monitoring: for example, annual monitoring of development decisions as a surrogate of market demand.
- Joint survey of development capacity: for example, industry support for a survey of individual mineral operations to provide market sensitive data on production rates.
- Consultative forum: for example, private sector interests have been involved as a key members of the Consultative Forum, with special briefings being given to such organisations as the Scottish Council for Development and Industry.

Implications for National Spatial Planning

In view of the above considerations, the role of national spatial planning must be seen as a critical element in the process of building institutional capacity. At present, strategic planning is weakened by the lack of clear national spatial perspectives on the range of issues listed in Table 9.3 below. It is not intended to set out the potential approaches to these issues, but the Joint Committee has seen it as part of its role to lobby for more effective national spatial planning. In this context, the new Scottish Parliament, established in 1999, is seen as an opportunity for radical change. In legislative terms, it can devote far more time for new planning legislation than the UK Parliament was able to do. The scale of the nation (5.6 million versus 57 million population) is more manageable than the UK as a whole. The specific Scottish dimensions (e.g. transport, natural resources, rural areas, urban form) can receive more relevant treatment. It will be necessary, however, to ensure that there is not a shift of power away from local communities towards over-centralisation within the Scottish Executive. The relationship to the UK Government needs also to be managed to avoid a lack of consistency with the rest of the UK.

Table 9.3   National Spatial Planning Dimensions

NPPGs (equivalent is PPG's in England & Wales) should give greater spatial guidance on: • safeguarding the national interest e.g. inward investment locations; • where the market operates at the national level e.g. opencast coal; • development choices between Structure Plan areas (the equivalent is Regional Planning Guidance in England & Wales) e.g. Housing and Economic Development; • identifying where sub-national planning is required; • consistency between policies of Local Planning Authorities and the Development Agency and its Local Enterprise Companies (the equivalent is Regional Development Agencies and Training and Enterprise Companies in England & Wales); • consistency between policies of Planning Authorities and Governmental Agencies with Spatial Planning implications eg. Scottish Homes.

Implications and Conclusions

A key factor that will determine the success of the strategic planning process in the Glasgow and Clyde Valley area will be the strength of the institutional relationships that have been put in place. This has been based upon two primary considerations. The first is based upon establishing a 'third way' in defining the role of the planning system and the planner. The second is the need for a structured approach to networking which recognises the differing requirements for partnership than those that are traditionally encompassed.

In terms of the first of these considerations, the Joint Committee was, and is still, concerned to make planning more relevant to the wider corporate agenda being pursued by central and local government. This particularly applies to the four core objectives of economic regeneration, social inclusion, environmental quality and integrated transportation systems. If historic trends continue, planning is in danger of becoming marginalised from these issues. At the opposite end of the spectrum, there is a desire by some to reclaim the role of the planner by making the development plan the central policy document from which others would cascade. Political experience, derived from practical operation of the Planning system, could render this an unlikely scenario.

Reflecting these polarities, the Joint Committee is pursuing its 'third way' whereby the structure plan is presented as a 'resource' or vehicle to assist others (Government, Agencies etc.) to achieve their objectives. This has been reflected in the format of the plan as well as in the process that has been described in this review of experience. It is epitomised by the fact that the new structure plan does not have the same emphasis on development control policies as characterised many former plans, but focuses on what the planning system (at a strategic level) can contribute to the four key objectives for the economy, society, the environment and transport. As a result, the structure plan has only ten policies, contrasting with the plethora (often in excess of 100) of policies in previous generations of plans.

In terms of the second consideration, a structured approach to networking, it was evident at the outset of the new joint planning process that was established for the Glasgow and Clyde Valley area that a reliance upon the traditional approach to 'partnership' and institutional capacity which had not been related well to the needs of long-term strategic planning, would not achieve the wider strategic objectives set within the new plan. Partnerships are normally based upon alliances of like-minded organisations with common objectives, clear outcomes and performance measures. The context of joint strategic planning, however, requires partnership over the longer-term between potential 'competitors' with very diverse objectives. This has implications for the nature, management and operation of the partnership. These differences are summarised on Table 9.4.

There are also critics of the planning system as set up in 1996, in that it relies upon the co-operation of eight councils who still remain individually responsible for planning their own areas.[9] There is also a fear which has been expressed by some commentators that this will result in a 'lowest common denominator' approach to making decisions. The current system is very new and has not been applied before. As such the 'Jury is still out'. The experience to date has however been one in which there has been a genuine desire, by both politicians and officials, to ensure an effective strategic plan. If nothing else has been achieved by the change, however, at least a radical reassessment of the institutional arrangements and capacity to undertake strategic regional planning has resulted. This will hopefully make a more permanent contribution to the future of the planning system, irrespective of any changes that may be made to its legal arrangements.

A Strategic Approach to Community Planning 189

Table 9.4   The Characteristics of Partnership

FACTOR	SHORT TERM PROJECTS	LONG TERM INITIATIVES
Incentive for Partnership	*Threat or Prize* immediate or short term gain relative to the input	*Hearts and Minds* a belief that acting together delivers more than the sum of the parts
Leadership	*High Profile* influence tends to be related to the pedigree of the lead organisation	The *'Boston Box'* Necessary leadership qualities need to be related to the 'maturity' & 'stage' of the partnership
Resources	*Diversionary* resources tend to be abstracted, at least in part, by diversion from elsewhere - 'bending the spend'	*Additional* combined resource 'streams' leverage of additional resources to mainstream programmes
'Condition of Entry' to Partnership working	*Adherents* The partners have shared objectives and/or mutually reinforcing agenda	*Friends and Foes* all with a related agenda, even if differing, must be 'partners'
Nature of Alliances	*Opportunistic* for early/quick progress existing linkages and networks have to be 'tapped'	*Structured* a systematic approach to engage all necessary partners
Relationship to Strategy	*Liaison* strategic context already tends to be set	*Co-producers* partners have their hand on the pen
Output	*Asserted* impacts are asserted	*Demonstrated* impacts are open to real monitoring
	Project Oriented impact measurements are internal to the scheme because of lead times for wider impacts	*Cumulative/Aggregate* net additionality of benefits is key to success
	Status Quo	*'Moving the Goal posts'* advocacy of legislative/policy change is part of action
	Fashionable Elite? 'Are you one of us?' - often used as a career promotion activity.	*Corporate* inclusive of all, even /especially the sceptics. The 'baton' has to capable of being handed on and the lessons disseminated

The general need for a closer and more transparent alignment of the policies and programmes at and between all levels of government is essential to maximise the benefit of the resources and talents that are being devoted to achieving sustainable economic growth, greater social equity and a secure environmental future. The development of community plans offers a practical vehicle for co-ordinating a diverse range of local action. The experience of the Glasgow and Clyde Valley Structure Plan Joint Committee is that a new approach can be developed in the preparation of strategic land-use plans to achieve collective and collaborative action at a strategic scale of government. This will, in doing so, provide confidence to the more local community-based plans.

Notes

[1] The Structure Plan is the statutory plan that all local authorities in Scotland are required to prepare for the whole of the area. This plan is approved by Scottish Ministers after full public consultation, and if necessary, public examination. The plan sets out locational strategy and policies for the long term development of the economy, housing and other main land uses. It also is required to identify those environmental resources that require protection and enhancement, and the transportation systems required to serve this development strategy.

[2] See www.scotland.gov.uk/library/documents5/cp-01.htm.

[3] More details of the planning arrangements can be reviewed on the web site www.gcvcore.gov.uk.

[4] 'Blue-sky' thinking refers to high-level theoretical thinking unconstrained by the boundaries of a current reality and in particular, by any possible future application of the result of that thinking.

[5] Sections 4, 5, 6, 6A and 8.

[6] The Scottish Executive's front-line economic development agency is the Scottish Enterprise network. This comprises the Scottish Enterprise National (SEN) with responsibility for strategy, and a network of Local Enterprise Companies (LECs) with responsibility for economic development and project implementation within their area, working under the overall strategy set by the SEN.

[7] www.gcvcore.gov.uk.

[8] A colloquial term used to indicate positive qualities in a bid for funding.

[9] Town and Country Planning (Scotland) Act, 1997, Part II, p 3.

10 Sustainable Institutional Capacity for Planning: The West Midlands

ALAN WENBAN-SMITH

Introduction

Within the framework set out in Chapter 1, this contribution looks at the pressures that help sustain or degrade institutional capacity for collaborative action in urban governance. The thesis is that there are powerful forces driving the decay of institutional capacity. It follows that, unless active steps are taken to build and maintain institutional capacity, it will decline. The views expressed are based primarily on experience as a local government officer within the urban and regional planning and transport policy scene in the West Midlands between 1981 and 1995,[1] but also on observation (both as an official and as a consultant) in other regions and as a policy adviser at national level.[2]

Context and Issues

The West Midlands Region is close to being the geographical centre of England and Wales (Figure 10.1). Roughly half the 5m population lives in the West Midlands Metropolitan County, the densely urbanised industrial conurbation at its core. For purposes of local administration, the Metropolitan County is divided into seven Metropolitan Districts (Birmingham, Coventry, Dudley, Sandwell, Solihull, Walsall and Wolverhampton), which are now responsible for all local government services. Between 1974 and 1986, however, there was an upper tier Metropolitan County Council (MCC) responsible for strategic planning, highways, public transport, fire and police services, but relatively little else.

Outside the conurbation, two tiers of local government have been the norm for the whole of the twentieth Century. Over the period under review four 'shire'[3] county councils (Hereford and Worcestershire, Shropshire, Staffordshire and Warwickshire) were responsible for a similar range of strategic planning, transport, fire and police services as metropolitan counties, but also education and social services, financially a much larger scale of activities. The lower tier 'shire' district councils had a more limited range of functions than the metropolitan district councils, and were much more clearly 'junior partners'. In recent times, a few of the more urban districts in the shires have achieved 'unitary' status, becoming responsible for all local services, like the metropolitan districts.

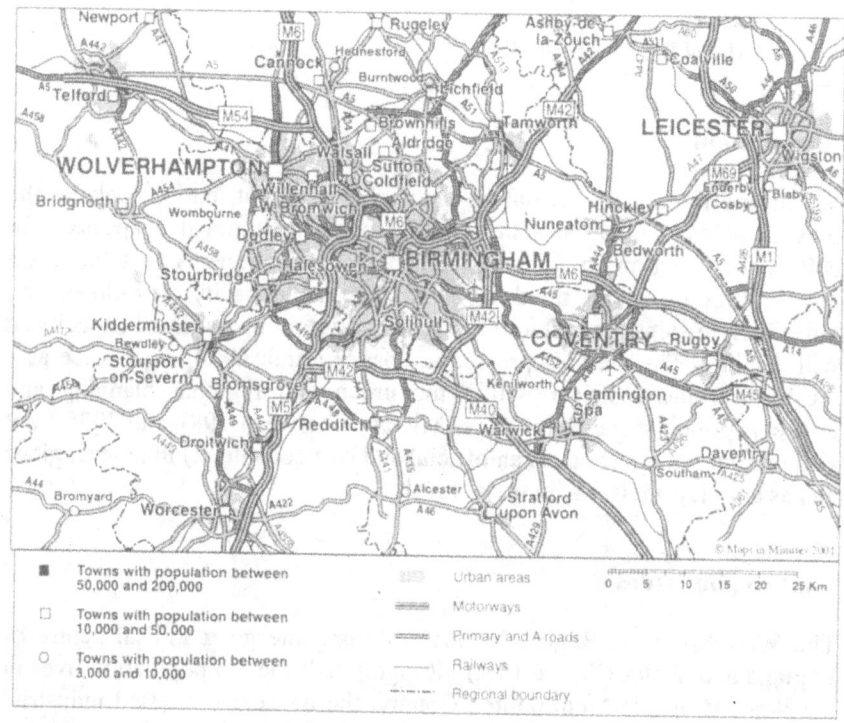

Figure 10.1   The West Midlands Area

The West Midlands is a particularly interesting case, because in the late 1970s and through the 1980s its local institutional capacity was placed under great strain by a combination of its particular structure and external events:

- Until the mid-1960s it had enjoyed a high measure of relative prosperity, based on its economic specialisation on manufacturing, particularly mechanical engineering and the motor industry with the highest per capita GDP of any region except the South East. This turned to relative disadvantage with increased international competition, the failure to reinvest and hostile regional policy. Between 1975 and 1985 Birmingham alone lost more jobs than Scotland and Wales put together. Huge swathes of industrial land became vacant and derelict and there was intense concentration of deprivation in both inner areas and outer estates.

- The long period of economic prosperity and slum clearance had led to rapid expansion of the urban area. In response, the planning system was used to set in place one of the earliest provincial green belts, together with a major programme of new and expanded towns and overspill estates. By the 1970s, the edge of the built up area, the boundaries of the urban local authorities and the green belt boundary were the same line along most of the conurbation's periphery. Provision for housing demand generated in the conurbation, always a major issue with neighbouring shire counties, had become acute.
- The Metropolitan County, established in 1974 had barely begun to grapple with these issues when it was abolished in 1986. Initially it adopted a conventional approach, attempting to focus industrial investment in older industrial areas by preventing it elsewhere and seeking large scale housing provision in the shire counties. More innovatively, it established an Enterprise Board to provide a local source of industrial investment funds. Both positive and negative measures were undermined by the national government of the time, which was ideologically committed to market initiative rather than planning or public intervention. Retail development rather than industry took place on the vacant factory sites (especially in the enterprise zones), exacerbating the problems of the older centres and making no net contribution to employment. Industrial and housing development was concentrated on greenfield sites in the shires (including the new and expanded towns, especially after the new town of Telford was linked to the M54 in 1984, see Figure 10.1). Urban exodus increased, with more return-commuting to city centre service jobs. The conurbation became increasingly car-dependent, congested and socially polarised.

The abolition of the metropolitan counties in 1986 meant that shire county councils and metropolitan districts faced each other directly on a range of contentious and urgent planning issues, in particular:

- Structure plan housing provisions ran to 1991. Unless reviewed and rolled forward, the 5-year minimum land supply requirement imposed by central government would place both shire and metropolitan planning authorities at risk of losing control of the location of

development. As a result, greenfield land releases would be permitted by the appeal mechanism rather than through development plans;
• the distribution of industrial development was following the pattern of good quality industrial land, overwhelmingly taking place on greenfield land beyond the Green Belt, and not on the large supply of inner urban brownfield land.

There were deep-seated conflicts, dating from over a century of rapid urban expansion. The metropolitan area had traditionally sought 'lebensraum', whilst the shires were defensive and suspicious, having consistently lost territory on the urban periphery and been forced by national government to host formal and informal urban encroachments on 'their' countryside.[4]

Institutional Development

The institutional arenas for dealing with these issues had been the West Midlands Forum of County Councils at the regional level and the West Midlands Metropolitan County Council at conurbation level. The former had never been particularly effective in overcoming fundamental distrust and hostility. Its attempts at reconciling regional policy conflict never amounted to much more than soggy compromises which collapsed as soon as placed under any strain. From 1986, the Metropolitan County no longer existed.

The abolition of the metropolitan counties in 1986 reflected the political philosophy of the Thatcher government. In a market economy there was no need for a strategic social or economic role at the local level. Such macro-economic functions as are necessary would be performed by central government. Local government should be concerned solely with enabling the delivery of local services, not with the larger issues of social change and economic growth and decline, which should be left to market forces.

From this unpromising starting point, over the next ten years, the West Midlands became a leader in developing the theory and practice of strategic planning at regional and conurbation levels, the first with Strategic Planning Guidance to replace the Metropolitan County Structure Plan,[5] the first major city Unitary Development Plan (Birmingham City Council 1993), the first Metropolitan Integrated Transport Studies (MVA Consultancy 1989) and Transport 'Packages',[6] and the first of a more holistic approach to regional planning guidance.[7] In each case, the West

Sustainable Institutional Capacity for Planning 195

Midlands was not only first in time, but also made major methodological and policy advances. The key factors in this turnaround were:

- *Political leadership*: a deliberately low key approach by Birmingham to its role amongst the metropolitan districts, although by far the largest, eschewing 'big brother' roles and attitudes. Partly this was an expression of comradely solidarity amongst Labour authorities facing sustained hostility from a Conservative government, but it went further than this: the only Conservative metropolitan district (Solihull) was given the role of coordinating planning and transport policy within the conurbation. Although the outcome of political horse-trading, in which what were seen as larger prizes (public transport, police services, etc) went to Labour authorities, this turned out to be an inspired decision. It ensured that joint policy was developed in non-ideological terms[8] and also built bridges with the shire counties (similar interests and outlook) and government (same party). In spite of the explicitly *political* motivation for abolishing metropolitan county councils, this outcome owed more to 'practical politics' than to the debate about the role of political leadership at local level. Crisis management also had a part to play, as discussed next.
- *An outside threat*: the combination of a serious lack of attractive industrial sites with increasing housing and transport pressures were substantial threats to vital interests of the new unitary authorities. The simultaneous deregulation of local public transport was an additional and linked complication of the newly acquired responsibilities of metropolitan districts. Having gained their 'independence' from the Metropolitan County, the metropolitan districts needed to demonstrate to a sceptical Government and development world that they could actually deliver.
- *Existing institutional capital*: the Chief Engineers and Planning Officers' Group of the metropolitan districts had been in existence for several years by the time of abolition. Originally conceived as a means for districts to combine against the County's strategic power, the common need to deal with a hostile government meant that it latterly came to include both county and districts. Meeting monthly, it dealt mainly with planning matters, drawing on work by a group of planning officers at 'principal assistant' levels. Over a period of 6 or 7 years, this built intellectual and social capital at officer level. Metropolitan district chief planners and engineers knew each other personally and had debated many of the strategic issues. There were also both inter-personal networks and a substantial body of expertise and information at operational level. On abolition of the Metropolitan County, this

intellectual and social capital became available to the new joint political arrangement, and continuity of service was maintained.

In many ways, these informal collaborative arrangements within the conurbation were *more* effective than the formally-constituted Metropolitan County. Agreements about strategy were being made by those also responsible for implementation and the (often bitter) internecine disputes between the County and the metropolitan districts were ended. This more effective metropolitan arrangement led to greater effectiveness at regional level. Shire counties found themselves faced with a more coherent and powerful conurbation[9] and had to evolve an effective response. Dealing with shared problems built *informal* institutional capital. Successful collaboration reinforced this in a 'virtuous cycle' until it became stronger than the pre-existing *formal* institutional arrangements. These points are returned to in the conclusion.

This was reflected in greatly enhanced information-sharing. Regional industrial land information had been put onto a common basis in 1985[10] and housing land followed soon after.[11] Hitherto, questions of data reliability and compatibility had tended to fog discussions and turn off political engagement. Shared information meant that shires counties and metropolitan districts could address the real issues between them. There was early recognition that the sea-change that had occurred in the regional economy (and the impact of this on housing needs) required new policy responses. Changes in long-standing, almost traditional, policy stances took place, and *real* deals were done. For example, the shires accepted loss of green belt in return for 'premium industrial sites' close to the conurbation[12] and a united front in dealing with the housebuilders' demands for greenfield land deep into the shires. There was a sound technical rationale for these shifts in position. But they could not have happened politically without the growth of shared institutional capital.

The effectiveness of metropolitan arrangements for delivery of the new transport planning agenda have been the subject of recent research (Vigar, Steele et al. 2000). The case study of the West Midlands demonstrates the significance of the shared institutional capital of the metropolitan districts in taking a national lead. A wider regional consequence was that, in 1995, the West Midlands region was the first to initiate an integrated approach to preparing a regional transport strategy, which has since become the national norm.[13]

Institutional Decline

The informal structures for voluntary metropolitan collaboration have proved more effective than the formally-constituted Metropolitan County Council, and this has fed through to the regional level, as described above. In spite of these very real achievements, there were (and continue to be) powerful countervailing forces. In the West Midlands, a key factor is the culture of government (local and central), which shifted decisively during the 1980s away from strategic planning in any form (DoE 1985). By the time of the revived interest in regional planning in 1990 (DoE 1990), the reintroduction of a 'plan-led system' in 1991[14] and greater emphasis on integration on transport and land-use planning in 1994 (DoE 1994), there was little remaining institutional capacity to deliver these at local level. At central government level, the appropriate form of discourse was viewed in terms of 'top down' direction rather than collaboration or consensus building.[15] As discussed in Chapter 8, the overwhelming imbalance of power in favour of the centre continues to inhibit the development of local capacity, encouraging local fatalism and buck passing and confirming central assumptions of superiority in a vicious circle.

A further countervailing force is that, for those engaged (particularly on the metropolitan district and shire district side), regional collaboration is seen as an addition to their 'day job' rather than as part of it. Few local politicians rate it highly compared with their more immediate day-to-day concerns, even though it sets the context for many of these. This places considerable personal and career strains on those involved.

Competitive bidding has also increasingly become the preferred means of distribution of funding by government and the European Commission, displacing needs-based funding through general revenue and capital support. The benefits of such competition are seen primarily in terms of achieving greater value for money by focusing attention on the capacity to deliver outputs. Unfortunately such capacity is not necessarily (or even mainly) found in the places with the greatest need for help Moreover the concomitant focus on measurement of outputs brings its own attendant dangers and distortions (see Chapter 6). Such programmes typically have short lives and rapid turnover, leading to an emphasis on short-term outputs (such as can be measured within the administrative timescale of the programme, demonstrating performance against the award criteria) at the expense of longer-term outcomes. Evaluation methodologies have developed to meet the narrow and short-term focus of such approaches, thus confirming and sustaining them at the expense of longer-term strategic concerns.[16] While the original purpose of competitive bidding, to build local capacity, remains valid, a different approach to performance measurement and management may be needed to avoid perverse incentives.

A further factor undermining local institutional capacity are the institutional arrangements around such bids. These may be called 'partnerships', but are sometimes little more than marriages of convenience, failing to develop new ways of working and real new *community* capacity. In other cases, much effort may be expended on setting up special joint arrangements, only to find that 'transaction costs' become excessive and benefits not commensurate with costs. Such experiences can be aversive, undermining collaboration even where it would clearly be productive. Indeed there is much anecdotal evidence of increasing 'partnership fatigue'.

Efforts to extend the range of stakeholders involved in strategic regional and subregional issues run into similar problems. There is difficulty in engaging more than a limited group of 'usual suspects' because of limited resources to support participation and scepticism about the influence of local or regional agreements on an essentially centralised decision-making process. This confirms the findings of American research.[17]

A further, more subtle, effect of these institutional pressures has been a loss of shared intellectual capital. The increasing understanding during the 1970s of strategic planning as a process requiring continuous management of uncertainty (Friend and Jessop 1969) has been supplanted by a focus on 'end-point' planning, with methodologies borrowed from the plethora of shorter-term action plans, often having a very strong property development bias. Longer-term 'visions' are pursued by means of strategies defined in physical and quantitative terms, which (once set) can only be adjusted by wholesale plan review, itself made lengthy and cumbersome by the same quantitative emphasis[18] (especially when taken together with more legitimate concerns for integration and participation). Strategic planning needs to be approached in a different way from shorter-term initiatives. A more sophisticated approach (eg 'plan, monitor and manage') has different requirements for institutional infrastructure and information. These are not more costly or difficult in principle, but the loss of understanding of the difference is a major obstacle in the way of an appropriate response.

Conclusions

There is increasing recognition that the capacity of a *place* to engage a wide range of stakeholders in collaborative endeavour is crucial to its competitiveness. Increasingly specialised companies are linked in global supply chains, but draw upon local infrastructure and resources, especially labour markets. Sustainable growth depends upon meeting personal and environmental needs as well as conventional requirements for physical infrastructure. This implies institutional capacity for strategic collaborative planning, as summarised in Figure 10.2.

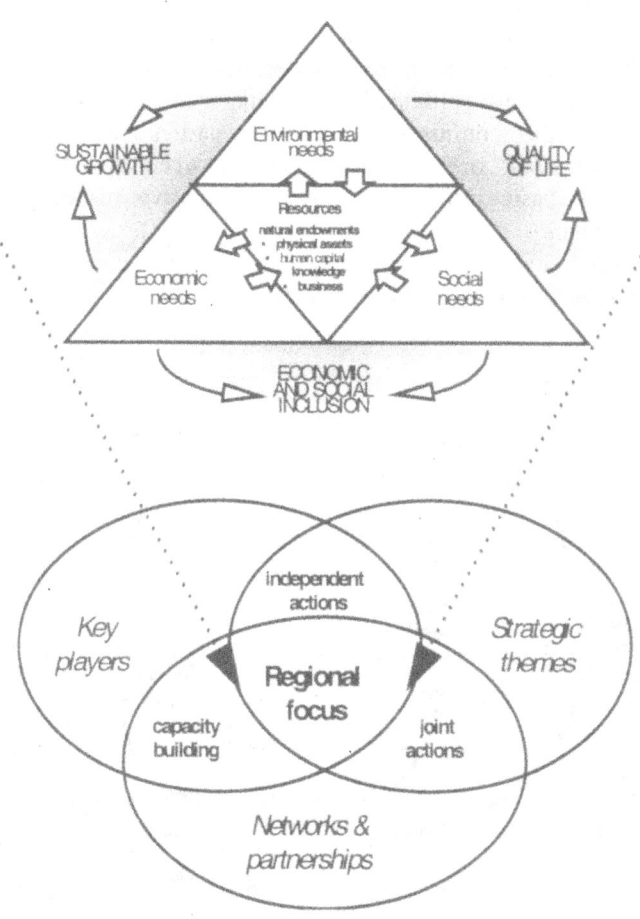

Figure 10.2   Range and Focus for Strategic Regional Collaboration

Building *sustainable* institutional capacity for strategic planning at regional and subregional levels involves strengthening the processes of institutional development and counter-acting the processes of institutional decline. These can each be thought of as cyclical processes, in which a range of factors reinforce each other in a cumulative way, as either a 'vicious' or a 'virtuous' circle.

Factors that help *build* local institutional capacity (see Figure 10.3) include:

- internal: shared intellectual, social and political capital, which is expressed in the ability to widen the search for consensus beyond the immediate issue, grounded in understanding of basic community values and perceptions; sufficient trust in other stakeholders to negotiate trade-offs in the confidence that other parties will deliver on their commitments; organisational and resource support for continuing contact, basic information and collaborative responses to external challenges;
- external: a style of government that recognises and rewards 'joined-up thinking' and local collaborative effort.

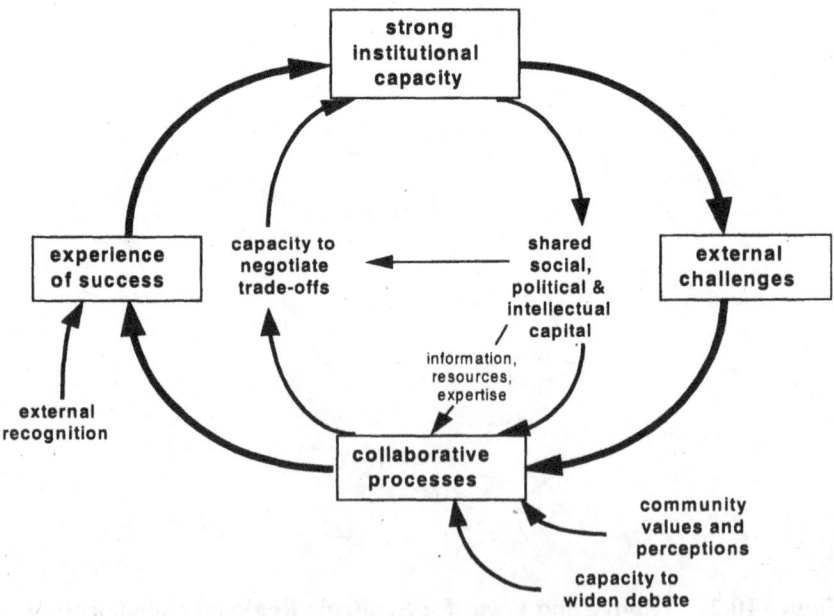

Figure 10.3   Developing Institutional Capacity

Sustainable Institutional Capacity for Planning 201

Factors that tend to destroy local institutional capacity (see Figure 10.4) include:

- internal: lack of investment of time and staff resource in building social and political relationships between local stakeholders and developing common information bases; collaboration narrowly focused on specific issues; lack of a strong base in community values;
- external: a top-down style of government in which connections across departmental boundaries are not recognised; appraisal and performance measurement regimes which allocate funds on the basis of sectional and short-run outputs rather than strategic and cross-sectoral outcomes.

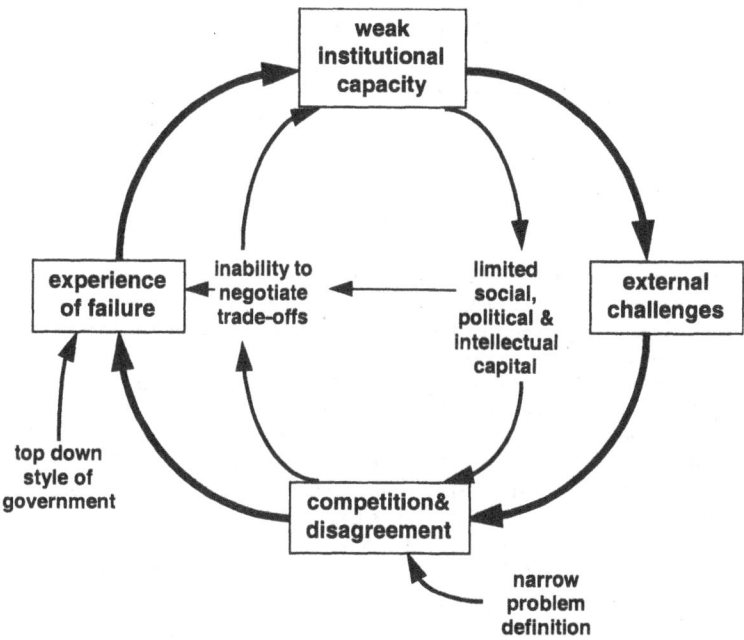

Figure 10.4   Declining Institutional Capacity

The differences between the 'virtuous' and 'vicious' cycles illustrated are felt at each point. The lessons of the West Midlands experience suggest that quality of political leadership is the key consideration. However, this may not take a conventional form. In the West Midlands, the attitude of a few leading politicians in recognising and respecting less powerful and minority interests was more significant than any explicit policy. At the same time, the ability to frame issues in terms clear enough to permit the necessary political deals and trade-offs to be struck between these interests depended on good quality information and analysis, a technical capability. The keys to realising and mobilising the positive dynamic of Figure 10.3 seem on the basis of this experience to lie in the following areas of action:

- fostering shared social capital *within* both political and technical domains – and communication *between* them;
- fostering the development of shared resources of information and expertise;
- fostering the capacity to widen debate across conventional topic and sectoral boundaries, increasing scope for resolving problems by widening the range of potential trade-offs between interests that can be considered. To be politically robust, this requires underpinning by good understanding and communication with community interests and values.

Notes

1. Responsible for planning (1981 on) and transport (1986 on) policy for Birmingham, city's officer representative at Metropolitan and regional level (1991 on), Chairman of both Metropolitan and Regional officer adviser groups for planning, transport and economic development 1994 and 1995.
2. Strategic transport and planning policy roles in Newcastle upon Tyne and Tyne and Wear, and consultancy in Northern, London, South East, Merseyside, West Midlands and Yorkshire and Humberside regions; external adviser on research to DOT and DOE 1993-97 and transport adviser to Shadow Transport Secretary 1996-7.
3. The term 'shire' is used to distinguish *non-metropolitan* district and county councils.
4. Described graphically in Richard Crossman's Diaries during his period as Minister for Housing and Local Government in the late 1960s.
5. '*PPG10: Strategic Planning Guidance for the West Midlands*' (Feb 1988), prepared under Section 5 of DoE Circular 30/85 on the basis of advice given by West Midlands MDCs in May 1987.
6. '*West Midlands Transport Package 1992*' – the basis of the national system initiated by DOT Circular 2/93.
7. '*Advice on RPG for the West Midlands: 1991-2011*', WM Forum of Local Authorities, 1993, leading to '*RPG11: Regional Planning Guidance for the West Midlands*' (Sept 1995).
8. Not the same as being technically-dominated or value-free: a coalition of interest had to be identified.
9. Partly a matter of arithmetic having been 4 shires and 1 metropolitan County, the regional Forum was reconstituted on the basis of equality of representation (reflecting the population split).
10. Birmingham and Warwickshire jointly managed the Regional Industrial Land Study (RILS), at Birmingham's urging. This (for the first time) included quality, preparation costs and market segment information on a consistent basis across the region. The first

report, reviewing the situation as at April 1986, was published in January 1987 and has continued as a base information source for economic development ever since.
[11] Coordinated by Hereford and Worcester County Council.
[12] Eg the West Midlands Premium Industrial Sites Study (1989) by Birmingham, Hereford & Worcester, Solihull and Warwickshire.
[13] West Midlands Forum of Local Authorities (1998), *'Accessibility & Mobility: an Integrated Transport Action Plan for the West Midlands Region'*; DETR (Feb 1999), *'Planning Policy Guidance Note 11: Regional Planning – public consultation draft'*.
[14] Planning and Compensation Act 1991.
[15] The way in which housing provision in RPG and Structure Plans is still cascaded down from national household projections provides a particularly clear example of the persistence of this kind of thinking.
[16] A particular case in point concerns transport evaluation which continues to be based on transport outcomes, ignoring possibly larger and more important social and economic impacts on patterns of activity and settlement.
[17] Innes 992 suggests four conditions for success: 1) The group must include representatives of interests affected and those who can make it successful; 2) The group must know that the agreements they reach will matter; 3) Group processes must be conducted so that all members have an equal voice, even if they do not have equal power outside the group (this may require training and skilled facilitation; 4) The group must include experts to bridge the gap between technical and everyday knowledge.
[18] The most striking case in point being the use of long-term household projections as the foundation of provision for housing land, leading to loss of control over the use of greenfield land (see Wenban-Smith 1999).

11 Urban Governance Capacity in Complex Societies: Challenges of Institutional Adaptation

PATSY HEALEY, GÖRAN CARS, ALI MADANIPOUR AND CLAUDIO DE MAGALHÃES

In this Chapter, we draw together the contributions of the book and return to some of the arguments opened up in Chapter 1. In the first section, we summarise the main conclusions which emerge as to the changes underway in governance capacities. In the following three sections, we review the three propositions put forward in Chapter 1, in the light of the various contributions. In the final section, we draw together the implications for those involved in urban governance, both generally and as regards specific suggestions for those seeking to develop collective action capacities and programmes in the dynamic and complex realities of urban places in the new century.

Institutional Inheritance and Transformative Effort

Urban Governance in Complex Contexts

The contributions in this book have discussed transformative efforts directed at urban governance capacity in a range of different situations – different national cultures, local realities, geographical and administrative scales and policy emphases. They all illustrate the challenges facing the transformation of institutional capacities in complex and dynamic contexts, where inherited practices interact with new organizational priorities and principles, and where alternative concepts of possible trajectories conflict with each other. They emphasise the importance of understanding the interplay between changes in formal law, procedure and organisational structure, and the accretion of cultures and practices that build up around the institutional sites of governance activity. Chapters 9 and 10 show well how the abolition of a formal layer of government liberated energies for informal alliances, which could become freer and more inventive, though hampered by the continual struggle to maintain persuasive power in a fragmented institutional context. Chapter 6 illustrates how the formal task of writing resource allocation rules at national level subverted political intentions for more community-responsive and empowering forms of local governance. Chapter 4 charts how historically-formed cultural antagonisms created a social milieu which counteracted the efforts of formal government representatives to re-build and re-position a collective identity for a divided city. The Chapters also provide examples of the challenge experienced by key actors within urban governance contexts to re-position their localities in a changing geography of economic, political and cultural relations.

The contributions also show that the driving forces of these processes are neither singular nor unilinear in direction. They impact on localities as a complex mix of the changing dynamics of economic relations, changing social needs and cultural referents and changing expectations about what constitute appropriate and legitimate forms of collective action. Although, as the regulation theorists have argued (see Chapter 1), the rhetoric of much policy exhortation in Europe in recent years has emphasised the need for more flexible, innovative and responsive governance, sensitive to the shifting dynamics of globalising capitalist economic relations, the recognition and mobilisation as active pressure groups of a whole range of social groups also demands flexibility, innovation and responsiveness, often in ways which conflict with each other and with the demands of economic groups. Cross-cutting this new economic and political landscape are changes in technology and lifestyle, with their new patterns of information flow, discussion and political mobilisation, which generate alternative 'public arenas' to the traditional 'public realms' of urban politics. These multiple driving forces imply that the evolutions underway in the milieux in which urban governance processes play out are not just about struggles over access to material resources, which so pre-occupied the builders of mid-twentieth century welfare states. They also involve struggles over re-conceptualising identities, of individuals, groups and qualities of places, as Matthiesen brings out in Chapter 4.

Thus the interplay of structure and agency in institutional capacity-building needs to be understood as an ever-present multi-dimensional and mutually constitutive process, as we argue in Chapter 1. Simple linear models of policy-implementation, or stimulus-response, or the interplay of utility-maximising individuals, are inherently unable to capture such dynamics, in which the structuring forces are themselves constituted and re-composed as their effects play out in particular times and places. This re-composing effort applies not just to the 'external forces', whose pulses and waves flow through and across the social relations and mindsets of those in particular places. It also applies to the qualities of the social milieux in which these social relations are located. The interaction between 'external forces' and internal processes that Wenban-Smith describes in Chapter 10 is thus an ongoing, co-evolving process, as we argued in Chapter 1. As a consequence of the complexity of these interactions, transformations in governance capacity do not flow along predictable pathways. Transformations occur and transformative initiatives have impacts, but what these are emerge over time. The full impacts of actions in complex, dynamic situations cannot therefore readily be forecast through technical analysis. Awareness of their effects lies as much in the realm of strategic conceptualisation.

Inevitably, as these driving forces play out in localities, in complex interplay with local histories and geographies, the result is diversity and conflicting impulses in local institutional dynamics, both as between areas, and as between different foci of governance attention within areas. Chapter 10 illustrates this interplay in its discussion of how removing layers of formal government released innovative mobilisation energy, but destroyed knowledge resources. Chapter 8 berates the confusion of national government initiatives that seek to encourage empowering local collaborative processes while burdening them with all the paraphernalia of control and compliance processes. Most of the contributions point the finger at governance capacity for its failures of adaptation to these complex and dynamic forces. Allen, Cars, Taylor, Lambert, Oatley and Stewart emphasise failures in the parameters of structural institutional design, in legislation and procedure, in the distribution of competences, in the formal processes governing resource flows. De Magalhães et al. and Matthiesen stress failures in the design of practices, and in particularly the way those involved in urban governance are culturally 'locked in' to older ways of doing things. Yet, in a context of complex dynamics, the notion that there are ideal structural institutional parameters and appropriate designs for local practices must itself be questionable, as we note in Chapter 1.

Intellectual Perspectives

How do the contributors suggest analysing these complex dynamic processes of governance change and transformation? They all follow the 'institutionalist' emphasis in examining governance process through the interplay of actors and networks engaged in collective action. Most also stress the importance of analysing collective action in the context of its specific institutional setting, a key point also made in the literature on business organisation in complex contexts (Kickert, Klijn et al. 1997). Beyond this commonality, the contributions represent different intellectual angles of vision. Chapters 2 and 3 explicitly take up the challenge of an institutionalist focus on what Gualini calls the 'generative' qualities of collective action efforts as these deploy, maintain, change and build new institutional capacities. Others take a more structural view of transformation processes. In Chapter 4, Matthiesen develops a model of transformation pathways and levels in which formal structures and everyday cultures are brought into interaction. Allen and Cars set their discussion of the situations facing distressed neighbourhoods in the context of regulationist concepts of the transition from Fordism. Other intellectual strands are also drawn into the discussion, particularly in Chapter 8, where Stewart makes reference to Williamsonian concepts of transaction costs (to challenge the design of national neighbourhood renewal initiatives) and to notions of 'whole systems' (to focus efforts in institutional re-design on the 'whole person' in their social milieux, challenging sectoralised delivery systems).

The significance of intellectual perspective lies not just in its role in framing the conceptualisations of governance activity and capacities. Perspectives also direct the foci of analytical attention. All the contributions look beyond what individual actors and power elites do, to focus on interactions, relations and networks. They emphasise the processes through which actions are performed and the generation of the capacity to act collectively, rather than merely what gets done and its material consequences. They also emphasise the tensions which arise between alternative modes of acting and the struggles that may occur over institutional design principles. Such struggles emerge particularly clearly in Chapter 3, in the tension between the practices of a traditional local authority and its own arms-length agency; in Chapter 4, in the contrast between a local history of governance and the sudden imposition of the 'NordRhein Westfalen governance model' transported from Western Germany; and in Chapter 8 in the tense co-existence between compliance and collaborative modes of governance in English policy for neighbourhood renewal. The contributions also throw light on what it takes to construct a 'public sphere', arenas where legitimate and accountable collective action initiatives are designed and implemented. If, as Stone (1989) argues, the traditional model of representative democracy seems inadequate for the demands of accountability and legitimacy placed on it, that of partnership may also fail in its capacity for focus and responsiveness. This suggests that an important development of institutionalist analysis should lie in examining the social processes through which accountable and responsive collective action arenas are created. The contributions in this book suggest that this involves as much a mental effort in re-framing conceptions of legitimacy and accountability an organizational effort in designing incentive structures and procedures. It involves not single arenas and levels of government, but many operating in interaction. It also requires attention to the daily routines and 'bodily practices' of performing governance work as well as to the rhetorics of political manifestoes, policy 'guidance' and formal plans.

Transformation for What?

These conclusions have considerable implications for the design of interventions intended to speed up governance adaptation in complex, dynamic situations and to encourage innovation. The Chapters in Part 3 all address this challenge and how this relates to the interaction between the design of the structuring parameters of urban governance activities and the design of institutional practices in specific contexts.

But what is the purpose of all this effort in adaptation and transformation? Much of the policy rhetoric demanding governance change seems to value adaptation in its own right. The British government's continual initiatives to change the landscape and practices of local government have been positioned by the New Labour administration of 1997 under the banner of 'modernisation' (DETR 1998a). Such rhetoric seems to confirm the regulationist thesis that new modes of accumulation demand new modes of regulation, including at the urban governance level. Another interpretation is that such initiatives merely seek a more 'efficient' relation between the costs of urban governance and the range and quality of its material outputs. All these ideas share a functionalist notion of 'goodness of fit' between context and governance activity. But if the context is understood as complex and dynamic, with power diffused through all kinds of relations and arenas, then any 'fit' is likely to be partial, temporary and contested. Perhaps instead what is being recorded in the analyses of institutional capacity-building processes in this book is a speeding up of the 'restless search' for a resolution to the inherently contradictory demands on the contemporary state, which Offe described in the 1970s (Offe 1977).

Beyond such a functional model of 'fit', there are a number of substantive objectives behind efforts to transform urban institutional capacity. A strong motive is the drive to re-position cities and urban regions in a new economic geography and/or policy landscape, as in the Guben/Gubin case in Chapter 4, or the examples of informal sub-regional strategy-development discussed in Chapters 9 and 10. The contributions also illustrate a goal of improving living conditions, particularly for those in poor neighbourhoods (see Chapters 5, 6 and 8). This orientation has been generalised in the UK at national level, with local authorities now charged with paying attention to the 'well-being' of their citizens (DETR 1998a), a phrase resurrected from a century ago (Stewart, J. 2000). It is as yet impossible tell whether this will be quietly interpreted into established local meanings or whether it will act as a Trojan Horse, forcing major changes in local governance agendas and practices. Along with many other interventions, it is a piece of formal institutional design thrown into the ongoing dynamic flow of complex relations and interactions.

However, the dynamic, diffused power contexts of urban governance activity imply that, while actors may have clear transformative purposes, the connection between purposes, actions and outcomes will never be easy to establish. Policy actions are a kind of 'risky bet'. In this context, policy actors, and researchers on urban governance, need some kind of 'evaluative stance' from which to identify and judge emerging patterns. As editors, we have taken our own evaluative position, as we outline in Chapter 1. We are interested to know what kinds of urban governance in what kinds of context have the potential to spread access to opportunities and material welfare and to sustain community well-being over the long-term. In this statement, we deliberately locate concerns with economic performance, with social well-being and with environmental qualities, within an orientation to citizens as they live their lives and care about particular issues and phenomena within the contexts of their living, working and imagined places of being.

Evaluated in this way, it is not difficult to identify what is wrong with much of urban governance in Britain. It fails to respond to citizens' needs as citizens perceive them. It responds only to well-articulated voices or those accepted among elites, not to those of ordinary daily life experiences. Particularly in recent years, a focus on material economic performance measures has tended to crowd out concerns for the quality of local environments and the cultivation of a sense of collective identity which could act as a positive resource to enrich people's individual lives. In Sweden, a similar critique is expressed. The emergence of new governance structures has to a large extent benefited the interests of established power elites. Policy agendas have not reflected the issues most urgent to the general public; issues such as technical and economic performance have had priority over social, environmental and cultural concerns. Often citizen involvement and citizen participation are explicitly expressed objectives, but they seldom amount to more than rhetoric. These problems seem to be commonly present in Europe. Pierre (2000) suggests that we need to rethink the notion of democratic government to fit the realities of today's organisational society. Governance arrangements need to be subject to local democratic control and internal practices conducive to democratic manners.

However, to move from such evaluation to propose models of good governance is to fall into the trap of an expectation that 'goodness of fit' can be designed-in to governance systems. What looks like a 'good design' in one place and one time could have quite different effects in other times and places. Instead, an evaluative stance provides a position from which to generate strategic imagination as to the possible consequences of innovations, to monitor emerging patterns as governance processes play out and to alert governance arenas to upsides to encourage and downsides to avoid if possible. From this vantage point, a critical tension to emerge from the contributions in this book is that between encouraging the capacity for flexible adaptation while at the same time generating sufficient resources of moral obligation and collective responsibility to maintain an inclusionary ethic and provide the stability within which to attend to long-term environmental and social cohesion considerations. The examples of city centre governance and the building of regional governance arrangements in South West England, the Glasgow region, and the West Midlands all emphasise flexible adaptation. They could probably be developed further through exploring ideas of self-regulating processes in open, dynamic, self-learning and self-organising systems (Christensen 1999, Innes and Booher 1999, Kickert, Klijn et al. 1997). These address issues of co-ordination through developing notions of mutual dependence and interest. But without the cultivation of cultural resources around collective responsibility, grounded in identification with people and places, with their particular histories and geographies, it is very difficult to develop and sustain sufficient commitment to recognising the diversity of situations people find themselves in and a sufficiently rich understanding of environmental care to allow the management of 'common pool resources'.

This argument suggests that the agendas of urban governance need to focus as much on culture and identity formation as on material demands and needs. However, there is no single institutional design, either of a strategic instrument or a governance practice, which could be guaranteed to make this happen and in ways which avoid the very real dangers of cultural domination. There is no substitute for situated local design of governance practices. There are merely ideas about possible ways of releasing pent up energies and creating moments within which local transformations can progress. What is the implication of these conclusions for our concerns with the nature of urban governance, with place and territory, and the significance of governance form to the wider society, which we raised in Chapter 1?

The Dimensions of Urban Governance

Government and Governance

Our first proposition argued that explicit attention to ways of involving actors and networks of the wider society in the business of urban government would continue to pre-occupy analysts and orient policy-makers. The contributions provide rich illustrations of the practical effort that this involves, drawing in particular on notions of 'network' and 'social capital'. Developing new networks offers the promise of drawing in new knowledge resources and new mobilisation capacities to strengthen and re-legitimise the activities of formal government, as de Magalhães et al. argue in Chapter 3. Such strategies offer a way of tapping into neighbourhood level understandings of issues and re-composing the relations between citizen and state, particularly in poor neighbourhoods experiencing alienation and exclusion, as Allen, Cars and Taylor argue in Chapters 5 and 6. Goodstadt and Buchan in Chapter 9 and Wenban-Smith in Chapter 10 illustrate the ways in which wider networks can be drawn into collective will formation to strengthen a co-ordinated approach to strategic territorial management. In these cases, social capital built up over decades under different institutional conditions provided a key resource on which new network-building efforts could build. Lambert and Oatley in Chapter 7 show how local history and its inheritance of conflictual social capital may undermine such mobilisation possibilities. Their contribution reminds us that the development of new governance arrangements is more than a technical exercise. As local realities often are characterised by strongly divergent interests and conflicts, considerations concerning 'new' modes for governance must take issues of conflicts and conflict resolution into account.

Some of the contributors treat 'network governance' as a normative model, appropriate for contemporary times and for a more bottom-up and participatory democratic mode of governance, in contrast to the top-down, bureaucratic hierarchy and privatised, market delivery of public services. Given its late twentieth century history of top-down government oriented by neo-liberal principles, it is not surprising that this model is very attractive to analysts from Britain. Often top-down and bottom-up models are presented as opposite and exclusive. One approach is presented as excluding the other. Ultimately the question to be analysed is how far these modes of governance are mutually exclusive, and how far they can be seen as complementary. Networks and social capital are not new phenomena in urban governance, and they may have many forms and qualities. The formal structures of government have always been accompanied by their policy communities and networks, their traditions of discourse and their modes of behaviour. They have always been embedded in particular social milieux which connect them to wider networks and particular resources of social capital. What is different now is that the overt struggles for dominance over agenda formation and action programmes are being pulled out of the internal workings of government departments and agencies, to be played out 'in the open' in new arenas and practices (partnerships, joint forums etc). It is not the existence of networks which the contemporary emphasis on 'governance' encourages but a deliberate effort to try to reconfigure them. This emerges in the way the contributors discuss both the relations between 'formal' and 'informal' activity, and 'levels' of governance.

Formal and Informal

This distinction is widely used by the contributors but in different ways. Matthiesen in Chapter 4 distinguishes between what government organisations do (the formal) and the informal practices of the wider society, between state and civil society. Allen and Cars similarly refer to the formal networks of government agencies and the rich and varied informal networks of residents in distressed neighbourhoods. Both are concerned about the gap between the two. In Chapter 8, Stewart argues that bridging the gap requires recognition that social capital resides not merely in the social milieux in which government agencies operate. He takes the UK Social Exclusion Unit to task for failing to recognise the nature of the social capital tied up in government agencies themselves, inhibiting their ability to respond to calls for more citizen-responsive governance. Other contributors use the formal/informal distinction to move inside the working practices of government agencies as they face pressures to re-structure themselves. This is clearest in Chapters 9 and 10, where the authors contrast the formal procedures and structures of the public sector with the informal arrangements and practices which participants create. Both examples discuss the way new arrangements were constituted based on mutual consent rather than formal institutional rules.

However the distinction is used, the examples discussed illustrate important qualities of contemporary urban governance. The first is an ongoing struggle between new institutional design principles and those inherited from the past, with their accretions of discourses and practices. As Matthiesen puts it in Chapter 4, new initiatives continually 'bump up' against the old. The second, consequential on the first, is the effort to create new network morphologies – challenging vertical, sectoral policy networks with 'horizontal', territorial networks, with tentacles reaching to and linking together all kinds of stakeholders, in attempts to mobilise a collective 'voice' for territory, city and neighbourhood. The third quality is the search for negotiated, collaboratively-arrived at rules and practices, rather than reliance on formal legal and procedural rules embedded in established organisations. The fourth quality is a continual and complex interaction between formalised law, procedure and organisation, and the power relations which surround these, and the invention of rules and practices for specific contexts. The formal parameters can never be ignored. They structure the invention of new practices, while the struggles to escape their parameters generate mobilisation campaigns to 'change the law'. Taylor in Chapter 6 and Stewart in Chapter 8 both seek to change the national level regulatory procedures through which so much targeted funding is dispersed, because it inhibits the achievement of the government's own social exclusion objectives. Finally, the attempts to escape the constraints of old governance forms, because they focus so much on informal invention of ways of going on, are chronically deficient in formal procedures for legitimacy and accountability. One route out of this dilemma is to formalise them in some way, as in the way urban regeneration partnerships are tied to local authority decision-making bodies, with all the difficulties this may generate (see Chapter 3). Another is the formation of collaborative strategies, where legitimacy is given by the consent of all stakeholders to the process, if not to the strategy itself. As all these qualities evolve, in different ways in different places, they re-mould the social milieux for urban governance in localities. As Gualini argues in Chapter 2, 'the social capital' available in localities is thus not a geological 'soil' that constrains what can be cultivated, but a continuously re-produced resource generated by the interaction between formalised structures and procedures and informal governance practices.

Levels of Governance

A characteristic of the organisation of the welfare states designed in the mid-twentieth century was hierarchy and sectoralisation, combined with clear distinctions between public and private spheres. There were clear formal divisions of responsibilities between levels of government, firm divisions of policy communities along sectoral lines and limited overt linkage between the public sector and the wider society. Critiques have argued that post-war welfare states have failed to deliver because they have relied too heavily on traditional, vertical functionally-organised structures (Burgess, Hall et al. 2001). The new governance forms and dynamics are seeking to break out of this model not merely by blurring the distinction between public and private spheres, formal and informal, state and civil society, state and business. They also imply a change in conceptions of the levels and scales of activity. In the 1970s, urban political economists argued that the functional division between levels reflected functional roles in relation to the capitalist economy. The nation state took care of economic policy and production issues, while the local state was responsible for 'collective consumption' matters (Saunders 1981). Always too simplistic to capture what urban governance activities were really up to, such a distinction was difficult to maintain as city governments became increasingly involved in economic development programmes and national governments had to respond to voter concern with the quality of public services and with environmental conditions. The contributions point to a different way of thinking about how other arenas of governance, at other levels or in other places, get drawn into the shaping of urban policy agendas and processes.

De Magalhães et al. show in Chapter 3 how local, regional and national actors interacted routinely in the evolution of a small city centre partnership. In Chapter 7, Lambert and Oatley illustrate the struggles going on between national level actors and policy agendas and local actors in the construction of a 'missing' regional level in South West England. Goodstadt and Buchan in Chapter 9 argue that the Strathclyde area has been fortunate in its tradition of 'multi-level governance'. The discussion of regional spatial planning in Chapters 7 and 10 both illustrate the tensions in the continuing 'top-down' nature of the English planning system, which results in the paradox of spatial policies which have little spatial content (see also Murdoch, Abram et al. 2000, Vigar, Healey et al. 2000). The discussions of the situation of 'distressed' neighbourhoods in Chapters 5, 6 and 8 show all too clearly how national government activity impacts on, and slices up, the life experiences of residents. The contributors to this latter discussion seek to invert the 'top-down' perspective of national governments to give greater power to grassroots voices. However, this tends to replicate the hierarchical metaphor.

An alternative approach to the issue of levels lies in concepts such as 'multi-level governance' and multi-scalar governance. As Gualini argues, governance settings are these days multi-dimensional, trans-sectoral and trans-scalar. This means that, in any one setting, many dimensions, sectors and scales are likely to be represented at the same time. Just as in a neighbourhood, some residents will have access through their social networks to relatives, friends and others in many different areas while others will know little more than their street, so in a city centre partnership, discussions about the quality of street paving become linked both to limiting traffic noise for residents and to experiences of what a city centre should be like from across Europe (Healey, de Magalhães et al. 2001). The implication is that no level has necessarily a privileged perspective, or privileged knowledge or networks. Where hierarchy remains in governance processes, it is because one level controls significant powers, access to resources, or the definition of regulatory rules. Given the way contemporary economic and social relations are articulated in space, there is no longer a functional logic or 'superior' capacity which locates a particular level 'above' another. There is only a logic of continually contested power relations. This shifts conceptions of government organisation away from vertical hierarchy to a plurality of arenas, or institutional sites where governance activity is focused, each with its own spatial reach and its own power to act and to influence others. In each arena, multiple scales are in play at the same time. As Stewart, J. (2000) argues, the arenas of national government in Britain are just as much a parochial 'Whitehall Village' as those of a county or district council. How arenas relate to each other, and obtain and retain power, both within and between them, is thus a matter of continual contestation and re-negotiation.

Modes and Cultures of Governance

In an attempt to describe the general patterns arising from the dynamic institutional adaptations going on in urban governance, the contributors offer various models expressing the overall modes in which governance is performed. The concept of 'mode' combines conceptions of the span of involvement (which actors and which networks), the relation between formal structures and procedures and informal practices, and the ways in which different levels and scales are drawn into governance. The concept of culture highlights the combination of frames of reference and routines which become normalised in the performance of governance activity. Taylor in Chapter 6 and Stewart in Chapter 8 use a contrast between three broad modes – hierarchy, with a culture of compliance; market, with a culture of competition; network, with a culture of collaboration. Lambert, Oatley and Taylor, distinguish between regulatory and juridified governance cultures and inventive, experimenting cultures. Goodstadt, Buchan and Wenban-Smith emphasise the importance of developing a culture of knowledgeability, especially as regards technical analysis of regional dynamics, to inform regional strategic policy-making.

What these comments on modes and cultures of governance imply is that transforming governance practices and building new governance capacities is a multi-dimensional enterprise. It is likely to happen at different speeds and in different forms in different parts of urban governance (see, for example, Painter and Goodwin 2000). The evolutions may be so slow as to be imperceptible except over long time spans. Some changes may have the appearance of revolutions, dramatically replacing one political regime with another, as in East Germany and Poland. Even here, as Matthiesen shows in Chapter 4, some cultural elements will live on in the accretion of inherited cultural referents and practices. As a result, governance capacities are built by the continual interaction of multiple modes as these co-exist and co-evolve, framing each other. Thus there may well be a shift to more 'horizontal' broad span networks, and to a more open and diverse governance culture compared to that linked to the vertical, sectoral hierarchies of traditional welfare states, a shift to Jessop's 'heterarchies' (Jessop 2000). But these may take many forms, each with their own integrating nodes and areas of exclusion and blindness. 'Joined-up' government in a comprehensive sense is inherently impossible. What is being negotiated are different ways of dividing up the work of governance and different modes and cultures through which the business of governance, of collective action, is performed.

This implies that a critical capacity for urban governance innovations which have the mobilisation power to 'make a difference' in fluid, evolving situations, where different models as to how to do governance are struggling to get articulated and to become dominant, is a strategic capability to 'read' the evolving situation, to take risks in selecting what mode of governance to deploy, and to be prepared to 'switch' out of bad judgements quickly without leaving behind too much 'poisonous sediment' which could inhibit future capacity to adapt and change. But this is a huge challenge for urban governance actors, embedded as they are in milieux created by past practices. It requires not merely the capacity to build networks which can mobilise for collective action and help to access all kinds of knowledge resources. It involves major collective efforts in 'frame reflection', reviewing the accumulated baggage of discourses, routines and practices. One of the reasons for the attraction of 'collaborative' modes of governance, as promoted by Stewart in Chapter 8 and to an extent illustrated in Chapters 9 and 10, is that they offer ways of collective frame reflection. But the promise of such collaborative governance has less to do with creating a broad consensus around new agendas and modes of governance, which can stabilise fragmented, confused and conflictual urban governance landscapes. It has more to do with developing a capacity to learn, to monitor, to experiment, to re-frame and to invent, and with generating the energy for building the capacity to act as a collective actor.

Place and Territory as Integrating Concepts

In Chapter 1, we argued that place and territory would come to play a significant role as a focus of policy attention in the contemporary period, compared to the sectoral foci of much public policy in the second half of the twentieth century. The European discussion of a 'Europe of the Regions', the academic and policy talk of cities in competition in Europe, the initiatives in several European countries to strengthen the regional level and, in the UK at least, the emphasis on the qualities and governance of cities and of neighbourhoods all suggests that such a shift is underway. However, the contributions in this book, as reviewed above, also emphasise the power of older conceptions to live on and to resist changes. Nor is it clear that a place focus will emerge as a key 'integrating concept' around which new modes of governance could cluster. What do the contributions suggest may be significant driving forces promoting a focus on place and territory? How powerful are these likely to be against the bastions of vertical, sectoralised governance organisation? How likely is a place focus to be able to liberate the capacities for the kind of innovative, knowledgeable strategic action in complex contexts discussed above?

One factor promoting a place focus raised by both de Magalhães et al. in Chapter 3 and Matthiesen in Chapter 4 is the recognition that a city now exists in a different geography than the one previously taken-for-granted. City centre promotion initiatives in Newcastle seek to re-position the city in a landscape of European cities, with a distinctive ambience for leisure and lifestyle, rather than in continual competition with its neighbouring cities in the Tyne and Wear conurbation. Guben/Gubin, a city once divided by a global geo-political boundary now finds itself on the soon-to-be-overtaken edge of the European Union. These changing geographies not only to re-configure change the networks and political relations of cities and their governance elites. They also challenge the identities of cities, as constructed in local politics, by the media, in citizen's consciousness and in business perceptions.

A second factor promoting a place focus is the recognition that, when economic relations and cultural aspirations and referents are globalising, it is the material qualities, cultural heritage and social milieux of territories which attract companies, migrants and visitors, and the investors which seek to meet their needs. This encourages attention to place qualities, their potentials and deficiencies. This concern was an important driving force behind building enhanced regional institutional capacity in the West Midlands. In the South West, the pressure for some kind of place focus, perhaps around a sub-region, reflected the difficulties of maintaining place qualities in the face of a vigorous growth dynamic. But in this case, the region as a whole was too varied to provide an appropriate context for building such a place focus, and the hostile attitudes among municipalities in the Bristol and Bath sub-region provided a 'poisonous sediment' which inhibited the development of a sub-regional territorial focus. This experience emphasises the importance of developing concepts of place quality which are not just about materialities – development sites, physical infrastructure investments, well-designed city centres. Place quality also lies in the nature of the social milieux, in terms of attitudes and values as much as the objective qualities of social life, cultural expression, the business environment and the natural environment.

A third factor promoting a place focus relates to policy delivery. This message comes through strongly in the discussion of policies for 'distressed neighbourhoods' in Chapters by Allen, Cars, Taylor and Stewart. In their role in delivering and regulating a whole array of services that support social life, city governments are increasingly being persuaded to co-ordinate and integrate their activities so that they are provided in ways which are appropriate and helpful to citizens who want and need to access these services. For those with plenty of time and/or easy internet access, as well as plenty of choice about transport mode where relevant, delivering services in bits tailored to individual requests, increasingly over the internet, may be an appropriate response. For many others, the ability to access services and to go about daily life is seriously compromised if they have to face complex journeys, costly technology or multiple outlets for services (Speak and Graham 2000). Business interests are making similar points about the provision of different kinds of business support (Illsley, Lloyd et al. 2000). A first response to this issue of 'bundling' service delivery in ways relevant to users is to coordinate the location of services in some way. A second is to shift the whole focus of policy design and delivery to a 'whole system' which is relevant to the user, as Stewart argues in Chapter 8. However, there is no 'whole system fits all' resolution to this challenge, and the result of initiatives which successfully demand attention to 'whole systems' is rather a shift in the focus of policy organisation from the perspectives of individual service providers to that of the user/consumer rather than the individual service producer. In making this shift, some localities will find a place focus helpful. It is certainly a significant strand behind the recent British government initiatives to promote neighbourhood governance (DETR 2000d, 2001).

A fourth factor is the role of place and territory as a locus for the mobilisation of collective action and the construction of people's identities as citizens concerned about the public sphere. This has always been the justification for a sustained role for local government, providing a basis for the defence of local government units and local services. This defence of locality has been enlarged in recent years by an increasingly vigorous mobilisation around the promotion and protection of local environments. The examples of initiatives such as Local Agenda 21, around which people can express their concerns about local environmental qualities (Selman 2001), and of the way residents and environmental groups have used the procedures of land use planning systems to voice their concerns (Rydin 1999), show a vigorous and lively local politics of place. As Gualini suggests in Chapter 2, efforts to create an integrated territorial focus may be considered as experiments to discover the ground upon which a collective actor *for* a city or region can be formed.

These factors in combination suggest that resurrecting a place focus from beneath the weight of vertical sectoralism will continue to be an important dimension of the ongoing struggles to transform urban governance agendas and practices. However, such shifts will need significant injections of intellectual capital, to help participants evolve new ways of understanding place qualities, as well as building the organisational structures, procedures, discourses and practices which could support such an integrative focus. The accounts in the Chapters by Goodstadt, Buchan and Wenban-Smith illustrate the kinds of effort that may be involved in generating a 'voice' for place and maintaining a collective actor with sufficient power to 'speak clearly'. In Chapter 7, Lambert and Oatley suggest that, where there is no tradition of conceptions of an area to draw on, it may be very difficult to create a momentum for such strategic effort. Certainly, there is no guarantee that formal spatial planning systems necessarily provide an intellectual or social capital to be mobilised for the task. As Lambert and Oatley argue, the British planning system locks participants into narrow, sectoralised debates and has few resources for the imaginative construction of the spatiality of territorial dynamics.

However, in localities where urban governance stakeholders are able to generate concentrated institutional attention on place quality, there will always be dangers of rigidity. Once new frames of reference and new organising principles have been identified and found to work in the short term, it is all too easy to defend them. The North American local government literature, which responds to the very powerful legal position of local jurisdictions in the US, is replete with examples of municipal 'regimes' which defend 'their place' against intrusions of all kinds, or which boost development in their territory long after the adverse consequences of rapid development have become obvious (Logan and Molotch 1987, Stone 1989). The implication is that developing a focus on place quality – a vision for a city, developing ideas about city futures, organising governance around key place quality priorities rather than sectoral service delivery principles, will not necessarily achieve sufficient adaptability to produce any of the outcomes implied by the above four factors and may be counterproductive to goals of social inclusion, enhancing human well-being and fulfilling moral obligations for environmental care. So a place focus as an approach to integrating urban governance is no magic formula. There is no 'whole system' which can be encompassed within it just as there is no ideal mode for urban governance. Rather, it provides a position from which to challenge how things are done now, to encourage co-ordinating attention, and to generate new intellectual resources and social networks which could enrich and make more inclusive local institutional capacity. It provides a critical angle for experimentation in building institutional capacity which cuts across the hierarchical sectoralism inherited from the mid-twentieth century models of governance.

Transforming Governance Capacities

The Chapters amply illustrate our third proposition, that the quality of the governance capacity of a locality makes a difference to the experience of citizens, of businesses and to the quality of the natural environment. In more stable times, this reality may become so much part of the institutional landscape that it becomes taken-for-granted and invisible. In the late twentieth century, however, these taken-for-granted parameters have been vigorously challenged. This is not merely a matter of ideology, neo-liberal versus social democratic. Many people experience their urban governance as 'not working'. Key actors are 'bumping up' against inherited cultures and practices, while many stakeholders suffer from the lack of governance capacity to attend to their concerns as they see them. People notice bits of the institutional fabric which do not work. It is in this context that the political pressure to change governance capacity builds up.

But, as we have argued above, the extent and trajectory of transformations in governance capacity are not inevitable or unidirectional pathways. Not only is there enormous diversity in the situations and contexts of urban governance activity. The range of forces acting on and across the terrain of localities is so multi-dimensional and variable, with so many transecting, intersecting and separate relations of interaction, that complexity, uncertainty, conflict and the dispersal of power are the characteristic qualities of context. In this situation, a dualist contrast between co-ordinated, technocratic 'managerial' governance and pro-active, risk-taking 'entrepreneurial' governance fails to capture the dynamic, inventive and inherently variable way in which urban governance trajectories are being moulded. The trajectories of institutional capacity building for urban governance vary in their historical inheritance, their positioning in diverse global relations, the availability of critical resources upon which to build new resources of intellectual and social capital, and the availability of human resources and action repertoires through which to mobilise stakeholders to focus on building urban governance capacity.

Nor does the dualistic contrast take into account that any such effort to transform governance capacities involves struggles at all kinds of levels, from the finegrain of neighbourhood organisation and partnership dynamics through strategies to which aim to re-imagine localities and position them in a new geography, to efforts to change national or EU legislation and create new structuring parameters. The way these struggles play out through and within the flowing dynamics of socio-cultural, economic and environmental forces not only generates evolving patterns of resource distribution, changing power to define governance agendas and the meaning of the public interest and the public realm, the privileging of particular modes and styles of governance and the cultural frames which support them. It also creates the potential for all kinds of 'tragedies of the commons', with respect to shared environmental resources (degradation rather than enhancement), shared human values (deterioration rather than enhancement in the conditions for sections of a polity) and shared material costs and benefits (loss of efficiency in provision of material services).

Faced with these variable realities, it is not surprising that attempts are made to produce ideal models for 'modern' urban governance. However, as we have argued above, the idea of a 'one size fits all' governance model has little leverage in a world of complex, intersecting relations operating at multiple scales and in multiple timespans. Further, as Stewart argues in Chapter 8, such an approach to forcing transformation *on* local governance may crowd out local invention and inhibit building new institutional capacity. Instead, the most effective levers to encourage transformation may be the provision of challenges and tools through which those involved in urban governance arenas can access their taken-for-granted routines and practices and develop new mobilisation repertoires through which to create new ways of doing things. Among these 'tools for change', the speeding up of local struggles, tensions and conflicts may be at least as productive of transformation efforts as hierarchical exhortation to build consensual partnerships. As Taylor argues in Chapter 6, the smoothing out of conflicts in attempts to find some short-term consensus among key players may be counter-productive to long term transformation, as this strategy may fail to recognise the value of a vigorous local culture of challenge and conflict in maintaining diversity, clarifying issues and promoting learning (see also Healey 2001). Wenban-Smith in Chapter 10 also emphasises the value of conflict in promoting the building of new intellectual and social capital.

Developing the Policy Implications

Our analysis in 'conversation' with the contributions in this book indicates a very different model of strategic urban governance than that suggested by the model of a city government 'steering' the ship of the city through choppy waters to calm prosperity.[1] Instead, actors involved in governance arenas in and around a locality find themselves swimming along, or often merely floating, swung about in the eddies and whirlpools of multiple tidal flows. How, in this situation, can individual actors 'hold on' to enough others to make a difference to the direction of flow? How can a strategic capacity to act as a collective actor be created and sustained?

There are many policy ideas about urban governance trajectories to encourage and to resist, from Gualini's concern in Chapter 2 with the renewal of democratic theory and practice to Taylor's concern in Chapter 6 with promoting learning processes, which can combine authority structures with innovative flexibility. Faced with the evolving complexity, Gualini suggests more action research and policy experimentation.

Matthiesen argues for more attention to 'informal processes', the dynamic relation between formal governance initiatives and the cultures of their wider social milieux. Allen and Cars also suggest more attention to the interconnection between citizens' networks and how these connect to those built around governance processes. They suggest that a way forward would be to develop processes which could help form a collective local actor between politicians, professionals and residents, strengthening residents' social networks and enlivening formal ones. Both De Magalhães et al. in Chapter 3 and Taylor in Chapter 6 argue for caution in the introduction of 'partnerships'. While particular forms may liberate energies for change and mobilise local resources in one instance, they may crowd out local initiative in others, or merely increase the 'transaction costs' through which governance outcomes are produced. Stewart in Chapter 8 urges national government to be consistent in the models of change it encourages. Goodstadt and Buchan in Chapter 9 and Wenban-Smith in Chapter 10 stress the importance of enhancing the intellectual capital for territorial governance, particularly as regards understanding the complex dynamics through which territories are being shaped. Goodstadt and Buchan call for the development of four elements of institutional capacity: technical capability, institutional competence, inclusive processes and connections to national policy frameworks. Wenban-Smith emphasises the way internal capacity-building can challenge and change the external context. He also calls for more attention to the delicate work of combining technical and political domains in creating a collective voice for a regions and sub-regions.

These specific suggestions carry a more general message. If governance capacity is formed in continual interaction with its social milieux, then it is important to focus on the relation between urban governance processes and the evolving qualities of milieux. Governance capacity serves as a form of social infrastructure, a 'soft infrastructure' to set alongside the 'hard infrastructures' of physical networks, welfare facilities and public and private law (Healey 1997, Chapters 8 and 9). But making connections between governance activity and the wider society is a long-term process, with all kinds of possible trajectories. It involves changing perceptions and behaviours in diverse positions in governance arenas, while simultaneously re-moulding who participates in governance, in what arenas, and around what agendas.

What then does this add up to in terms of ideas to help those involved in seeking to shape and change the trajectories of urban governance capacity? One option, reflecting the dynamic complexity of urban contexts, is to experiment with isolated initiatives and to let governance capacities emerge. This implies the kind of focus on the particular – a project or a specific service delivery activity – which characterised many urban governance interventions in the 1980s and 1990s. But it is this strategy, with its resultant fragmentation and conflicts among initiatives which has focused attention on the quality of the 'soft infrastructure' of urban institutional capacity, on how this enlarges the scope for collective actor formation and on how to re-configure the relations between key governance actors and wider social milieux, as discussed in Chapter 1. Faced with this kind of analysis, what should those participants in urban governance arenas seek to do to enhance the capacity of their localities to operate as some kind of collective actor, and to do so in ways which have a chance of promoting well-being in inclusive, socially-just and environmentally careful ways? The discussion in this book highlights several actions, attitudes and conceptions which could help those seeking to encourage the emergence of new governance capacities.

Firstly, it is important to know your milieu, strategically and in its fine grain. This involves knowing its dimensions, its inherited intellectual, social and political capital, the relations between governance arenas and wider social and economic relations, its dynamics, potential trajectories, key arenas and windows of opportunity for change.

Secondly, it is helpful to assess critical structuring parameters in play in a specific instance. How stable are they? What conflicts do they produce? How do they affect emergent trajectories, the potential for expanding different pathways, the tensions with local trajectories and the institutional 'cracks' and 'windows of opportunity' through which changes can be inserted. How can reflexivity on taken-for-granted assumptions, values and practices help to enhance awareness of the way these parameters are shifting?

Thirdly, it is usually helpful to build on what is already present. This should avoid displacement, and unintentional trampling on people's existing networks and values. This requires a capacity to pursue mobilisation work at the fine grain and the strategic scale at the same time, in parallel, and in small steps which can accumulate through time to support bigger shifts in efforts to shape trajectories.

Fourthly, building inclusive governance capacity should seek to foster diversity and innovation and encourage all kinds of self-regulation. A helpful governance role is to support such activity by making available intellectual, social and political capital which could help release the energies of many stakeholders, while encouraging inclusiveness, protecting some people's networks and mobilisation initiatives from being destroyed by the actions of others, and fixing bits of connectivity which seem to have got stuck.

Fifthly, it will often be productive to foster collaboration and learning by encouraging initiatives when they pop up. This might involved making arenas available, offering technical resources to facilitate understanding, and opening channels from one learning arena to the central nodes of collective actor formation. In doing so, it is likely to be helpful to avoid depressing such processes with too many compliance rules.

Sixthly, it may be helpful to focus collective attention on a few key qualities which many stakeholders can relate to and use to build their own identities and trajectories, for example, a voice for 'place'. In doing so, transient marketing images are probably best avoided. Instead, efforts to promote new identities may be more productive if they focus on building a 'public realm resource' which can endure.

Seventhly, it makes sense to adopt a critical attitude towards the portfolio of mobilisation and intervention tools available. Given the complexity of urban governance situations, using repertoires of action and intervention tools experimentally is likely to be productive, if accompanied by a capacity for monitoring at the fine grain of the 'street' and at the level of strategic positioning. The important emphasis should be on the generative power of each tool, rather than simple output achievement or the ability to reach defined outcome targets.

Finally, it is likely to be valuable to find ways to promote and sustain collaboration and collective argumentation as a practice, as a way to challenge retrenchment into narrow bureaucratic practices, technocratic dominance, the powerplay of politics and the dominance of one group over others in the formation of a collective actor. This implies developing collaboration processes in such a way as to promote learning, innovation and the development of a stronger public realm. An indicator of a rich and lively public realm is likely to be as much reflected in the degree of conflict and struggle over collective agendas as in the capacity to articulate and sustain some strategic direction.

In conclusion, we argue that urban governance needs a different kind of strategic competence to that built up in the comprehensive planning tradition of the 1960s and the competitive positioning projects and marketing visions of the 1980s and 1990s. Instead, a new kind of competence is required which aims to enrich the 'soft infrastructures' which connect governance activity to its milieux, and which relate a fine-grain understanding of the range and complexity of evolutions forming this milieux to a strategic understanding of the dynamics within the wider worlds in which the relations of urban areas exist. It demands a confidence to let precise policy agendas and the specific deployment of repertoires of policy tools evolve rather than defining them too tightly, while at the same time developing ways of monitoring how these play out over time and in different situations, so that experiments can be ended quickly and new mixes developed. This means that strategic urban governance becomes an evolving dynamic process, building institutional capacities in interaction with co-evolving milieux. Its task is not to predict a future and make it happen. Instead, it is to play a role in shaping the unfolding of trajectories emerging through complex social dynamics as they evolve in particular areas, with the hope of encouraging what seem like positive directions for keeping on the move while resisting entrapment in stagnant pools and poisonous waters or becoming dragged into destructive vortexes.

Note

[1] This metaphor was used of the planner in McLoughlin 1969.

References

6, P. (1997) The power to bind and loose: tackling network poverty, London, Demos.
6, P. Leat, D., Seltzer, K. and Stoker, G. (1999) Governing in the Round: strategies for holistic government, London, Demos.
Abercrombie, P. and Matthew, R.H. (1949) The Clyde Valley Regional Plan 1946, Edinburgh, HMSO.
Alexander, E.R. (1995) How organisations act together: interorganizational co-ordination in theory and practice, Luxembourg, Gordon and Breach.
Alexander, J.C. (1998) Real Civil Societies: dilemmas of institutionalisation, London, Sage.
Allen, J. Cars G. and Madanipour, A. (2000) Social exclusion in European neighbourhoods: Processes, experiences and responses Research report for the European Commission, Targeted Economic and Social Research, Contract No SOE2-CT97-3057 Brussels: Directorate General Science, Research and Development/Directorate F.
Amin, A. (1994) Post-Fordism – a Reader, Oxford, Blackwell.
Amin, A. and J. Hausner, eds (1997) Beyond market and hierarchy: inter-active governance and social complexity, Cheltenham, Edward Elgar.
Amin, A. and Thrift, N. (eds) (1994) Globalisation, Institutions and Regional Development in Europe, Oxford, Oxford University Press.
Amin, A. and Thrift, N. (1995) Globalisation, 'institutional thickness' and the local economy, P. Healey, S. Cameron, S. Davoudi, S. Graham and A. Madanipour (eds) Managing Cities, Chichester, UK, John Wiley, pp 91-108.
Anastacio, J., Gidley, B., Hart, L., Keith, M., Mayo, M. and Kowarzik, U. (2000) Reflecting Realities: participants' perspectives on integrated communities and sustainable development, Bristol, The Policy Press.
Asheim, B. (1996) Industrial districts as learning regions: a condition for prosperity? European Planning Studies, Vol 4 (3), pp 379-400.
Atkinson, R. (1999) Discourses of partnership and empowerment in contemporary British urban regeneration, Urban Studies Vol 36 (1) pp 59-72.
Atkinson, R. and Cope, S. (1997) Community participation and urban regeneration in Britain, in ed. Hoggett, P. Contested Communities, Bristol, Policy Press, pp 201-221.
Axelrod, R. (1984) The Evolution of Cooperation, New York, Basic Books.
Bagnasco, A. (1994) Regioni, tradizione civica, modernizzazione italiana: un commento alla ricerca di Putnam, Stato e Mercato, Vol 40, pp 93-104.
Bagnasco, A. (1999) Tracce di Comunità, Bologna, Il Mulino.
Bagnasco, A. (2000) Trust and Social Capital, in Nash, K. and Scott, A. (eds) Blackwell Companion to Political Sociology, Oxford, Blackwell.
Bailey, N. (1995) Partnership Agencies in British Urban Policy, London, UCL Press.
Barjak, F. And Heimpold, G. (1999) Development Problems and Policies at the German Border with Poland Regional Aspects of Trade and Investment. Institute for Economic Research Halle, Discussion Papers Nr. 101.
Barnes, J.A. (1969) Networks and Political processes, in Mitchell J.C. (ed.) Social Networks in urban situations, Manchester, University of Manchester Press, pp 51-76.

Barrett, S. and Fudge, C. (1981) Reconstructing the field of analysis in Barrett, S. and Fudge, C. (eds) Policy and Action: essays on the implementation of public policy, London, Methuen, pp 249-278.

Bauman, Z. (1999) In search of politics, Cambridge, Polity Press.

Begg, I. Moore, B. Altunbas, Y. (2000) Long-run trends in the competitiveness of British cities, paper presented to ESRC Cities, Competitiveness and Cohesion research programme, Symposium on Competitiveness, South Bank University, April 2000.

Belussi, F. (1996) Local systems, industrial districts and institutional networks: towards a new evolutionary paradigm of industrial economics? European Planning Studies, Vol 4 (3), pp 5-26.

Berger, P. and Luckmann, T. (1967) The Social Construction of Reality, Harmondsworth, Penguin.

Birmingham City Council (1993) The Birmingham Plan, Birmingham, Birmingham City Council.

Blackstone, T. and Plowden, W. (1988) Inside the Think Tank, London, Heinemann.

Blotevogel, H. (2000) Rationality and Discourse in (Post) Modern Spatial Planning, in Salet W. and Faludi, A (eds), The Revival of Strategic Spatial Planning, Amsterdam, Koninklijke Nederlandse Akademie van Wetenschappen, pp 121-134.

Blowers, A. and Evans, B. (eds) (1997) Town Planning into the 21st Century, Routledge, London.

Boddy, M. (1999) Geographical economics and urban competitiveness, Urban Studies, Vol 36, (5/6), pp 811-842.

Boddy, M., Lambert, C. and Snape, D. (1997) City for the 21st Century: globalisation, planning and urban change in contemporary Britain, Bristol, Policy Press.

Bott, E. (1971) Family and Social Network, London, Tavistock.

Bourdieu, P. (1977) Outline of a Theory of Practice, Cambridge, Cambridge University Press.

Bourdieu, P. (1979) La distinction. Critique sociale du jugement, Paris, Editions de Minuit.

Bourdieu, P. (1986) The forms of capital, in Richardson, R. ed, Handbook of Theory and Research for the Sociology of Education, New York, Greenwood Press, pp 241-258.

Bramley, G (1998) Measuring planning: indicators of planning restraint and its impact on the housing market, Environment and Planning B, Planning and Design, Vol 25 (1), pp 31-58.

Bramley, G. (1999) The influence of planning on housing supply and economic performance, paper presented at ESRC Property and Competitiveness Colloquium, University of Reading, May 1999.

Bramley, G. and Lambert, C. (1998) Regulation entrenched: planning for housing, in Allmendinger, P. and Thomas, H. (eds) Urban Planning and the British New Right, London, Routledge, pp 87-113.

Bramley, G., Bartlett, W. and Lambert, C. (1995) Planning, the Market and Private House Building, London, UCL Press.

Breheny, M. (1991) The renaissance of strategic planning? Environment and Planning B: Planning and Design, Vol 18, pp 233-249.

Breheny, M. (1992) The contradictions of the compact city: a review of sustainable development and urban form, in Breheny, M. (ed.) Sustainable development and urban form. London, Pion, pp 138-159.

Breheny, M. (1999) The People: where will they work? London, TCPA.

Brennan, A., Rhodes, J. and Tyler, P. (1998) Evaluation of the Single Regeneration Challenge Fund Budget: A Partnership for Regeneration: An Interim Evaluation, London, Department of the Environment, Transport and the Regions.

Brown, G. (2000) Address to the National Council for Voluntary Organisations, January, London, The Treasury.

Brusis, M. (1999) Re-Creating the Regional Level in Central and Eastern Europe: Lessons from Administrative Reforms in Six Countries, in von Breska, E. and Brusis, M. (eds), Central and Eastern Europe on the Way into the European Union: Reforms of Regional Administration in Bulgaria the Czech Republic, Estonia, Hungary, Poland and Slovakia, München, Universität München.

Bryson, J.M. and Crosby, B.C. (1992) Leadership for the Common Good. Tackling Public Problems in a Shared Power World, San Francisco, Jossey-Bass Publishers.

Burgess, P., Hall, S., Mawson, J. and Pearce, G. (2001) DeVolved approaches to local governance policy and practice in neighbourhood management, York, John Rowntree Foundation.

Cabinet Office (1998) Bringing Britain Together: a national strategy for neighbourhood renewal Cmnd 4045, London, HMSO.

Cabinet Office (2000a) Reaching Out: The Role of Central Government at Regional and Local Level, Performance and Innovation Unit, Cabinet Office, London, The Stationery Office.

Cabinet Office, (2000b) Wiring it Up, Performance and Innovation Unit, Cabinet Office, London, The Stationery Office.

Calhoun, C. (1993) Habitus, Field and Capital: The question of historical specificity, in Calhoun, C., LiPuma, E., Postone, M., (eds) Bourdieu: critical perspectives, Polity Press, Cambridge, pp 61-88.

Cars, G. and Engström, C.-J. (1997) Current Trends in Swedish Planning, in Swedish Planning Towards Sustainable Development, Gävle, Sweden, Föreningen för samhällsplanering, pp 19-25.

Castells, M. (1996) The Rise of the Network Society. Cambridge, Massachusetts, Blackwell Publishers.

Central Policy Review Staff (CPRS) (1975) A Joint Approach to Social Policy, London, HMSO.

Challis, L., Fuller, M., Henwood, M., Klein, R., Plowden, W., Webb, A., Whittigham, P. and Wistow, G. (1988) Joint Approaches to Social Policy: Rationality and practice, Cambridge, Cambridge University Press.

Champion, A.J., Atkins, D., Coombes, M. and Fotheringham, S. (1998) Urban Exodus, London, CPRE.

Christensen, K. (1999) Cities and complexity: Making intergovernmental decisions, London, Sage.

Cohen, J. and Rogers, J. (1992) Secondary associations and democratic governance, Politics and Society, Vol 20 (4), pp 393-472.

Coleman, J. (1988) Social capital in the creation of human capital, American Journal of Sociology Vol 94 Supplement S95-120.

Coleman, J. (1990) Foundations of Social Theory, Cambridge Mass, Harvard University Press.

Collinge, C. and Srbljanin, A. (2001) Is there a network paradigm in urban governance?, in Hambleton, R., Savitch, H. and Stewart, M. (eds) Globalism and Local Democracy London, MacMillan.

Commission for the European Communities (CEC) (1997) Towards an urban agenda in the European Union, Communication from the Commission, COM (97)197 final, Brussels.

Committee for Spatial Development (1999) European Spatial Development Perspective, Luxembourg, CEC.

Connerton, P. (1989) How Societies Remember, Cambridge, Cambridge University Press.

Cooke, P., Davies, C. and Wilson, R. (2000) Urban networks and the New Economy: The Impact of Clusters on Planning for Growth, paper presented to ESRC Cities, Competitiveness and Cohesion research programme, Symposium on Competitiveness, South Bank University, April.

Cooke, P. and Morgan, K. (1993) The network paradigm: new departures in corporate and regional development, Environment and Planning D Society and Space, Vol 11, pp 543-564.

Coulson, A. (ed.) (1998) Trust and Contracts, Bristol, The Policy Press.

Cowell, R. and Murdoch, J. (1999) Land Use and the Limits to (Regional) Governance: Some Lessons from Planning for Housing and Minerals in England, International Journal of Urban and Regional Research, Vol 23 (3), pp 654-669.

Crespi, F. (1992) Social Power and Action, Oxford, Blackwell.

Crouch, C., Le Galès, P., Tregillia, C. and Voelskow, H. (2001) Local Productive Systems: Rise and Demise, Oxford, Oxford University Press.

Crow, G. (1997) What do we know about the neighbours, in Hoggett, P. (1997) Contested Communities, Bristol, Policy Press, pp 17ff.

Dahl, R. (1961) Who Governs?, New Haven, Conn Yale University Press.

De Groot, L. (1992) City Challenge: Competing in the Urban Regeneration Game, Local Economy, Vol 7 (3), pp 196-209.

De Leonardis, O. (1990) Il terzo escluso. Le istituzioni come vincoli e come risorse. Milano, Feltrinelli.

De Leonardis, O. (1997) Declino della sfera pubblica e privatismo, Rassegna Italiana di Sociologia, Vol 38 (2), April-June, pp 169-193.

Department of the Environment (DoE) (1985) Circular 14/85: Development and the Environment, London, HMSO.

Department of the Environment (DoE) (1990) Planning Policy Guidance 15: Regional Planning Guidance, Structure Plans and the Content of Development Plans, London, HMSO.

Department of the Environment (DoE) (1994), Planning Policy Guidance 13: Transport, London, HMSO.

Department of the Environment, Transport and the Regions (DETR) (1998a). Modern Local Government: In touch with people, London, DETR.

Department of the Environment, Transport and the Regions (DETR) (1998b) Planning for the Communities of the Future, London, The Stationery Office.

Department of the Environment, Transport and the Regions (DETR) (1999) Planning Policy Guidance Note 11: Regional Planning, Consultation Draft, London, DETR.

Department of the Environment, Transport and the Regions (2000a) Modernising Local Government London, DETR.

Department of the Environment, Transport and the Regions (2000b) The Co-ordination of Area-based Initiatives Research Working Paper 1, London: DETR.

Department of the Environment, Transport and the Regions (2000c) Collaboration and Co-ordination in Area-based Initiatives Research Working Paper 2, London: DETR.

Department of the Environment, Transport and the Regions (2000d) Joining It Up Locally, Report of Policy Action Team 17, London, DETR.

Department of the Environment, Transport and the Regions (2000e) New Deal for Communities and the Single Regeneration Budget: Project Appraisal and Approval, London, DETR.

Department of the Environment, Transport and the Regions (2000f) Planning Policy Guidance Note 3: Housing, London, The Stationery Office

Department of the Environment, Transport and the Regions (2000g) Planning Policy guidance Note 11: Regional Planning, London, The Stationery Office.

Department of the Environment, Transport and the Regions (2001) Local Strategic Partnerships: Government Guidance London, DETR.

Di Maggio, P.J. and Powell, W.W. (1991) Introduction, in Powell, W.W. and DiMaggio, P.J. (eds) (1991) The New Institutionalism in Organizational Analysis Chicago, University of Chicago Press, pp 1-38.

Donolo, C. (1997) L'intelligenza delle istituzioni, Milano, Feltrinelli.
Douglas, M. (1986) How Institutions Think, Syracuse NY, Syracuse University Press.
Douglas, M. (1992) Risk and Blame, London/New York, Routledge.
Dowding, K. (1995) 'Model or Metaphor' A critical review of the policy network approach, Political Studies, Vol XLIII (1), pp 36-158.
Dowding, K., Dunleavy, P., King, D., Margetts, H. and Rydin, Y. (2000) Understanding urban governance: the contribution of rational choice, in Stoker, G. (ed.) The New Politics of British Local Governance, London, Macmillan, pp 91-116.
Du Gay, P. (ed.) (1997) Production of Culture/Culture of Production, London, Sage.
Dunleavy, P. and O'Leary, B (1987) Theories of the State: The politics of Liberal Democracy London, Macmillan.
Dürrschmidt, J. (1997) The Delinking of Locale and Milieu: On the situatedness of extended milieux in a global environment, In Eade, in Living in the Global City, London, Routledge (ed) pp 56-72.
Dyrberg, T. (1997) The Circular Structure of Power, London, Verso.
Easton, D. (1965) A Systems Analysis of Political Life, New York, John Wiley.
Ebert, R., Gnad, F. and Kunzmann, K. R. (ed.) (1992) Partnerschaften für die Kultur: Chancen und Gefahren für die Stadt, Dortmund, Universität Dortmund, IRPUD.
EDAW (1996) Grainger Town Regeneration Strategy, Glasgow, EDAW Consulting.
Edwards, R. and Foley, M. (1998) 'Civil society and social capital beyond Putnam', American Behavioural Scientist, Vol 42 (1), pp 124-139.
Elander, I. and Blanc, M. (2000) Partnerships and democracy: a happy couple in urban governance? in van Kempen, R. and Andersen, H. T. (eds) Governing European Cities. Volume III: Social Fragmentation and Governance, Aldershot, Ashgate, pp 93-124.
Emirbayer, M. and Goodwin, J. (1994) Network Analysis, Culture, and the Problem of Agency, American Journal of Sociology, Vol 99 (6), pp. 1411-1454.
Esping-Andersen, G. (1990) The Three Worlds of Welfare Capitalism, Cambridge, Polity Press.
Evans, B. and Rydin, Y. (1997) Planning, Professionalism and Sustainability, in Blowers, A. and Evans, B. (eds) Town Planning into the 21st Century, Routledge, London, pp 55-69.
Evers, A. (1995) Part of the welfare mix: the third sector as an intermediate area between market, economy and community, Vol 6 (2), pp 159-182.
Fainstein, S. (2000) New Directions in Planning Theory, Urban Affairs Review Vol 34(4), pp 451-476.
Fassmann, H. (1997) Die Rückkehr der Regionen regionale Konsequenzen der Transformation in Ostmitteleuropa: Eine Einführung, in Die Rückkehr der Regionen. Beiträge zur regionalen Transformation Ostmitteleuropas, Vienna, Österreichische Akademie der Wissenschaften, pp 13ff.
Flyvberg, B. (1998) Rationality and Power, Chicago, University of Chicago Press.
Fordham, G. (1995) Made to Last: creating sustainable neighbourhoods and estate regeneration, York, Joseph Rowntree Foundation.
Fothergill, S. and Gudgin, G. (1982) Unequal Growth: Urban and Regional Employment Change in the UK, London, Heinemann.
Foweraker, J. and Landman, T. (1997) Citizenship Rights and Social Movements: a comparative and statistical analysis, Oxford, Oxford University Press.
Friend, J. and Jessop, N. (1969) Local Government and Strategic Choice, London, Tavistock.
Fukuyama, F. (1992) The End of History and the Last Man, London, Hamish Hamilton.
Fukuyama, F. (1995) Trust: the social virtues and the creation of prosperity, London, Penguin.
Fukuyama, F. (1999) The Great Disruption: Human nature and the reconstitution of social order, London, Profile Books.
General Register Office for Scotland (GRO (S)) (1999) Mid-1998 Population Estimates, Scotland, Edinburgh, GRO, www.gro-scotland.gov.uk.

Giddens, A. (1984) The Constitution of Society, Cambridge, Polity Press.
Giddens, A. (1994) Beyond Left and Right: The Future of Radical Politics, Stanford California, Stanford University Press.
Giddens, A. (1998) The Third Way: the renewal of social democracy, Cambridge, Polity Press.
Giddens, A. (2000) The Third Way and its Critics, Cambridge, Polity Press.
Giglioli, P.P. (1989) Teorie dell'azione, in Panebianco, A. (ed.) L'analisi della politica. Bologna, Il Mulino.
Gilchrist, A. (2000) The well-connected community: networking to the edge of chaos, Community Development Journal Vol 35 (3), pp 264-275.
Gilchrist, A. and Taylor, M. (1997) Community Networking: Developing Strength through diversity, in Hoggett, P. Contested Communities. Bristol, Policy Press, pp 165-179.
Glasgow and Clyde Valley Structure Plan Joint Committee 1998 A Common Development Framework for the next 20 years - The Strategic Issues Glasgow, GCVSPJC.
Goodwin, M. and Painter, J. (1996) Local governance, the crisis of fordism and the changing geographies of regulation. Transactions of the British Institute of Geographers, Vol 21, pp 635-648.
Grabher, G. Stark, D. (ed.) (1997a) Restructuring Networks in Postsocialism, Oxford University Press, Oxford.
Grabher, G. Stark, D. (ed.) (1999) Organizing Diversity: Evolutionary Theory, Network Analysis and Postsocialism, Regional Studies, Vol 31 (5), pp 533-544.
Granovetter M. (1973) The Strength of Weak Ties American Journal of Sociology, Vol 78, pp 1360-1380.
Granovetter, M. (1985) Economic Action and Social Structure:The Problem of Embeddedness, American Journal of Sociology, Vol 91 (3), pp 481-510.
Gregersen, B. and Johnson, B. (1997) Learning Economies, Innovation Systems and European Integration, Regional Studies, Vol 31 (5), pp 479-490.
Griffiths, R. (1998a) Making Sameness: Place Marketing and the New Urban Entrepreneurialism, in Oatley N. (ed.) Cities, Economic Competition and Urban Policy London, Paul Chapman Publishing, pp 41-57.
Griffiths, R. (1998b) The National Lottery and Competitive Cities, in Oatley N. (ed.) Cities, Economic Competition and Urban Policy, London, Paul Chapman Publishing, pp 181-198.
Gruber, J. (1993) Coordinating Growth Management through Consensus Building: Incentives and the Generation of Social, Intellectual and Political Capital, Working Paper 617, Berkeley Cal., IURD, University of California.
Gualini, E. (2001) Planning and the Intelligence of Institutions. Aldershot, Hants, Ashgate.
Habermas, J. (1984) The Theory of Communicative Action, Cambridge, Polity Press.
Habermas, J. (1987) The Philosophical Discourse of Modernity, Cambridge, Policy Press.
Haldane, J. (1918) Report of the Machinery of government Committee (The Haldane Report), CMND 9230, London, HMSO.
Hall, S. and Mawson J. (1999) Challenge Funding, contracts and area regeneration, Bristol, Policy Press.
Hall, P. and Taylor, R. (1996) Political Science and the three Institutionalisms Political Studies XLIV, pp 936-957.
Hall, P. Thomas, H. Gracey, R. and Drewett, R. (1973) The Containment of Urban England, London, Geo Allen & Unwin.
Hall, S. and Mawson, J. (1999) Challenge Funding, contracts and area regeneration, Bristol, The Policy Press.
Hannerz, U. (1996) Transnational Connections, Routledge, London/New York.
Harding A, (1995) Elite theory and growth machines, in Judge, D. Stoker, G. and Wolman, H. (eds.), Theories of Urban Politics. London, Sage, pp 35-53.

Harding, A. (1997) Urban Regimes in a Europe of the Cities? European Urban and Regional Studies, Vol 4 (4), pp 291-314.
Harding, A. (2000) Regime Formation in Edinburgh and Manchester, in Stoker, G. (ed) The New Politics of Local Governance, Houndsmill, Macmillan, pp 54-71.
Hardy, C. Phillips, N. and Lawrence, T. (1998) Distinguishing Trust and Power in Inter-Organisational Relations: Forms and Facades of Trust, in Lane, C. and Bachman, R. (1998) (eds) Trust within and between Organisations Oxford, Oxford University Press, pp 64-87.
Harloe, M. (1995) The peoples' home? Social rented housing in Europe, Oxford, Blackwell.
Harvey, D. (1989). From managerialism to entrepreneurialism: the formation of urban governance in late capitalism, Geografisker Annaler, Vol 71, pp 3-17.
Hassink R, (1997) Localised industrial learning and innovation policies. European Planning Studies, Vol 5 (3), pp 283-298.
Hastings, A., MacArthur, A. and MacGregor, A. (1996) Less Than Equal? Community organisations and regeneration partnerships, Bristol, Policy Press.
Haughton, G. (1999) Searching for the Sustainable City: competing philosophical rationales and processes of 'ideological capture' in Adelaide, South Australia, Urban Studies Vol 36 (11) pp 1981-1906.
Haynes P. (1999) Complex Policy Planning: the Government strategic management of the social care market, Aldershot, Ashgate.
Healey, P. (1997) Collaborative Planning: Shaping Places in Fragmented Societies, London, Macmillan.
Healey, P. (1998a) Collaborative planning in a stakeholder society, Town Planning Review, Vol 69 (1), pp 1-21.
Healey, P. (1998b) Building institutional capacity through collaborative approaches to urban planning, Environment and Planning A, Vol 30, pp 1531-1546.
Healey, P. (1999) Institutionalist analysis, urban planning and shaping places, Journal of Planning Education and Research Vol 19 (2), pp 111-122.
Healey, P. (2000) Planning in relational space and time: responding to new urban realities, in Bridge, G. and Watson, S. (eds.) A companion to the city, Oxford, Blackwell, pp 517-530.
Healey, P. (2001), Place, identity and governance: transforming discourses and practices, in ed. Hillier, J. and Rooksby, E., Habitus: A sense of place, Aldershot, Ashgate.
Healey, P., Purdue, M. and Ennis, F. (1993) Gains from Planning? Dealing with the impacts of development, York, Joseph Rowntree Foundation.
Healey, P., Cameron, S., Davoudi, S., Graham, S. and Madanipour, A. (eds) (1995) Managing Cities – The New Urban Context, London, John Wiley.
Healey, P., Khakee, A., Motte, A. and Needham, B. eds. (1997) Making strategic spatial plans: innovation in Europe, London, UCL Press.
Healey, P., Magalhães, C. de. and Madanipour, A. (1999) Institutional capacity-building, urban planning and urban regeneration projects, in M Sotarauta, (ed.), Urban Futures: A Loss of Shadows in the Flowing Spaces?; special issue of Futura, Vol 18 (3), pp 117-137.
Healey, P., Magalhães, C. de., Madanipour, A. and Pendlebury, J. (2001) Shaping City Centre Futures: Conservation, Regeneration and Institutional Capacity, Newcastle upon Tyne: Centre for Research in European Urban Environments, University of Newcastle (forthcoming).
Healey, P. Magalhães, C. de. Madanipour, A. and Pendlebury, J. (forthcoming) Place, identity and local politics: analysing partnership initiatives, in Hajer, M. and Wagenaar, H. (ed.) Deliberative Policy Analysis: Understanding Governance in Network Societies, Cambridge, Cambridge University Press.
Hellmer, F. Friese, C. Kollros, H. and Krumbein, W. (1999) Berlin, Mythos Netzwerke, Edition Sigma.

Hirst, P. (1994) Associative democracy, Cambridge, UK, Policy Press.
Hirst, P. (2000) Democracy and Governance. in Pierre, J. (ed) Debating Governance - Authority, Steering and Democracy. Oxford, Oxford University Press, pp 13-35.
Hoggett, P. (ed.) (1997) Contested Communities. Bristol, Policy Press.
Hollingsworth, R. and Boyer, R. (ed.) 1997 Contemporary Capitalism - The Embeddedness of Institutions, Cambridge University Press, Cambridge.
Honneth, A. (1995) The Fragmented World of the Social, Albany, NY, SUNY Press.
Hubbard, P. and Hall, T. 1998 The Entrepreneurial City and the 'New Urban Politics, in Hall, T. and Hubbard, P. (ed.) The Entrepreneurial City: geographies of politics, regime and representation, London, John Wiley, pp 1-30.
Hull A. (1997) Restructuring the debate on allocating land for housing growth, Housing Studies, Vol 12 (3), pp 367-382.
Hunter, F. (1953) Community Power Structure, Chapel Hill, North Carolina Press.
IBA (1999) Vorbereitungsgesellschaft mbH: Fürst-Pückler-Land 2000 bis 2010, IBA Vorbereitungsgesellschaft, Großräschen.
Illsley, B. Lloyd, G and Lynch, B (2000). 'From Pillar to Post?' A One Stop Shop Approach to Planning Delivery, Planning Theory and Practice, Vol 1 (1), pp 111-122.
Imrie, R. and M. Raco (1999) How new is the new local governance?, Transactions of the Institute of British Geographers, Vol 24 (1), pp 45-63.
Ingold, T. (2000) The perception of the environment: essays on livelihood, dwelling and skill, London, Routledge.
Innes J, (1990) Knowledge and Public Policy: The Search for Meaningful Indicators. New Brunswick, Transaction Books.
Innes, J. (1992) Group processes and the social construction of growth management, Journal of the American Planning Association, Vol 58 (4), pp 440-453.
Innes, J. (1996) Planning through Consensus Building: a new view of the comprehensive planning ideal, Journal of the American Planning Association, Vol 62 (4), pp 460-472.
Innes, J. and Booher, D. (1999) Consensus-building and complex adaptive systems: a framework for evaluating collaborative planning. Journal of the American Planning Association, Vol 65 (4), pp 412-423.
Innes, J., Gruber J, Thompson R and Neuman M. (1994) Co-ordinating growth and environmental management through consensus-building, Report to the California Policy Seminar, University of California, Berkeley.
Jenkins, R. (1996), Social Identity. London, Routledge.
Jenks, M., Burton, E. and Williams, K. (1996) (eds) The Compact City: a sustainable urban form? London, E&F Spon.
Jessop, B. (1991) The welfare state in the transition from Fordism to Post-Fordism, in Jessop, B, Kastendiek H, Nielsen K and Petersen IK (eds.) The Politics of Flexibility, Aldershot Hants, Edward Elgar, pp 135-161.
Jessop, B. (1995a). Towards a schumpeterian workfare regime in Britain? reflections on regulation, governance and the welfare state, Environment and Planning A, Vol 27, pp 1613-1626.
Jessop, B. (1995b) The regulation approach, governance and post-fordism: alternative perspectives on economic and political change, Economy and Society, Vol 24 (3) pp 307-333.
Jessop, B. (1997) Governance of complexity and the complexity of governance: preliminary remarks on some problems and limits of economic guidance, in Amin, A. and Hausner, J. (eds) Beyond market and hierarchy: interactive governance and social complexity, Edward Elgar Cheltenham, pp 95-108.
Jessop, B. (2000) Governance Failure, in Stoker, G. (ed.) The New Politics of British Local Governance, London, Macmillan, pp 11-32.

John, P. and Cole, A. (2000) Policy networks and local political leadership in Britain and France, in ed Stoker, G. The New Politics of British Local Governance, Houndmills, Macmillan, pp 72-90.
Judge, D., Stoker, G. and Wolman, H. (eds) (1995) Theories of Urban Politics, London, Sage.
Keane, J.(1988) Democracy and Civil Society, London, Verso.
Keeble, D. (1980) Industrial decline, regional policy and the urban-rural manufacturing shift in the United Kingdom, Environment and Planning A, Vol 12, pp 945-962.
Keim, K-D. and Matthiesen, U. 1998 'Globalocal': Regionale Netze und locale Milieus im Prozess der europäischen Metropolitanentwicklung, WGL – Journal, Bonn, pp 6ff.
Kickert, W. J. M., E.-H. Klijn, et al. (1997), Managing Complex Networks, London, Sage.
Klijn E-H., Koppenjan J., and Termeer K. (1995) Managing networks in the Public Sector: a theoretical study of management strategies in policy networks, Public Administration Vol 73, pp 437-454.
Kooiman, J (ed.) (1993) Modern Governance – New Society Government Interactions London, Sage.
Korcelli, P. (1997), Regionale Muster der Transition: Polen, in Fassmann, H. (ed.), Die Rückkehr der Regionen. Beiträge zur regionalen Transformation Ostmitteleuropas, Wien: Österreichische Akademie der Wissenschaften, p 187 ff. (Beiträge zur Stadt- und Regionalforschung, Band 15).
Kotkin, J. (2000) The New Geography. New York, Random House.
Kramer, R.N. and Tyler, T.T. (eds.) (1996) Trust in Organisations: Frontiers of Theory and Research London, Sage.
Krätke, S. (1998) Problems of Cross-Border Regional Integration: The Case of the German-Polish border area, European Urban and Regional Studies, Vol 5 (3), pp 249-262.
Kumar, A. and Paddison, R. (2000) Trust and Collaborative Planning Theory: The case of the Scottish planning system, International Planning Studies Vol 5 (2), pp 205-223.
Labrousse, A. (1999) Der komplexe Wandel von Institutionen und Organisationen in der ostdeutschen Transformation, in Thomas, H. (ed.), Institution: Lebenswelt und Ökonomische Rationalität, Berlin, BISS publications, pp 105 ff.
Lang, R. and Hornburg, S. (1998) Editors Introduction: What is social capital and why is it important to public policy? Housing Policy Debate, Vol 9 (1), pp 1-16.
Lanzara, G.F. (1993) Capacità negativa. Competenza progettuale e modelli di intervento nelle organizzazioni, Bologna, Il Mulino.
Latour, B, (1987) Science in Action, Cambridge, Mass., Harvard University Press.
Lauria, M. ed (1997) Reconstructing Urban Regime Theory: Regulating Urban Politics in a Global Economy, London, Sage.
Law, J. (1998) Power, action and belief: a new sociology of knowledge? Sociology Review Monographs, No.32.
Le Galès, P. (1998) Regulation and Governance in European Cities, International Journal of Urban and Regional Research, Vol 22 (3), pp 482-506.
Le Galès, P. and Mawson, J. (1995) Contracts versus Competitive Bidding Journal of European Policy, Vol 2 (2), pp 207-241.
Leadbetter, C. and Christie, I. (1999) To Our Mutual Advantage, London, Demos.
Leitner, H. and Sheppard, E. (1998) Economic uncertainty, inter-urban competition and the efficacy of entrepreneurialism, in Hall, T. and Hubbard, P. (eds) The Entrepreneurial city: geographies of politics, regime and representation London, Wiley, pp 285-308.
Levi, M. (1996), Social and Unsocial Capital. A Review Essay of Robert Putnam's Making Democracy Work, Politics and Society, Vol 24 (1), pp 45-55.
Lindblom, C.E. (1965) The Intelligence of Democracy, New York, Free Press.
Lipietz, A. (1998) Rethinking social housing in the hour-glass society, in Madanipour, A. Cars, G. and Allen, J (eds) Social exclusion in European cities: Processes, experiences and responses, London, Jessica Kingsley, pp 177-188.

Logan, J. and Molotch, H. (1987) Urban Fortunes: The political economy of place, Berkeley and Los Angeles, University of California Press.
Low, N. Gleeson, B. Elander, I and Lidskog, R. (2000) Consuming Cities: The urban environment in the global economy after the Rio Declaration, London, Routledge.
Lowndes, V. and Skelcher, C. (1998) The dynamics of multi-organizational partnerships: an analysis of changing modes of governance, Public Administration, Vol 76, pp 313-333.
Lukes, S. (1974) Power: A Radical View, London, Macmillan.
Mackintosh, M. (1992) Partnership: Issues of Policy and Negotiation, Local Economy, Vol 7 (3), pp 210-224.
MacLeod, G. (1999) Place, politics and 'scale dependence': exploring the structuration of euro-regionalism, European Urban and Regional Studies, Vol 6 (3), pp 231-254.
Madanipour, A, Cars, G. and Allen, J. (1998) Social Exclusion in European Cities. London, Jessica Kingsley.
Madanipour, A., Hull, A. and Healey, P. (eds) (2001) The Governance of Place: Space and planning processes, Ashgate, Aldershot.
Malkin, J. and Wildavsky, A. (1991) Why the Traditional Distinction Between Public and Private Goods Should Be Abandoned, Journal of Theoretical Politics, Vol 3 (4), pp 355-378.
Malmberg, A. and Maskell, P. (1997) Towards an explanation of regional specialisation and industry agglomeration, European Planning Studies Vol 5 (1), pp 24-41.
March, J. (1994) A Primer on Decision-making, New York, Free Press.
March, J.G. and Olsen, J.P. (1989) Rediscovering Institutions: The Organizational Basis of Politics, New York, The Free Press.
March, J. G., and Olsen, J.P. (1995) Democratic Governance, New York, The Free Press.
Marsh, D. and Rhodes, R. (eds) (1992) Policy Networks In British Government, Oxford, Oxford University.
Marsh D. and Smith M. (2000) Understanding Policy Networks: towards a dialectic approach, Political studies, Vol 48 (4) pp 4-21.
Marshall, J. and Peters, M. (1985) Evaluation and Education: The Ideal Learning Community, Policy Sciences, Vol 18 (2), pp 263-288.
Martin, R. and Rowthorn, B. (eds) (1986) The Geography of De-Industrialisation, London and Basingstoke, Macmillan.
Massey, D. and Allen, J. (eds) (1988) Uneven Re-Development: Cities and Regions in Transition (Restructuring Britain), London, Hodder and Stoughton/The Open University.
Matthiesen, U. (1985) Das Dickicht der Lebenswelt und die Theorie des kommunikativen Handelns, Wilhelm Fink Verlag, Munich, 2nd edition.
Matthiesen, U. (1998a) Milieus in Transformationen, Positionen und Anschlüsse, in Matthiesen, U. (ed.) Die Räume der Milieus, Neue Tendenzen in der sozial- und raumwissenschaftlichen Milieuforschung sowie in der Stadt- und Raumplanung, Berlin, edition sigma, pp 17-79.
Matthiesen, U. (1998b), An den Rändern der deutschen Hauptstadt - Regionalkulturelle Suburbanisierungsprozesse im Märkischen Sand - zwischen 'Hightech-Kathedralen' und 'Nationalpark DDR', in Berliner Journal für Soziologie, Vol 2, pp 245-268.
Mawson, J. (1997) The English Regional Debate: towards regional government or governance? in Bradbury, J. and Mawson, J. (eds) British Regionalism and DeVolution, Jessica Kingsley, pp 180-211.
Mayer, M (1995) Urban Governance in the Post-Fordist City, in Healey, P. Cameron, S. Davoudi, S. Graham, S. and Madanipour, A. (eds) Managing Cities: The New Urban Context, London, John Wiley, pp 231-250.
Mayntz, R. 1993 Governing Failures and the Problems of Governability: Some Comments on a Theoretical Paradigm, in Kooiman, J (ed.) 1993 Modern Governance – New Society Government Interactions, London, Sage, pp 9-20.

McAuslan, J.W.P. (1980) The Ideologies of Planning Law, Oxford, Pergamon.
McCarthy, P. and Harrison, T. (1995) Attitudes to town and country planning, London, HMSO.
McLoughlin, J.B. 1969 Urban and Regional Planning: A Systems Approach London, Faber and Faber.
Meekosha, H. (1993) The Bodies Politic-equality, difference and community practice, in Butcher, H., Glen, A., Henderson, P. and Smith, J. (eds.) Community and Public Policy, London, Pluto Press.
Melucci, A. (1987) Sul coinVolgimento individuale nell'azione collettiva. Rassegna Italiana di Sociologia, Vol 28 (1) pp 29-53.
Melucci, A. (1988) Getting Involved: Identity and Mobilization in Social Movements, in Klandermans, B., Kriesi, H., and Tarrow, S. (eds) From Structure to Action: Comparing Social Movement Research across Cultures, Greenwich Conn., JAI Press, pp 248-329.
Melucci, A. (1996a) The Playing Self, Cambridge, Cambridge University Press.
Melucci, A. (1996b) Challenging Codes: Collective Action in the Information Age. Cambridge, Cambridge University Press.
METREX: Network for European Metropolitan Regions and Areas (1999) Metropolitan Spatial Planning and Development, Practice Benchmark, metrex.dis@strath.ac.uk.
Meulemann, H. (1998) Die Implosion einer staatlich verordneten Moral. Moralität in West- und Ostdeutschland 1990-1994, Kölner Zeitschrift für Soziologie und Sozialpsychologie, No. 50 (3), pp 411-441.
Meyer, M.W. and Zucker, L. (1989) Permanently Failing Organizations, Newbury Park Cal., Sage.
Michels, R. (1958) Political Parties: A Sociological Study of the Oligarchical Tendencies of Modern Democracy, New York, Free Press.
Miller C. (1998), Partnerships in Regeneration: constructing a local regime for urban management, Policy and Politics, Vol 27 (3).
Milofsky, C. (1987) Neighbourhood-based organisations: a market analogy in Powell, W.W. (ed.) The Nonprofit Sector: a research handbook, New Haven, Yale University Press, pp 277-295.
Mingione, E (1993) The new urban poverty and the underclass, International Journal of Urban and Regional Research, Vol 17 (3).
Minister for Transport and the Environment (1999) Speech to the Royal Town Planning Institute Scottish Executive, November 25, Glasgow.
Mitchell, J.C. (ed.) (1969) Social Networks in Urban Situations, Manchester, University of Manchester Press.
Modellprojekt (1999) Modellprojeckt Expo 2000, Brochure, Guben/Gubin.
Motte, A. (ed.) (1995). Schema directeur et project d'agglomeration: l'experimentation de nouvelles politiques urbaines spatialisees 1981-1993, Paris, Les editions Juris Service.
Mouffe, C. (1992) Dimensions of Radical Democracy: pluralism, citizenship, democracy, London, Verso.
Moulaert, F. (2000) Globalization and Integrated Area Development in European Cities, Oxford, Oxford University Press.
Muller, P. and Surel, Y. (1998) L'analyse des politiques publiques Paris, Montchrestien.
Mummert, U. (1999) Gradualismus versus Big Bang - Transformationsstrategien und institutioneller Wandel, in Thomas, M. (ed.) Institution; Lebenswelt und ökonomische Rationalität, BISS public, 2 Vols., Berlin, pp 41ff.
Murdoch, J., Abram, S. and Marsden, T. (2000) Technical Expertise and Public Participation in Planning for Housing: "Playing the Numbers Game", in Stoker, G. (ed.) The New Politics of British Local Governance, London, Macmillan, pp 198-214.
MVA Consultancy (1989) Integrated Transport Study, Birmingham, Birmingham City Council.

National Land Use Database (NLUD) (2000) Final estimates of previously developed land for England and Government Office Regions 1998, DETR, www.nlud.org.uk.

Neckel, S. (1999) Waldleben, Frankfurt/New York, Campus.

North, D. (1990) Institutions, institutional change and economic performance, Cambridge, UK, Cambridge University Press.

Oatley N, (1998) Cities, Economic Competition and Urban Policy. London, Paul Chapman.

Offe, C. (1977). The theory of the Capitalist state and the problem of policy formation. Stress and Contradiction in Modern Capitalism, in Lindberg, L.N. and Alford, A. (eds) Lexington, Massachusetts, D.C.Heath, pp 125-144.

Olson, M. (1965) The Logic of Collective Action: Public Goods and the Theory of Groups, Cambridge Mass., Harvard University Press.

Ostrom, E. (1990) Governing the Commons: The Evolution of Institutions for Collective Action, Cambridge, Cambridge University Press.

Ostrom, E. (1992) Community and the Endogenous Solution of Commons Problems. Journal of Theoretical Politics, Vol 4 (3), pp 343-351.

Ostrom, E. (1994) Constituting Social Capital and Collective Action, Journal of Theoretical Politics, Vol 6 (4), pp 527-562.

Painter, J. (1995) Regulation theory, post-Fordism and urban politics, in Judge, D., Stoker, G. and Wolman, H. (ed.) Theories of Urban Politics, London, Sage, pp 276-295.

Painter, J. and Goodwin, M. (1995) Local Governance and Concrete Research: Investigating the Uneven Development of Regulation, Economy and Society, Vol 24 (3), pp 334-356.

Painter, J. and Goodwin, M. (2000) Local Governance After Fordism: A Regulationist Perspective, in Stoker, G. The New Politics of British Governance, London, Macmillan Press, pp 33-53.

Panel Report (1999) Regional Planning Guidance for the South East of England, Public Examination May-June, Report of the Panel, Guildford, Government Office for the South East.

Pasquino, G. (1994) La politica eclissata dalla tradizione civica, Polis, Vol 8, pp 307-13.

Pearce, D. Markandya, A. and Barbier, E. (1989) Blueprint for a Green Economy, Earthscan, London.

Peck, J. and Tickell, A. (1994) Too many partners....The future for regeneration partnerships, Local Economy Vol 9, pp 251-265.

Pendlebury, J. (1999) The conservation of historic centres in the UK: the case of Newcastle upon Tyne, Cities, Vol 16 (6), pp 423-434.

Perkin, H. (1989) The Rise of Professional Society, Routledge, London.

Peters, G.B. (1996) The Future of Governing: Four Emerging Models, Lawrence, Kansas, Kansas University Press.

Peters, G.B. (1998) 'With a Little Help From Our Friends': Public-Private Partnerships as Institutions and Instruments, in Pierre, J. (ed.) Partnerships in Urban Governance – European and American Experience, London, Macmillan, pp 11-33.

Peters, G.B. (1999) Institutional Theory in Political Science: the 'New Institutionalism', London, Continuum.

Peters, G.B. (2000) Governance and Comparative Politics, in Pierre, J. (ed.) Debating Governance – Authority, Steering, and Democracy, Oxford, Oxford University Press, pp 36-53.

Peters, M. and Robinson, V. (1984) The Origins and Status of Action Research, Journal of Applied Behavioral Science, Vol 20 (2), pp 113-124.

Pierre, J. (ed.) (1998) Partnerships in Urban Governance – European and American Experience, London, Macmillan.

Pierre, J. (ed.) (2000) Debating Governance – Authority, Steering and Democracy, Oxford, Oxford University Press.

Pierre, J. and Peters, G. (2000) Governance, Politics and the State, London, Macmillan.

Pollack, D. 1996 Sozialstruktureller Wandel, Institutionentransfer und die Langsamkeit der Individuen. Untersuchungen zu den ostdeutschen Transformationsprozessen in der Kölner Zeitschrift für Soziologie und Sozialpsychologie, der Zeitschrift für Soziologie und der Sozialen Welt, Soziologische Revue, Vol 19, pp 413 ff.

Pollitt, C., Birchall, J., and Putnam, K. (1998) Decentralising Public Service Management, Basingstoke, Macmillan.

Powell, W.W. and Di Maggio, P.J. (eds) (1991) The New Institutionalism in Organizational Analysis, Chicago Ill., University of Chicago Press.

Power, M. (1997) The Audit Society, Oxford, Oxford University Press.

Pratt, J., Gordon, P. and Plamping, D. (1999) Working Whole Systems: putting theory into practice in organisations, London, The King's Fund.

Purdue, D., Razzaque, K., Hambleton, R., Stewart, M. with Huxham, C. and Vangen, S. (2000) Community Leadership in Area Regeneration, Bristol, Policy Press.

Putnam, R. (1993), Making Democracy Work: Civil Traditions in Modern Italy, Princeton, NJ, University of Princeton Press.

Putnam, R. (1998) Foreword. Housing Policy Debate, Vol 9 (1), pp V-VIII.

Putnam, R. (2000). Bowling Alone. New York, Simon and Schuster.

Raco, M. (1999). Competition, collaboration and the new industrial districts: examining the institutional turn in local economic development, Urban Studies, Vol 36 (5/6), pp 951-968.

Ramsay, M. (1996) Community, culture and economic development: the social roots of local action, Albany, State University of New York Press.

Regional Co-ordination Unit (RCU) (2000) Reaching-out Action Plan: Implementation of the Performance and Innovation Unit's Report on the Role of Central Government at Regional and Local Level, London, Regional Co-ordination Unit.

Rhodes R. (1996) The new Governance: governing without government, Political Studies, Vol 44, pp 652-657.

Rhodes, R. (1997) Understanding Governance – Policy Networks, Governance, Reflexivity and Accountability, Buckingham, Philadelphia, Open University Press.

Rhodes, R. (1999) Governance and Networks, in Stoker, G. (ed) The New Management of British Local Governance. London, Macmillan, pp xii-xxvi.

Rhodes, R. (2000) Governance and Public Administration. In Pierre, J. (ed.) Debating Governance – Authority, Steering and Democracy, Oxford, Oxford University Press, pp 54-90.

Riley, K. (1999) Networks in Post-16 Education and Training. in Stoker, G. (ed.) The New Management of British Local Governance, London, Macmillan, pp 168-180.

Rittel, H. and Webber, M. (1973) Dilemmas in a general theory of Planning, Policy Sciences, Vol 4, pp 155-169.

Roberts, P. (1999) Sub-regional planning: the missing link, Town Planning Review, Vol 70 (1) pp iii-iv.

Robson, B., Parkinson, M. and Robinson, F. (1994) Assessing the Impact of Urban Policy DoE Inner Cities Research programme, London, HMSO.

Robson, B., Peck, J. and Holden, A. (2000) Regional Agencies and Area-Based Regeneration, Bristol, Policy Press.

Room, G. (ed.) (1997) Beyond the threshold: The measurement and analysis of social exclusion, Bristol, The Policy Press.

Russell H., Dawson J., Garside P., and Parkinson M. (1996) City Challenge Interim Evaluation, London, HMSO.

Rydin, Y. (1999) Public participation in planning, in Cullingworth, J.B. (ed.) British Planning Policy: 50 years of regional and urban change, London, Athlone Press, pp 184-197.

Sabatier, P. A. and Jenkins-Smith, H.C. (1993). Policy Change and Learning: an advocacy coalition approach, Boulder, Colorado, Westview Press.

Salet, W. and Faludi, A. (eds) (2000) The revival of strategic spatial planning. Amsterdam, Koninklijke Nedelandse Akademie van Wetenschappen (Royal Netherlands Academy of Arts and Sciences).

Saunders, P. (1981) Social Theory and the Urban Question, London, Hutchinson.

Scharpf, F.W. (1989) Decision Rules, Decision Styles and Policy Choices. Journal of Theoretical Politics, Vol 1 (2), pp 149-176.

Scharpf, F.W. (1997) Games Real Actors Play: Actor-centered institutionalism in policy research, Boulder, Colorado, Westview Press.

Schelling, T. (1978) Micromotives and Macrobehavior, New York NY, Norton.

Schon, D. and Rein, M. (1994) Frame Reflection: Toward the Resolution of Intractable Policy Controversies, New York, Basic Books.

Schütz, A. and Luckmann, T. (1972) The Structures of the Life-World, Northwestern University Press, Evanston, Ill.

Scott, J.W. (1999) European and North American Contexts for Cross-border Regionalism, Regional Studies, Vol. 33 (7), pp 605-617.

Scott, J.W. and Collins, K. (1997) Inducing Transboundary Regionalism in Asymmetric Situations: The Case of the German-Polish Border, Journal of Borderlands Studies, Vol. XII, Nos. 1&2, pp 97 ff.

Seligman, A. (1992) The Idea of Civil Society, New York, Free Press.

Selman, P. (2001). Social capital, sustainability and environmental planning, Planning Theory and Practice, Vol 2 (1), pp 13-30.

Short, J.R., Fleming, S. and Witt, S. (1986) Housebuilding, planning and community action: the production and negotiation of the built environment, London, Routledge and Kegan Paul.

Simmie J. (1998) Reasons for the Development of "Islands of Innovation": evidence from Hertfordshire, Urban Studies, Vol 35 (8), pp 1261-1289.

Skelcher, K. McCabe, C. and Lowndes, V. (1996) Community networks in urban regeneration: 'It all depends who you know', York, Joseph Rowntree Foundation.

Snow, D.A., Burke Rochford, Jr. E., Worden, S.K., and Benford, R.D. (1986) Frame Alignment Processes, Micromobilization, and Movement Participation, American Sociological Review, Vol 51 (3) pp 446-481.

Snow, D.A., Zurcher, L.A., and Ekland-Olson, S. (1980) Social Networks and Social Movements: A Microstructural Approach to Differential Recruitment, American Sociological Review, Vol 45 (4), pp 787-801.

Social Exclusion Unit (SEU) (1998) Bringing Britain Together London, The Stationery Office.

Social Exclusion Unit (SEU) (2000) National Strategy for Neighbourhood Renewal: a framework for consultation, London, The Stationery Office.

Social Exclusion Unit (2001) A New Commitment to Neighbourhood Regeneration: The Action Plan, London, The Stationery Office.

South West Regional Planning Conference (SWRPC) (1999) Draft Regional Planning Guidance, Taunton, SWRPC, www.rpg-sw.gov.uk.

Speak, S. and Graham, S. (2000) Private sector service withdrawal in disadvantaged neighbourhoods, Bristol, Policy Press.

Spencer, K. (1982) Comprehensive Community Programmes, in Leach, S. and Stewart, J. (eds) Approaches to Public Policy, London, Allen and Unwin, pp 199-224.

Srubar, I. (1998) Lebenswelt und Transformation. Zur phänomenologischen Analyse gegenwärtiger Gesellschaftsprozesse, in Müller, K. (ed.) Postsozialistischen Krisen. Theoretische Ansätze und Befunde, Opladent, Leske & Budrich, pp 68-87.

Stewart, J. (2000). The Nature of British Local Government. London, Macmillan.

Stewart, M. and Taylor, M. (1995) Empowerment and Estate Regeneration: a critical review, Bristol, The Policy Press.

Stewart, M. (1999) The politics of interdependence: Risk and uncertainty in the city-region, in Blanke, B. and Smith, R. (eds) Cities in Transition: New challenges, new responsibilities, London, Macmillan, pp 19-36.

Stewart, M. (2000) Local Action to Counter Exclusion : a research review, in Joining It Up Locally - The Evidence Base Report of Policy Action Team 17, Vol 2. London, DETR.

Stewart, M., Gillanders, G., and Goss, S. (2000) Joining It Up in Practice in Joining It Up Locally - The Evidence Base Report of Policy Action Team 17, Vol 2. London, DETR.

Stewart, M. Goss, S. Clarke, R. Gillanders, G. Rowe, J. and Shaftoe, H. (1999) Cross-Cutting Issues Affecting Local Government, London, DETR.

Stoker, G. (1998) Public-Private Partnerships in Urban Governance, in Pierre J (ed.) Partnerships in Urban Governance – European and American Experience, London, Macmillan, pp 34-51.

Stoker, G. (2000a) Introduction, in Stoker, G. (ed.) The New Politics of British Local Governance, Houndmills, Macmillan, pp 1-10.

Stoker, G. (ed.) (2000b) The New Politics of British Local Governance, Houndmills, Macmillan.

Stoker, G. (2000c) Urban Political Science and the Challenge of Urban Governance, in Pierre, J. (ed.) Debating Governance: Authority, Steering and Democracy, Oxford, Oxford University Press, pp 91-109.

Stoker, G. and Mossberger, K. (1995) The post-Fordist local state: the dynamics of its development, in Stewart, J. and Stoker, G. (eds) Local government in the 1990s, Macmillan, Basingstoke, pp 210-227.

Stone, C. (1989). Regime politics: governing Atlanta 1946-1988. Lawrence, Kansas, University of Kansas Press.

Storper, M. (1997) The Regional World, New York, Guilford Press.

Strathclyde Labour Market Intelligence & Monitoring Service (SliMS) (1999) Labour Market Statement, 1999 - Glasgow & Clyde Valley Structure Plan Area, September, Hamilton, South Lanarkshire Council, www-slims.org.uk.

Susskind, L. (1990) A Negotiation Credo for Controversial Siting Disputes, Negotiation Journal, Vol 6 (4), pp 309-314.

Susskind, L. and Cruikshank, J. (1987) Breaking the Impasse – Consensual Approaches to Resolving Public Disputes, New York, Basic Books.

Susskind, L. and Field, P. (1996) Dealing With the an Angry Public - The Mutual Gains Approach to Resolving Disputes, New York, The Free Press.

Susskind, L., McKearnan, S. and Thomas-Learner, J. (eds) (1999) The Consensus-Building Handbook, Thousand Oaks, California and Sage, London.

Swidler, A. (1986) Culture in Action: Symbols and Strategies. American Sociological Review, Vol 51 (2) pp 273-286.

Tarrow, S. (1994) Power in Movement, Cambridge, Cambridge University Press.

Tarrow, S. (1996) Making Social Science Work Across Time and Space: A Critical Reflection on Robert Putnam's Making Democracy Work, American Political Science Review, Vol 90 (2), pp 389-397.

Taylor, M. (1987) The Possibility of Cooperation, Cambridge, Cambridge University Press.

Taylor, M. (1997) The Best of Both Worlds: the Voluntary sector and local government, York, Joseph Rowntree Foundation.

Taylor, M. (2000a) Communities in the lead: organisational capacity and social capital, Urban Studies, Vol 37 (5-6) pp 1019-1035.

Taylor, M. (2000b) Top Down Meets Bottom Up: neighbourhood management, York, Joseph Rowntree Foundation.

Taylor, M. and Hoggett, P. (1994) Trusting in networks? in 6, P. and Vidal, I. (eds.) Delivering Welfare: repositioning non-profit and co-operative action in western European welfare states, Barcelona: CIES.

Tester, K. (1992) Civil Society, London, Routledge.
Tewdwr-Jones, M. ed (1996) British Planning Policy in Transition: planning in the 1990s, London, UCL Press.
Tewdwr-Jones, M. (1997) Plans, policies and intergovernmental relations: assessing the role of national planning guidance in England and Wales, Urban Studies, Vol 34 (1), pp 141-162.
The Scottish Office (1995) Designation of Structure Plan Areas (Scotland) Order, 1995, Edinburgh, The Scottish Office.
The Scottish Office, Planning Division (1999) Land Use Planning Under a Scottish Parliament, Edinburgh, The Scottish Office.
Thomas, M. (ed.) (1999a) Institution: Lebenswelt und ökonomische Rationalität, 2 Vols, BISS public, Berlin.
Thomas, M. (1999b) Marktimplementierung und Tranformationsprozeß, in Thomas, M. (ed.) Institution: Lebenswelt und ökonomische Rationalität, BISS public, Berlin, pp 17-40.
Thompson, G. Frances, J. Levacic, R. and Mitchell, J. (1991) Markets, Hierarchies and Networks: the co-ordination of social life, London, Sage in association with the Open University.
Turok, I. and Edge, N. (1999) The Jobs Gap in Britain's Cities, Bristol, Policy Press.
Uphoff, N. Esman, M. and Krishna, A. (1998) Reasons for Success: learning from instructive experiences in rural development, West Hartford, Connecticut, Kumarian Press.
Urban Task Force (1999) Towards an Urban Renaissance, London, E&FN Spon.
Urry, J. (1981) The Anatomy of Capitalist Societies: The Economy, Civil Society and the State, London, Macmillan.
US Dept of Housing and Urban Development (1999) The State of the Cities 1999, Third Annual Report, Washington, HUD.
Vangen, S. and Huxham, C. (1998) Building Trust in Inter-organisational Collaboration, Synergy from Difference, Symposium, Academy of Management Annual Meeting, Toronto, 2000.
Vigar, G. Healey, P. Hull, A. and Davoudi, S. (2000). Planning, governance and spatial strategy in Britain, London, Macmillan.
Vigar, G. Steele, M. Healey, P. Nelson, J.D. Wenban-Smith, A. (2000) Transport Planning and Metropolitan Governance, London, Landor.
von Zon, H. (1999) The Variety of Development Paths in Central and Eastern Europe: The Cases of Ukraine and Poland, in Kuklinski, A. (ed.) The Changing Map of Europe. The Trajectory Berlin-Poznan-Warsaw, Warsaw, Friedrich-Ebert-Stiftung, pp 53ff.
Walzer, M. (1995) Toward a Global Civil Society, Providence, Berghahn.
Wann, M. (1995) Building Social Capital: Self help in a twenty-first century welfare state, London, Institute for Public Policy Research.
Webb, A. (1991) Co-ordination: a problem in public sector management, Policy and Politics, Vol 19 (4).
Webster, B. (1982) Area management and Responsive Policy-making in Leach, S. and Stewart, J. (eds.) Approaches to Public Policy London, Allen and Unwin., pp 165-198.
Weick, K.E. (1995) Sensemaking in Organizations, Thousand Oaks Cal., Sage.
Wenban-Smith, A. (1999) Plan, Monitor and manage: making it work, London, CPRE.
West Central Scotland Plan Team (1974) West Central Scotland: A Programme of Action, Glasgow, West Central Scotland Steering Committee.
Whyte, W.F. (1991) Social Theory for Action: How Individuals and Organizations Learn to Change, Newbury Park Cal., Sage.
Wilcox, D. and Mackie, D. (2000) Making the internet work for partnerships, Town and Country Planning, Vol 69 (5), pp 161-163.
Wilkinson, D. and Appelbee, E. (1999) Implementing Holistic Government, Bristol, Policy Press.
Williamson, O. E. (1975) Markets and Hierarchies, New York, Free Press.

Williamson, O.E. (1996) The Mechanisms of Governance, New York and Oxford, Oxford University Press.
Wilson, P. (1997) Building social capital: a learning agenda for the twenty-first century, Urban Studies, Vol 34 (5/6), pp 745-760.
Wilson, R. and Dissanayake, W. (eds) (1996) Gobal/Local, Duke Univ. Press, Durham/London.
Woolcock, M. (1998) Social Capital and Economic Development: Towards a theoretical synthesis and policy framework, Theory and Society, Vol 27, pp 151-208.
Wysocki, A. and Glante, N. (1999) Der Beitritt Polens zur Europäischen Union. Bedeutung für das Land Brandenburg. Potsdam, SPD-Europabüro N. Glante MdEP.
Zucker, L.G. (1991) The Role of Institutionalization in Cultural Persistence, in Powell, W.W. and DiMaggio, P.J. (eds) (1991) The New Institutionalism in Organizational Analysis, Chicago, University of Chicago Press, pp 83-107.

Index

6, P. 109
active policies, territorial 42-3
actor-network theory 24
administrative boundaries 136
agency relations 25
Alexander, J.C. 110
Amin, A. 27
Applebee, E. 118
Area Management 152
area-based initiatives (ABIs) 154-7, 166-7n2
asymmetries, border zones 74-5
'audit culture' 114

'Balcerowicz-type' transformation 73-4, 84
Bauman, Z. 111, 112
best practice, community participation 117-18
'Big Bang' transformation pathways 73
Birmingham *see* West Midlands
'black box' of governance 22, 23
Blanc, M. 9, 13
'blue-sky' approaches, strategic planning 173, 190n4
Booher, D. 12-13
border zones
    asymmetries 74-5
    Germany-Poland 72-5
    institutional capacity building 70-5, 80-8
    milieux 80-4
    peripheralisation processes 75, 87
    transformation pathways 72-4, 84
    see also Guben/Gubin
Bourdieu, P. 44n2
Bristol
    boundaries 136, 141n3
    edge-city developments 131-2, 136, 138
    inconsistencies in policy 139
    informal planning policy 135-6
    partnerships for planning 140-1
    place focus 218
    planning restraint 134-5
    short-term planning 137
Britain *see* United Kingdom
brownfield sites 51, 130

central government *see* government
Central Policy Review Staff 152
Centre for Civil Society 124n2
Centre for Voluntary Organisation 124n2
City Challenge 115, 122, 152
'civic society' 124n1
'civicness' 109
civil society
    concept of 29, 107, 108, 110-11
    and state 11-12, 111-12
Clyde Valley Plan 168
co-production 33
Cole, A. 13-14
Coleman, J. 34
collaborative governance 12-13
collective action
    analysis of 4, 206-7
    dilemmas 37
    institutional capacity building 36-8
    local actors 69, 100, 146
    organising 146
    place as focus 17-18, 218-19
    urban level 19-21
collective sense-making 40
colonisation-thesis, Germany 73
Common Perspectives 183-4
Common Purpose 165, 167n4
communicative planning theory 24
'communitarianism' 107, 108
community, meaning of 110-11
Community Empowerment Fund 165
Community Legal Service Partnerships 166n2
community participation
    best practice 117-18
    and government 112-14
    leadership 118-19

models 119-22
neighbourhoods 106-7
policy development 122-4
urban regeneration 66
Community Planning 149, 165, 169
Community Strategy 165
competition
between cities 6-7
for funding 197-8
Comprehensive Community
Programmes (CCPs) 152
consensus building 44n5, 54-8, 135-6, 140
consultation, and participation 181
contract management 160-1
Cowell, R. 128
Crime Reduction Programme 166-7n2
cultural development 17-18

De Leonardis, O. 39
decentralisation, edge cities 131-2
decision-making, forums 13-14
delivery systems, welfare state 66, 218
democracy, concept of 30
'democratic governance' 29, 33-4, 39-40
demographic projections, as planning targets 129, 137, 203n18
development
cultural 17-18
plan-led 137, 197
sustainable 133
development planning
Scotland 168-9, 186-7
South East England 132
United Kingdom 128
see also planning
development programmes, 'fast-track' 9
'distressed neighbourhoods'
barriers to change 96-9
micro-political structures 99-102
place focus 218
regeneration problems 103-5
social exclusion 66, 90-6
Douglas, M. 44n6
Dryberg, T. 26

East Germany
transformation pathways 73, 84
see also Guben/Gubin
Easton, D. 22
economic changes, European cities 6-7
economic systems, Fordist 91-2

'edge cities' 131-2, 133, 138
Education Action Zones 166n2
Elander, I. 9, 13
embedding structures 71, 80, 81, 85-6, 89n6
employment, service sector growth 92-3
employment geography 131-2
Employment Zones 166n2
English Heritage, Grainger Town 48, 49-50
English Partnerships, Grainger Town 49-50, 51
environmental movement, place quality 17-18
Etzioni, A. 108
'Euro-Model Town Guben-Gubin' 79, 80-1
Europe
East and West interface 72
localised services 16
place focus 217
urban governance 6-7, 209-10
European Union (EU)
cross-border initiatives 79
eastward expansion 70-2, 87-8
and local milieux 68
social exclusion 90-1
Evers, A. 111

'fast-track' development programmes 9
Fordham, G. 118
Fordist economy, transition from 8-9, 66, 69, 91-4
formal institution building 68, 79-80, 80-1, 212-13
Foweraker, J. 109
fragmentation, government structures 9
funding, urban regeneration 49

game theory 22
Gateshead 51
'geography matters' 17
Germany
Neue Bundesländer 73
Polish border zone 70-5, 88
see also Guben/Gubin
Giddens, A. 25, 109, 124n2
Glasgow and Clyde Valley Structure Plan
area 171-2, 175-6
complementary policy reports 183-5
implementation linkages 177-8

implications 187-90
Joint Committee 147, 169
legal powers 176-7
national implications 186-7
network creation 179-81
participatory planning 182-3, 185-6
'goodness of fit', governance systems 208, 210
governance
  concepts of 10-15, 31-3, 99-100, 126
  model 13
  modes of 146-7, 159-60, 215-16
  place-focused 15-18
  relational processes 25-6
  relations analysis 22-5
  transformation from government 7-10, 13-14, 32, 112, 126
  'whole-systems' approach 158-9, 218
  see also urban governance
governance capacity 21-2, 220-5
  see also institutional capacity
governance paradoxes 83, 89n4
government
  and civil society 11-12, 111-12
  and community participation 112-14, 115-16
  cross-cutting initiatives 153
  definition of 10-11
  and governance 163-6, 211-12
  local government connections 149-58, 163-6
  traditional 7
  transformation to governance 7-10, 13-14, 112, 126
gradualist transformation pathways 73
Grainger Town, Newcastle
  decline of 46-9
  Grainger Town Partnership 49-52
  institutional capacity building 52-62
  regeneration 49-52
  stakeholders 60
Granovetter, M. 109, 162, 163
Green Belts 129, 193, 194
Guben/Gubin
  city centre development 79
  formal institution building 68, 79-80
  history and development 76-80
  informal institution building 80-4, 88
  institutional capacity building 80-4, 86-8
  intermediary groups 82-3
  mayor 82-3

milieux networks 80-4
place focus 217
Polish administration reforms 89n3
trans-border institution building 67, 79-80

Hastings, A. 117
Healey, P. 99, 105, 113-14, 117, 118, 121-2, 123, 126-7
Health Action Zones 166n2
'heterarchy' 12
hierarchies
  administrative 191-2
  neighbourhood renewal 119, 159
Hirst, P. 104
housing, planning restraints 134-5
Huxham, C. 162-3

informality
  community partnerships 120-1
  institutional capacity building 71-2, 80-4, 88, 195-6, 212-13
Innes, J. 12-13, 203n17
institution building 35, 38, 40-1
institutional analysis 43-4n1
institutional capacity
  assessment of 45-6
  building *see* institutional capacity building
  concept of 3-5, 21-2, 35-6, 68-9, 126-7
  decline of 191, 197-8, 201
  Grainger Town, Newcastle 46-62
  intellectual perspectives 206-8
  sustainable 199-202
  transformation 204-10
  and urban planning 147-8
  West Midlands 194-202
institutional capacity building
  action-research perspective 39-43
  border zones 70-5, 80-8
  collective action 36-8
  concept of 21-2, 26-8, 68
  empirical model 85-7
  formal 68, 79-80, 80-1, 212-13
  Grainger Town 52-62
  Guben/Gubin 79-84, 86-8
  informal 71-2, 80-4, 88, 195-6, 212-13
  public sphere 38-9
  'virtuous' and 'vicious' circles 200-2
institutional capital 27, 37, 54-8

institutional change 36, 40
institutional competence 174-8
institutional design 36, 38, 40-1
institutional development, West Midlands 194-6
'institutional thickness' 27
institutionalist analysis 21-8
integrated working *see* 'joined-up working'
intellectual capital 27
intellectual perspectives, governance transformation 206-8
Inter-Metrex Benchmarking Report 174
international borders, Germany-Poland 70-5
interpretive policy analysis 24

Jessop, B. 12, 13, 31
John, P. 13-14
'joined-up thinking' 16, 115, 184
'joined-up working' 146, 148, 164, 216
  development planning 184
  disconnected 151-8
  governance system 158-61
  local governance 149-51
  social capital 161-3
  urban governance 8, 163-6
Joint Approach to Social Policy 152

Keane, J. 122
knowledge resources 27, 54-6, 57-8
Krätke, S. 74

Labour Government, 'joined-up working' 149-51
Landman, T. 109
language barriers, German-Polish border 75
Le Galès, P. 99-100
leadership, community participation 118-19
legal powers, strategic planning 176-7
levels of governance 213-15
lifeworld, transformation 86, 89n7
Local Agenda 21 219
'local collective actors' 69, 100, 146
local government
  amenity delivery 15-16
  central government connections 151-8, 163-6
  'joined-up working' 149-51

re-organisation 8, 129-30, 141n3, 168-9, 177-8, 208
Local Government Act 2000 158, 165
local milieux, Guben/Gubin 68, 80-4
local organisations, networks 69
Local Strategic Partnerships 149, 158, 165, 166
Lowndes, V. 122

McArthur, A. 117
Mackie, D. 121
markets, neighbourhood renewal 119-20
Mayntz, R. 7, 145-6
metropolitan counties, abolition 193, 194, 195-6
Michels, R. 120
'micro-political processes' 99-102
milieux
  development of 84, 89n5
  interaction 68, 80-4
  qualities of 20
  social milieux 4, 21-2, 148
Millennium Villages 51
Milofsky, C. 118
mobilisation 27, 40, 57, 58
modes, of governance 146-7, 159-60, 215-16
Mouffe, C. 117
Muller, P. 32
Murdoch, J. 128
mutuality 120

National Strategy for Neighbourhood Renewal 106, 114-16, 161
Neighbourhood Renewal Strategies 165
neighbourhoods
  barriers to change 96-9
  community participation 106-7, 114-19
  micro-political networks 100-2
  models for renewal 119-22, 159-60
  social exclusion 66, 69, 90-6, 103-5
neo-liberal policies 8, 9
networks
  central and local government 164
  Glasgow and Clyde Valley Structure Plan 179-81
  governance paradigm 159-60, 211-12
  Grainger Town Partnership 58, 60
  Guben/Gubin 80-4
  neighbourhood governance 100-2
  neighbourhood renewal 120

Newcastle 60-1
  stakeholders 54, 56
New Deal for Communities 106, 115, 116, 156, 161, 166n2
'new institutionalism' 22, 24, 36-7
New Start 166n2
new towns 129
Newcastle
  City Centre stakeholders 60, 61
  and Gateshead 51
  Grainger Town *see* Grainger Town
  networks 60-1
  office space 47-8
  place focus 217
  retailing 46-7
non-governmental actors 9
North, D. 22, 25

Offe, C. 14
Ostrom, E. 37, 44n4
'Ottomanisation' of society 104

paradox of consensus 96-9
participatory planning process, Glasgow and Clyde Valley Structure Plan 182-3
partnerships
  characteristics 188-9
  concept of 19
  performance of 146
  planning 140-1
  public-private 8, 9, 49-52, 185-6
  trust 162-3
  unsatisfactory 198
  urban governance 160
  see also community participation
'path dependency' 22, 25
'patterning power' 14
peripheralisation processes 75, 87
Pierre, J. 209-10
place
  focus on 15-18, 217-20
  management of 53
  territorial governance 41-3
'place wars' 6
plan-led development 137, 197
planning
  area of plan 175-6
  biases and weaknesses 133-8
  challenges to 131-3
  partnerships 140-1, 188-9
  regional economic development 132
  short-termism 137

strategic planning 147
see also development planning; strategic planning
planning agreements 129
Planning Policy Guidance Notes 130
pluralism 39-40
Poland
  German border zone 70-5, 88
  see also Guben/Gubin
political capital 27
'politics of scale' 42
population movements, German-Polish border 75
post-Fordism, welfare state 8-9, 93-4, 94-5
post-socialist transformation pathways 72-4
postmodernity, distressed neighbourhoods 104-5
power, forms of 26
Power, M. 114
private sector, participatory planning 185-6
'public good' 28, 31
public sector, participatory planning 182-3
public sphere 29, 38-9
public-private partnerships 8, 9
  Glasgow and Clyde Valley Structure Plan 185-6
  Grainger Town regeneration 49-52
Putnam, R. 21, 25, 31, 33, 44n2, 108, 109

regeneration *see* urban regeneration
Regional Assemblies 130
regional Co-ordination Unit 158, 166
Regional Development Agencies (RDAs) 51, 130, 139
Regional Industrial Land Study (RILS), West Midlands 202-3n10
Regional Planning Guidance 130, 132, 136, 139
regionalism, England 139
relational resources 27, 56, 58
retailing, Newcastle 46-7
Rhodes, R. 12
Rogers Report 130

Scotland
  development planning 168-9, 186-7
  see also Glasgow and Clyde Valley

Structure Plan
Scottish Enterprise Liaison Group 179, 183
Scottish Enterprise network 190n6
selective restraint, planning system 134-5
Seligman, A. 110
service sector, employment growth 92-3
services, local delivery of 15-16
Shengen Agreement 89n2
short-termism, planning 137
Single Regeneration Budget (SRB) 49, 50, 115, 122, 152, 166n2
Skelcher, C. 122
social capital
  concept of 27, 30-1, 33-5, 44n2, 107-11
  formation of 25
  and institutional capacity 3-4, 37-8, 212-13
  and urban governance 147, 161-3, 164
social changes, European cities 6-7
social exclusion
  barriers to change 96-9
  combating 99-100, 114-19
  community participation 106-7
  'distressed neighbourhoods' 66, 69, 90-6
Social Exclusion Unit 149, 152, 212
social milieux
  definition 4
  and institutional capacity 21-2, 148
social relations 25-6, 27, 56
South East England
  development disputes 127, 134
  development planning 132
  employment decentralisation 131
  inter-authority networks 140
space, and place 53
spatial planning, Scotland 186-7
'spatio-temporal fixes' 42
Spree-Neisse-Oder Euroregion 79
stakeholders
  consensus-building 54-8
  Grainger Town, Newcastle 60
  institutional capacity building 127, 198, 203n17
state *see* government
Stewart, J. 215
Stoker, G. 13, 19
Stone, C. 23-4, 207

Strategic Futures Group 179, 181-3
strategic planning
  Scotland 168-9, 186-7
  West Midlands 194-6
  see also Glasgow and Clyde Valley Structure Plan
Strathclyde European Partnership 183
Strathclyde Structure Plan 168
structural change
  policy responses 94-5
  post-Fordist 91-4
  social exclusion 95-6
structuration theory 25
Structure Plan
  Scotland 190n1
  see also Glasgow and Clyde Valley Structure Plan
supra-local forces, Newcastle 58, 61-2
Sure Start 106, 115, 156, 166n2
Surel, Y. 32
sustainability, institutional capacity 199-202
sustainable development 17, 133
Sweden, planning processes 8
SWOT analysis (strengths weaknesses opportunities threats) 182, 184

Tarrow, S. 57
Taylor, M. 162, 164, 165-6
technical capabilities, strategic planning 172-4
territorial innovation 17
territorial milieux 21
territory *see* place
The Newcastle Initiative (TNI) 49-51
'third way' 107, 108, 122, 187-8
Thrift, N. 27
'top-down' governance 197, 203n15, 211
trajectories, governance capacities 26-8, 220-1, 223-4
transaction costs 24, 160-1, 207
transformation, urban governance 6-7, 26-8, 204-10, 220-5
transformation pathways, Germany-Poland border 72-4, 84
transport strategy
  modelling 173-4
  planning policy 133
  Scotland 179
  West Midlands 196
trust

in partnerships 162-3
see also social capital
Tyne and Wear Development Corporation 47-8

United Kingdom
  community participation 106-7, 114-19
  critique of urban governance 209
  government policy changes 8, 45
  joined-up working 149-66
  local government re-organisation 8, 129-30, 208
  national policy changes 129-31
  neo-liberal policies 8, 9
  planning system 67, 69, 125-41
  regional planning 130, 131-3
  sustainable development 133
  urban growth 129-31
  see also Bristol; Newcastle; Scotland; West Midlands
urban containment 129, 130-1
urban governance
  collective action 19-21
  and government 163-6, 211-12
  levels of 213-15
  transaction costs 160-1
  transformation 6-7, 26-8, 204-10, 220-5
  see also governance
urban growth, planning 129-31
urban neighbourhoods *see* neighbourhoods
urban regeneration
  community participation 66

Grainger Town, Newcastle 49-52
  see also 'distressed neighbourhoods'
urban regimes 19
Vaatz, A. 73
Vangen, S. 162-3
'virtuous' and 'vicious' circles, institutional capacity 200-2

Walzer, M. 110
welfare state
  delivery systems 66, 218
  Fordist system 8, 92
  local focus 15-16
  post-Fordist 93-4, 94-5
'well-being' of citizens 8, 209
Wenban-Smith, A. 136
West Central Scotland Plan 168
West Midlands
  administrative hierarchy 191-2
  institutional decline 197-8
  institutional development 194-6
  planning issues 192-4
  political leadership 195
  Regional Industrial Land Study (RILS) 202-3n10
  sustainable institutional capacity 200-2
  transport strategy 196
whole-systems' approach 158-9, 207, 218
Wilcox, D. 121
Wilkinson, D. 118
Williamson, O. 24
Woolcock, M. 164